Roman Polanski

Roman Polanski

The Cinema of a Cultural Traveller

Ewa Mazierska

I.B. TAURIS
LONDON · NEW YORK

Published in 2007 by I.B.Tauris & Co Ltd
6 Salem Road, London W2 4BU
175 Fifth Avenue, New York NY 10010
www.ibtauris.com

In the United States and Canada distributed by
Palgrave Macmillan, a division of St. Martin's Press, 175
Fifth Avenue, New York NY 10010

ISBN (Hb):   978 1 84511 296 7
ISBN (Pb):   978 1 84511 297 4

A full CIP record for this book is available from the British Library
A full CIP record for this book is available from the Library of
Congress
Library of Congress catalog card: available

Typeset in Stone Serif by Dexter Haven Associates Ltd, London
Printed and bound in Great Britain by TJ International Ltd,
Padstow Cornwall

C O N T E N T S

LIST OF ILLUSTRATIONS

ACKNOWLEDGEMENTS

I wish to express my gratitude to Laura Rascaroli, Krzysztof Loska, Sarah Cardwell, George McKay, Robert Murphy, Dorota Ostrowska, Grażyna Stachówna, Susan Sydney-Smith and Glyn White for reading the whole or parts of the manuscript and for their insightful comments, and to Philippa Brewster at I.B. Tauris for her valuable editorial advice.

I am also indebted to Małgorzata Mazierska, Grażyna Stachówna, Krzysztof Loska, Adam Wyżyński and to the staff of Adlington Library who helped me to find the films, journals, books and stills used in the book, to Iwona Sowińska and George McKay for giving me access to their unpublished work, to Roman Włodek for providing me with information about the use of jazz in prewar Polish films, and to Margaret Kerr for helping me with translation.

My special thanks goes to Roman Polanski who granted me permission to use the stills I chose for my book. All stills were provided by the National Film Archive in Warsaw.

The study leave, funded by the University of Central Lancashire, allowed me to embark on this project and to finish it on time.

A preliminary version of Chapter 1 was published with the title 'The Autobiographical Effect in the Cinema of Roman Polanski' in *Film Criticism*, 3, 2005.

INTRODUCTION:
AN ELUSIVE FILMMAKER

Few viewers doubt Polanski's fame or question his talent. He is one of only a handful of directors from Europe who achieved success in America without losing their European connection. His name even rings a bell of recognition in the ears of people who are not interested in cinema. However, the same people find it difficult to describe his cinema, perhaps with the exception of pointing to the director's predilection for violence. Even critics and film historians have problems establishing what constitutes a 'Polanski film', while at the same time including him in the category of *auteurs* and masters of cinema.

There are several reasons for his elusiveness. Firstly, his oeuvre is very heterogeneous in terms of themes, settings, characters and genres; which gives the impression to the uninformed viewer that his films are made by different directors. Secondly, unlike typical *auteurs* who embark on personal projects, Polanski rarely writes scripts for his films; and external factors such as commercial pressures or the literary tastes of his wives play a major part in his choices. He also seems to be less faithful to his collaborators than many other old masters of cinema such as Jean-Luc Godard, Woody Allen or Federico Fellini. Certain names reappear in the film credits, such as the scriptwriter Gérard Brach, composers Krzysztof Komeda and Wojciech Kilar, the editors Alastair McIntyre and Hervé de Luze, and the costume designer Anthony Powell, but only in the last decade Polanski has managed to assemble his own team of collaborators and create his own production company. Particularly interesting, taking into account that there appears to be more coherence among the visual styles of Polanski's films than among his narratives, is the fact that he never formed a lasting relationship with a cinematographer. Usually a different cinematographer has worked on each of Polanski's films and on one occasion, *Tess*, there were two different ones: Geoffrey Unsworth and Ghislain Cloquet. This apparent 'professional promiscuity' is partly due to non-artistic reasons such as the premature death of some of his closest contributors, particularly Krzysztof Komeda and Polanski's second wife,

Sharon Tate. However, it also reflects Polanski's way of approaching each film as a separate task, for which he assembles an appropriate crew, not a continuation of an earlier project or the next version of the same film.

Furthermore, because Polanski is a 'cinema kid' (as were the members of the French New Wave), and his cinema shows signs of being influenced by many cinematic trends and individual filmmakers such as Andrzej Munk, Alfred Hitchcock, Luis Buñuel, Federico Fellini, John Huston and Michael Powell, it is difficult to pigeonhole him to one movement or master. Like a magpie he seems to be interested in everything that he encounters on his way, but he easily discards his quarries and moves to another 'treasure'.

Another reason why Polanski eludes categorisation is the position of his cinema at the crossroads of two competing discourses: elitist and mass cinema. Not only does he move easily between artistic and commercial endeavours, low-budget and big-budget projects, America and Europe, but he caters simultaneously for the tastes of the mass audience and the art-house regular. His films follow the illusionist logic of mainstream cinema and always have (or at least attempt to have) high entertainment value by including such elements as mystery, violence and sex. At the same time, Polanski's emphasis on style, his almost obsessive attention to detail in order to achieve a particular visual effect, and consequently, his famous disregard for shooting schedules and budgets, distance him from the commercial cinema, making him resemble an archetypal artist who would rather die in poverty than compromise his art. Moreover, rather than providing the viewer with clear answers, Polanski's films invite competing readings. At their best, they are genuinely inexhaustible in their richness.

The next factor which helps to explain why it is so difficult to capture the specificity of Polanski's cinema is the wide interest in his biography, at the level normally granted to film stars. Discussing his films invariably strays into talking about his life. When I mentioned to a university colleague that I was writing a book about Polanski's films, his immediate comment was: 'What an interesting project. He had such a fascinating life.' Similar remarks were made by several others who assumed that I was either writing a biography of Polanski or treating his films as an extension of his biography. I will suggest that the perceived closeness or even inter-changeability between the text and the man on many occasions has prevented a serious examination of Polanski's work and has driven critics' attention away from other aspects of his films.

Finally, Polanski's elusiveness derives from his long artistic activity of over half a century. Few filmmakers made films over such a long time and even fewer in the later part of their activity have achieved so much interest and recognition as Polanski. Moreover, despite reaching retirement age, Polanski continues to look for themes and means of expression which he has not previously exploited. Certainly, if European cinema is taken into account, only the creators of the French New Wave, particularly Jean-Luc Godard and Eric Rohmer, can match Polanski's vitality.

This book attempts to account for the eclecticism, ambiguity and paradoxes of Polanski's cinema, while at the same time searching for common elements in his films. It mirrors (although it might be a distorted reflection) Polanski's tendency to look at reality from different angles by discussing his films from a number of perspectives and combining a variety of methods, belonging to broadly understood cultural and textual analysis. Rather than adopting the chronological approach, favoured by the vast majority of authors of previous monographs or extended essays on Polanski's cinema (such as Ivan Butler, Virginia Wright Wexman, Grażyna Stachówna, Mariola Jankun-Dopartowa and Herbert Eagle), I will devote each chapter to a different aspect of his work. I have adopted this structure in the conviction that it will allow a better test of whether and to what extent Polanski's cinema can be treated as an organic whole. Many of his films are therefore discussed more than once in different contexts. At the end of this book is an appendix with technical details of the films Polanski directed, as well as a collection of brief synopses. In the main narrative of my work I have avoided extended descriptions of the films' plots, in the knowledge that readers may refer to the appendix for further details.

My examination of Polanski's cinema begins with a discussion of the autobiographical effect of his films. I argue that we tend to regard the films of this director as an emanation of his life largely because his life, or at least a certain version of it, seems to be public property. Viewers think they know enough about Polanski to draw parallels between his life and his films. I concentrate on three enduring motifs in Polanski's films pertaining to his biography: violence, travel and voyeurism. Chapter 2 focuses on his characters and narratives. Recognising the influence of absurdist art on his cinema, I seek to establish what type of absurdity prevails in his films. My argument is that although absurd is a common denominator of Polanski's films, it affects his narratives in a variety of ways: sometimes causing conflict between his protagonists and those around them, on other occasions leading to inner turmoil. Accordingly, a useful category with which to examine changes in Polanski's narratives is the drama/melodrama dichotomy – dramas prevailing in the first part of his career, and melodramas in the second. Chapter 3 brings in another concept often applied to Polanski's oeuvre: surrealism. In my opinion surrealism most affected the visual side of Polanski's cinema: the way he represents human bodies and people's environment, including houses, cities and the sea. I use a concept of the 'double life' of things, which is largely the consequence of Polanski's preoccupation with subjective vision and playing it against an objective view. This chapter also tries to account for Polanski's interests in cultural history, especially his sensitivity to the meanings with which people furnish certain objects and how subsequently these meanings influence human interactions. I argue that Polanski's trajectory from dramatist to melodramatist is paralleled by his growing inclination to realist techniques at the expense of surrealism and expressionism. Chapter 4 discusses the types of music the director uses in his films and the purposes music serves, focusing on jazz as music conveying rebellion and madness, and on the relation between it and classical music, barbarity and civilisation. It gives particular attention to two Polish composers with whom Polanski collaborated: Krzysztof Komeda and Wojciech Kilar. Chapter 5 examines the ideologies conveyed in Polanski's cinema, and considers especially his treatment of religion, political power and authority, patriarchy and racism. Chapter 6 deals with literary adaptations, focusing on how using literary texts allows Polanski to develop themes and convey meanings that can be found in his 'original' work. It also discusses how Polanski's adaptations produce autobiographical effects and cater for the tastes of international audiences. The last chapter presents the ways in which Polanski conforms to and subverts conventions specific to film genres. Awareness of how different genres operate and what effect they have on the viewer has always played a large part in Polanski's approach to filmmaking. However, his attitude to genre is by no means monolithic. I suggest that up until the production of *Chinatown* (1974) the director tended to treat a genre only as a starting point from which to develop a new formula, while in the later part of his career he has been less willing to experiment with genres.

Throughout the book I look at Polanski's cinema from the perspective of film history, examining its links with Polish and European modernism, especially the Polish School and French New Wave, as well as post-modernism, and American genre cinema. Apart from Chapter 1, in which I consider different facets of Polanski's artistic personality my book is devoted to Polanski as a director; I have excluded examination of his career as an actor.

The image of Polanski's cinema that will emerge from this work will be one of coherence of themes and of approaches, but also of discontinuities and transformation: of travelling through styles and cultural traditions, as this book's title indicates. Some critics equate the transformation in his work with purging his films of the gimmicks which used to obscure serious content of his early films, acquiring a more classical form, more coherent ideological position and more sympathetic approach to characters and viewers. Others see it as losing the energy to experiment and challenge the audience, as a backward step, resembling the regression people experience in old age. The watershed, in the opinion of critics and Polanski himself, is *Tess* (1979). During the making of this film Polanski famously pronounced that the world had become too absurd and surreal for surreal films to be made. It is worth noting that there is a paradox in Polanski's position: his shift towards more realistic films results from his desire to escape reality. It seems like the thorny issue of realism in cinema is particularly difficult in relation to Polanski's films.

My favourites among Polanski's films were all made before *Tess*, the number one being *Cul-de-Sac* (which Polanski also regards as his best film), but in this book I try to discuss at some length all his movies and, if possible, not to obscure analysis through my own aesthetic predilections and my nostalgia. During my childhood and teenage years in communist Poland Polanski was my hero: the Pole who managed to achieve genuine fame in the West, a filmmaker whose films were watched abroad not because of viewers' curiosity about Eastern European culture but simply because they were good. Although from my current perspective I perceive this pride as not only belonging to my youth, but also as being immature, even mistaken, I still feel immense admiration for his courage to seek success abroad and respect for his talent and resilience. Moreover, as a Polish émigré I feel particularly attuned to Polanski's cinema, thanks to experiencing first-hand the discomfort one feels having a foreign accent and strange name, and because I understand the language spoken in his early films. It is worth mentioning here that although it is not my ambition to reclaim Polanski for Polish cinema and art in a wider sense, I think equally that his Polish links can not be overlooked. Firstly, his early shorts and his feature debut, *Knife in the Water*, as well as his recent film, *The Pianist*, constitute a significant part of his artistic output. For different types of viewers, *Knife in the Water* and *The Pianist* encapsulate what is best in his work. Secondly, certain features of his early work, such as absurdism, surrealism and his extraordinary craftmanship, can be traced back to his Polish roots. We can list such factors as the flourishing of absurdist theatre in Poland of the late 1950s and 1960s, studying at the Łódź Film School, where he acquired his versatile skills and began working with Andrzej Munk. In my book I also cite Polish critics and scholars, either because they were early witnesses of the phenomenon of Polanski and captured some features of his art earlier than their Western counterparts, or because of the depth of analysis they offered. This is particularly true of Aleksander Jackiewicz and Grażyna Stachówna. The former in his numerous essays on Polanski tried to account for the versatility and elusiveness of his oeuvre, especially his appeal to art-house and mainstream audiences, and his ability to create a distinctive style despite his 'magpie personality' – his affinity for pastiche, parody and literary adaptation (see Jackiewicz 1977; 1981; 1989). The latter is the author of the first Polish monograph which attempted not only to examine his films critically, but to address the 'Polanski phenomenon' in all its complexity (see Stachówna 1994).

I am aware that my sympathy for Polanski and, if not real, at least imagined proximity to the world he creates on screen might incline me to exaggerate certain marginal features of his films, blinding me to many which are more important or forcing me to adopt a submissive position towards them. My hope is that awareness of these dangers helps me to maintain a critical distance. This, does not mean however, that *Roman Polanski: The Cinema of a Cultural Traveller* is an objective or a final study of Polanski's films. I espouse Michel Foucault's view that such studies simply do not exist. The 'author' (and any book which has in its title 'the Cinema of so and so' assumes that the person mentioned in the title is an author) is a product of a particular discourse, in this case, of me writing a study of Polanski, not a pre-existing entity whom such a study attempts to uncover (see Foucault 1986: 284). I will regard it a success if my 'Polanski' resembles the 'Polanski' known to readers from elsewhere, but has some freshness about him too.

I

THE AUTOBIOGRAPHICAL EFFECT
IN THE CINEMA OF POLANSKI

Polanski's life and work on both sides of the Berlin Wall and in the Old and the New Worlds seems to cohere into nothing more or less than a demented imago of the latter half of the twentieth century. The fact that somewhere along the way this man has made some films seems to beggar the question. Perhaps the only surprise is that he has never been asked to helm his own auto-bio-pic.

Michael Eaton

It is a commonplace to say that there is as much interest in Polanski's life as in his cinema. Testimony to this is the proliferation of biographies and newspaper articles devoted to his life. More importantly, rarely are the films he directs or his performances analysed separately from his biography. For example, Harlan Kennedy asks: 'Why does *Bitter Moon* work?' and answers 'Because it's not so much by Polanski in crisis as *about* Polanski in crisis' (Kennedy 1994: 14). The distinguished Polish critic, Aleksander Jackiewicz, discussing Polanski's performance as Mozart in Peter Shaffer's play *Amadeus* in Na Woli theatre in Warsaw, claims: 'Polański...playing Mozart, also plays himself: an artist who follows his intuition and instinct. As an actor, even in film, he was always an amateur... He behaves now as in his youth: mystifying himself and others, changing the world which surrounds him into a circus' (Jackiewicz 1989: 269). A suggestion that there is an important connection between Polanski's personal experience and the content of his films is present even in the titles of film reviews, such as 'A *Tess* for child molestors' (Marcus 1981).

There are several intertwined reasons for this unrelenting interest in Polanski the real person and in the relationship between his films and his life. Firstly, as already stated, Polanski is not only a director but also an actor in his own films, as well as in the films of other filmmakers and in theatre plays. This makes his face more familiar than that of directors who limit themselves to staying behind the camera. According to Polanski's biographers, he has always been an actor in another, more fundamental sense: someone who likes to perform, be known and admired by the crowds. He started his career as a child actor in the Theatre for Young Viewers, on the radio and in the Kraków puppet theatre. However, as Barbara Leaming maintains, 'For Romek the real show was in the Kraków Market Square... Romek began to perform in the square, spinning out stories, cruelly mimicking passersby, attracting attention in whatever way he could. "They hated him in Kraków", said screenwriter Michał Ronikier. "He was little, loud and aggressive." But, whatever the reaction, Romek became a well-known street person, a familiar sight' (Leaming 1981: 20).

The urge to perform not only in theatre or in cinema, but in life as well, is also confirmed by one of his oldest and closest friends, René Nowak, who recollects Polanski's attraction to quarrels and hullabaloos, and his unrelenting need to be surrounded by people and be the centre

Roman Polanski (centre) in *Pokolenie* (*A Generation*, 1955)

of attention (see Piekarczyk 2000: 14–15). This is also documented by his career. For his early student film, *Let's Break the Ball*, he first arranged to film the annual student dance at Łódź, and then invited a group of local thugs to beat up the unsuspecting students, in order to make the reaction of his actors as authentic as possible (see Leaming 1981: 32; Stachówna 1994: 34). The 'performing' side of Polanski's career and personality, while allowing the public to have almost direct access to him, at the same time makes it difficult to establish who the 'real Polanski' is, to separate the mask from the person, or to concede that in his case the performer and the private person are indistinguishable – the mask is the man.

The second reason why the 'real' Polanski fascinates the public is the perception that his biography is more unusual than that of most filmmakers. Three periods of his life draw particular attention. The first is his childhood. Polanski was born in Paris in 1933, but in 1936 he came with his Jewish parents to Poland, his father's homeland (Polanski's mother was a Russian Jew). Soon after the war broke out, his parents were taken to concentration camps – his mother to Auschwitz, where she perished, his father to Mauthausen. Romek was hidden first in Kraków, then in the countryside, moving from one family to another and largely forced to provide for himself. The second event that attracts the interest of biographers and sparks the imagination of film critics and historians is the murder of Polanski's second wife Sharon Tate and three of his friends in 1969 by members of the Charles Manson cult. The third pivotal period of his life involved his arrest in Los Angeles in 1979 on charges of sexual intercourse with a thirteen-year-old girl and his subsequent decision to flee the United States to avoid arrest.

The first two of these three episodes encourage us to see Polanski predominantly as a victim, although we can also register an undertone of guilt on the part of Polanski, a common feature among those who survived while others members of the same nation or family perished (see Adorno 1973: 361–5; Levi 1988). In the case of Polanski's mother's death the guilt was exacerbated by Polanski's father; even after the war, when he was miraculously reunited with his son, he held the boy responsible for her disappearance (see Kiernan 1980: 49). Polanski himself admitted to feeling guilty for not being with his wife when the Manson gang attacked her in their rented house (see Polanski 1984: 282–3). Thomas Kiernan in his rather unsympathetic biography of Polanski tries to play down Polanski's victimhood and emphasises his guilt by drawing attention to the fact that he is a lucky survivor who deserves no pity; while those around him perish, he stays alive and goes from strength to strength (see Kiernan 1980). In the third pivotal episode from Polanski's life his role is predominantly that of a paedophile predator, although for many years following the incident Polanski himself refused to recognise his act as immoral. Instead, he pointed out the adult appearance and behaviour of his sexual partner and claimed to be a victim of her and her mother's greed (see Kiernan 1980: 90–100; Leaming 1981: 110–41; Polanski 1984: 329–41).

On the whole, Polanski does not fit the model of a 'suffering artist' in the manner of Van Gogh, for example. Neither can we compare him to the murderous Caravaggio. Instead, he uniquely combines the qualities of a victim and a perpetrator, thus constituting a category of his own. But even saying that does not explain Polanski's puzzling uniqueness. Equally interesting is his attitude to these events. One gets the impression that his reaction to them is somehow muted or impenetrable to an outsider. Hence, although we know much about Polanski's biography, we know very little about his inner life and character.

Unable to find a real artist whose biography and attitude remind me of Polanski, I searched for a fictitious character of similar qualities in literature and encountered one in *Life: A User's Manual*, the renowned novel by Georges Perec, a fellow Jew and Parisian, whose parents, like Polanski's, were taken to the concentration camp. The character similar to Polanski is Vera Beaumont (maiden name Orlova), an immigrant from Russia who became a famous opera singer and travelled all over the world giving recitals before settling in Paris with her two granddaughters. She took care of the girls after their parents, Vera's only daughter and her son-in-law, were murdered in horrific circumstances. This was not the only sudden death in her life – twenty-five years earlier her archaeologist husband had committed suicide and even earlier she had lost her father and siblings.

Polanski, as his biographies and his films reveal, shares with Vera Beaumont not only a deep desire to perform and be admired, a nomadic nature which made both of them spend long periods away from their closest family (with some dire consequences), and a fair share of personal tragedy, but also an unsentimental attitude to the world and to themselves. Although the author of *Life: A User's Manual* avoids psychological analysis, he sheds some light on Vera's apparent indifference to misfortune, and it may also partly explain Polanski's stance in life. Perec describes how during the October Revolution the aristocratic Orlov family was almost entirely wiped out by members of the Red Army. It happened in front of little Vera, who, with her mother, managed to escape after months of exhausting travel to reach Austria (see Perec 2003: 150). Perec suggests that experiencing utter tragedy in early life teaches one to be prepared for disasters of the same magnitude in the future and to regard them not as an anomaly to individual and social history, but as the recurrent pattern of one's life. Perhaps it also instils an appreciation of one's life and a need to regard it as the greatest asset, a gift that should not be squandered.

The third and most problematic motivating force behind the interest in Polanski's life and the predilection to make connections between his films and his biography is seeing Polanski's films as stories about his life and reflections of his character. Following the concept of Russian formalist Boris Tomashevsky, Grażyna Stachówna describes Polanski as an 'artist with a biography' – as opposed to artists without a biography – and puts him in the same category as Erich von Stroheim, Federico Fellini and Woody Allen (see Stachówna 1994: 28). According to Tomashevsky, the artist with a biography inscribes it into his art (consciously or not); his work is autobiographical (Ibid.: 28–9). Thus knowledge of the artist's life is an important condition for understanding his work.

How does one establish that the artist is indeed writing his life into his art? In the book about the cinema of Nanni Moretti, which I co-wrote with Laura Rascaroli, we drew attention to various problems that resulted from applying the term 'autobiography' to art and to film in particular (see Mazierska and Rascaroli 2004: 14–22). Dictionaries define autobiography as a work of art, whose subject is the author's own life. Yet many critics argue that all art is autobiographical, because even if it does not represent

Adam Fiut and Roman Polanski in *The Bicycle* (1955)

facts from an artist's life, it reveals his inner life: his own ideas, experiences and emotions. If we accept this claim, then the very concept of autobiography ceases to be methodologically viable. The only way out from this conundrum seems to be by putting further restrictions on the concept of autobiography or discriminating between autobiography in a wider sense (in which all art is autobiographical) and in a narrower sense, when only some novels, paintings, films, or certain aspects of them are considered as autobiographical. The second, opposing argument claims that no work of art can be autobiographical, because it is impossible to represent oneself completely and truly; representations are the product of selection and abstraction, and are therefore inevitably always subjective and partial.

There are also philosophical problems with human 'life' and 'identity'. As Szymon Wróbel observes, '"Life", in common with a narrative, is a construct of human imagination in the same way as any other narrative. When somebody tries to relate his life to us, it is always a certain cognitive achievement, not a statement of things which simply happened. It is also a narrative achievement. From a psychological point of view, life as such does not exist; those who relate it, select the events and interpret them at the same time. From a philosophical perspective, one cannot be a naive realist regarding one's own life' (Wróbel 2001: 149). Wróbel also suggests regarding human 'life' and 'identity' as products of narrating one's life, not the other way round – stories about one's life being a consequence of living a particular life and having a particular identity. If we use his approach, then establishing if a work of art is an autobiography ultimately means matching one partial and subjective representation (autobiography) with another one which is also partial and subjective (life). A similar argument is presented by Stuart Hall, who maintains: 'Rather than speaking of identity as a finished thing, we should speak of *identification*, and see it as an on-going process. Identity arises, not so much from the fullness of identity which is already inside us as individuals, but from a *lack* of wholeness which is "filled" from *outside us*, by the ways we imagine ourselves to be seen by *others*. Psychoanalytically, the reason why we continually search for "identity", constructing biographies which knit together the different parts of our divided selves into a unity, is to recapture this fantasised pleasure of fullness (plenitude)' (Hall 1992: 287–8).

Accepting the aforementioned arguments of Wróbel and Hall leads to the conclusion that the relation between life and autobiography is symmetrical. Just as the artist's autobiography is shaped by his actual life, so his life, or what is regarded as his life, is shaped by his autobiography. Indeed, critics who discuss autobiography in Polanski's work operate a concept of 'Polanski' which is influenced by his films.[1] For example, after the premiere of *Bitter Moon* opinions about the state of his marriage with Emmanuelle Seigner were based largely on the assumption that the film reflected the director's personal life (which Polanski robustly denied). Interestingly, the work of Roland Barthes who announced the 'death of the author' (see Barthes 1977) and other poststructuralists made the search for authorial traits in an author's work look old-fashioned, methodically flawed and even futile. At the same time some biographies, based on analysis of the writer/painter's work, such as Walter Benjamin's essays on Kafka and Proust (see Benjamin 1999a; 1999b), Deleuze and Guattari's study of Kafka (see Deleuze and Guattari 2000) and Susan Sontag's work on Benjamin (see Sontag 1983b), proved persuasive and captivating. Consequently, the practice of reconstructing the artist's life by using his work is now more legitimised. Susan Sontag in her essay on Benjamin famously said: 'One cannot use the life to interpret the work. But one can use the work to interpret the life' (Sontag Ibid.: 111).

I will be considering Polanski's films as a reflection of his life (as it is known to me) and looking at them as a way to gain access to his life and persona, but with the awareness that both methods cannot be fully satisfactory. Grażyna Stachówna also shows awareness of the problems which result from naively assuming that a film can accurately mirror somebody's life and character. For this reason, instead of declaring Polanski's films as autobiographical, she uses the term Polanski's 'biographical legend' as both reflected in his films and created through them (Stachówna 1994: 34). 'Biographical legend', as understood by Stachówna, is the version of Polanski's biography which the viewer/reader constitutes from any available material about his life. Because of the mythical undertones of the term 'biographical legend', I opt for the 'autobiographical effect' – the viewer's impression of watching the life of the film's author, or that what on screen in an important sense pertains to the author's life. In my opinion this effect is produced by several intertwining discourses the director uses in his films. The first one, which should receive precedence over others by the law of chronology, is the discourse on violence. As was established earlier, in his off-screen life Polanski was regarded as both a victim and a victimiser. Similarly, the most common theme of his films is violence and victimisation. This applies to Polanski's first film, *The Bicycle* (1955); it was the only film he made which did not survive; and it was based on a real event in the director's life. The teenage Roman, who was then obsessed by cycling, was lured to an out-of-town bunker by a well-known Kraków crook who promised to sell him a bicycle for a bargain price. There the thug robbed Polanski and beat him so severely that the future author of *Knife in the Water* narrowly escaped death. Ironically and meaningfully, from the perspective of the blurred boundary between victim and predator in Polanski's life and cinematic character, and his fondness for doppelgangers, the man who attacked Polanski shared with him his first name. His full name was Roman Dziuba (Ibid.: 32). In *The Bicycle*, as one might expect, Polanski himself played the victim. In his later career he cast himself both as perpetrator and victim, hinting that he identifies with both types. Among roles belonging to the first type we could list the nameless thugs in *Two Men and a Wardrobe* and *Chinatown*, in the second, the lean man in *The Fat and the Lean*, Trelkovsky in *The Tenant* and Alfred in *Dance of the Vampires*. The character of a vampire deserves special attention here, because a vampire is a victim and perpetrator in one entity: someone who becomes a bloodsucker after being attacked by another bloodsucker. It could be argued that in Polanski's biography we could also detect a vampiric trajectory: from an abused child to a paedophilic abuser. In some cases of violence, represented by Polanski, it is not easy to establish who is the oppressor and who is the oppressed because many of his characters use physical force against other people in (however displaced) self-defence. Moreover, acts of violence often have an ambiguous status: they might just be taking place in the character's mind.

Violence in Polanski's films is directed towards children and women and often takes the form of sexual abuse. Examples are incest in *Chinatown*, rape in *Repulsion*, *Rosemary's Baby*, *Tess* and *Death and the Maiden*, the rejection by society of a crippled or monstrous child in *The Tenant*, and the neglect and economic exploitation of an orphan in *Oliver Twist*. Polanski is also associated with these two types of violence as a private person: being an orphaned child traumatised by war experiences, the husband of a woman brutally murdered and the alleged abuser of a teenage girl. Critics have tried to explain Polanski's preoccupation with violence by referring to such concepts as catharsis and psychotherapy (see Stachówna 1994: 32) and atonement (see Wexman 1987: 109), which are also cited as the most important reasons to produce an autobiography (see Wróbel 2001).

It is worth noting that in the last three films that Polanski directed the problem of sexual violence is not present. Interestingly, this has also been the period when Polanski's tragic loss of his wife and his notorious behaviour lost its appeal to journalists and was almost forgotten. My present students, even those who know Polanski's earlier films, regard him almost exclusively as 'the man who escaped death during the

Holocaust' – which is obviously the result of making *The Pianist* and the publicity surrounding this film, which links the story of Władysław Szpilman to Polanski's own past. This shift not only in its emphasis, but in the very content of Polanski's 'biography' as known to the general public, excellently confirms the opinion that the relation between the life and autobiography is symmetrical. The artist's autobiography is shaped by his actual life, but his life (or what is generally regarded as his life) is also shaped by his autobiography.

The second discourse that encourages us to consider Polanski's films as autobiographical refers to national culture and travel. As was established earlier, Polanski was a Jew born in Paris who spent his formative years in Poland. After that he lived in several different countries, including Britain, Italy, the USA and, longest of all, France. His decision to leave Poland for good after completing *Knife in the Water* was not political (as one might assume), or at least its political dimension was not very significant. It rather reflected Polanski's restless personality and his outlook on life. In the interviews he gave we can find such pronouncements as 'I am glad that I am a nomad... I have always regarded that significance given by people to borders as ridiculous' (Polański 1980: 15) or 'When I was young and studied at the Łódź Film School, I had only one thought in my head: to leave. I had never imagined my future in Poland. I always wanted to leave for the world, to get to know other countries, meet new people. I always assumed that the Earth belongs to me as much as to other people' (Ibid.: 58).

The nomadic character of Polanski's life and, accompanying it, shifts of identity are excellently reflected in the changes of his name. He was born as Raymond Polanski, because his father had discarded his own original name, Liebling. In Poland his surname was written Polański, with softened 'n' as in Spanish 'ñ'. For most of the Nazi occupation he was known as Roman Wilk (Wolf), a suitable name for the little Catholic he would become when hidden by Polish families (see Leaming 1981: 2). Following his first successes as a filmmaker and his emigration to the West, virtually everywhere except Poland he became known as Roman Polanski – the Polish 'ń' in his surname changed into the much easier to spell and pronounce 'n'.

Polanski's films reflect his Jewishness and Polishness, as well as testifying to his nomadic character and lifestyle. For example, *The Fat and the Lean* is the reworking of a Jewish story in which a rabbi advises a man suffering from overcrowding to get a goat, and later to get rid of it when his life becomes intolerable. *Dance of the Vampires* is set in a village populated by Jews and alludes to various Jewish customs and idiosyncrasies. Eventually, *The Pianist*, regarded as the most autobiographic of Polanski's films, features a Polish Jew and Holocaust survivor, Władysław Szpilman, as the main character. There are also references to Polish culture in Polanski's films. In particular, the memories of the main character of *When Angels Fall*, an old woman who works as an attendant in a men's room, narrated in flashbacks, are full of events and figures very familiar to Poles. Among them we can list the figure of a girl looking through a window at passing soldiers or the mother parting with the son who goes to war. Together they allude to the dominant view of Polish history as being heroic and doomed.

Yet, what is more striking than the presence of citations from Jewish and Polish history and culture is their relative scarcity and the way of conveying them which is rather different to that of the 'accented cinema' of such exilic or diasporic directors as Andrei Tarkovsky, Atom Egoyan or even Polanski's compatriot, Krzysztof Kieslowski (see Naficy 2001). These references are more than balanced by allusions to cultures and histories of other nations. Moreover, Polanski's representations of Polishness and Jewishness are always mediated by earlier representations, such as the paintings of Marc Chagall in *Dance of the Vampires* and the art of Artur Grottger and Jacek Malczewski in *When Angels Fall*. It feels as if Polanski has no personal experience or memory of the respective traditions, but in order to depict them he must rely on someone else's testimonies. Furthermore, in his films the director reveals no yearning for his Jewish or Polish past or cultural roots. On the contrary, he underscores the lack of personal involvement in these cultures by using very stylised acting and mise-en-scène which often produces a comical effect. For example, Alfie Bass's Chagal in *Dance of the Vampires*, with his 'goatie' beard, long kapota, exaggerated gestures and poor hygiene (he disapproves of his daughter's frequent baths), looks and behaves like an archetypal Jew or even a caricature of a Jew from Eastern European folklore (which was largely anti-Semitic). In *When Angels Fall* Polanski himself plays a Polish icon of femininity: a Polish Mother who gives away her son to fight and die for his country. The fact that a man appropriates this role can be regarded as an insult to Polish tradition. On some occasions Polanski even makes the point that Polish or Jewish culture, as indeed any other culture, is just one among many traditions competing for the place in modern, cosmopolitan or global consumer world. Take an episode in *A River of Diamonds* in which the Dutch suitor of a young French woman invites her to an Indian restaurant where they are served over ten dishes and he asks her if she was ever served more meals; she answers 'yes', but adds that she cannot remember whether it was in a Chinese or Jewish restaurant.

Such a nonchalant, unsentimental or even critical attitude to cultures that we can regard as Polanski's own betrays his experience as somebody who has travelled widely and who in his work and life has taken advantage of appropriating elements of various traditions. At the same time, it could be argued that this attitude testifies to the director's Polish and Jewish roots, or at least to his closeness to some strands of these cultures, as embodied by such figures as Franz Kafka, Susan Sontag, Witold Gombrowicz[2] and Andrzej Munk. Susan Sontag argues that Jews (or at least the most outstanding and innovative representatives of this ethnic group) tend not to identify themselves with any community, be it religious or national. They are individualists, whose spiritual motherland is a moral cause or an intellectual value, and not a piece of land or the community where they grew up (see Sontag 1983a: 88). Sontag herself was an excellent example of this attitude: an American Jew, accused of utter lack of loyalty and hatred of both America and Israel because she was critical of the aggressive, anti-Arab ideologies and policies of the governments of these two countries.

In their analysis of the work and life of Franz Kafka, Gilles Deleuze and Félix Guattari ascribe to him a similar attitude as that which Sontag identified as particularly Jewish. They represent Kafka's protagonists, particularly the hero of the autobiographical 'Letter to the Father', as someone who suffers from 'an exaggerated Oedipus [complex]'. He dreams of escaping his father and everything the father stands for: his culture and history, Jews, Czechs and Germans; by entering a completely different level of existence, for example through becoming an animal (see Deleuze and Guattari 2000: 9–15).

Isaac Deutscher (1907–1967), the Jewish Marxist writer, was born and educated in Poland, and emigrated to Great Britain in 1939. He coins the term 'the non-Jewish Jew', describing him as somebody who transcends Jewry and Jewishness to live on the edge of various religions and national and cultural traditions. He mentions, among others, Heine, 'torn between Christianity and Jewry, and between France and Germany', Marx whose 'thought was shaped by German philosophy, French socialism and English political economy', and Freud whose 'mind matured in Vienna in estrangement from Jewry and in opposition to the Catholic clericalism of the Habsburg capital' (Deutscher 1968: 29–30). Paradoxically, Polanski's 'non-Jewishness', marked by the scarcity of references to and a distance from Jewish culture, can be regarded as a sign of his Jewishness, as defined by Sontag and Deutscher. It is also worth noting here that the only Jewish character who is placed in the central position of the narrative and treated with the utmost sympathy by the director, Władysław

Szpilman, fits well the paradigm of the 'non-Jewish Jew'. Although he is loyal towards his Jewish community, he does not identify very strongly with the traditions of his ancestors. In particular, he is not a religious Jew; neither is he an ardent Polish patriot (despite having many Polish friends) as was, for example Korczak, both in reality and in the film *Korczak*, directed by Andrzej Wajda in 1990 (see Mazierska 2000). Szpilman's main spiritual homeland seems to be music – his love of music assures his survival, and in his behaviour he is guided primarily by his desire to stay alive and by basic human decency, not by patriotism. Furthermore, in *The Pianist* Polanski does not idealise Jews, instead showing that the population of the ghetto included the whole spectrum of moral attitudes. While some Jews showed courage and altruism even when facing their own death, others were prepared to betray their compatriots to Germans to repossess their property and increase their power within the community. Szpilman's whole story contains a condemnation of nationalism and works as a testimony to the solidarity of people transcending language, religion and national culture, and to the good people can do if they overcome their nationalistic prejudices.

Polanski's even less frequent references to Polish culture and his mocking attitude to national myths reveals a similar position on Polishness as to Jewishness. This attitude can be also found in the work of Witold Gombrowicz, the Polish absurdist writer who emigrated from Poland in 1939 and to whom Polanski is often linked. Their similarities will be discussed in greater detail in Chapter 2, but here it suffices to say that Gombrowicz was very critical of Polish literature and art as parochial and preoccupied with the community/nation rather than with an individual. For example, in his *Diaries*, in the spirit of ridiculing Polish nationalists who regard everything that is Polish as best, he quotes Galeazzo Ciano: 'Kraków. Monuments and palaces, which for them [Poles] appear as magnificent, for us, Italians, have little value' (Gombrowicz 1997: 11). In the same volume we also encounter such derogatory remarks as 'Good Polish literature, both contemporary and earlier, was not very useful for me and did not teach me very much – because it never had the courage to notice an individual human being' (Ibid.: 108). Gombrowicz not only points out that the standard of some of Poland's greatest achievements is somehow below that of some other nations, but notes that the Polishness of some of the greatest Poles, such as Copernicus and Chopin, is somehow problematic (Ibid.: 14). He is critical of any boastful approach to one's culture by saying that, paradoxically, it is not a sign of identification with one's culture, but an alienation from it. 'Nothing which one regards as one's own, should impress him. Therefore if we are impressed by our greatness or our history, it is proof that they are not in our blood' (Ibid.: 16). In common with Gombrowicz, Andrzej Munk in his films, particularly *Eroica* (1957) and *Zezowate szczęście* (*Bad Luck*, 1959), is very derogatory about Polish patriotism and the tendency to focus on society/nation/community and overlook the individual. He perceives it as damaging to individuals (of whom, after all, the nation consists) and irrational. In short, like Gombrowicz, Munk advocates individualism.

As far as individualism (understood as an alternative to patriotism) is concerned, there is little disparity between Polanski's stance on- and off-screen. In his interviews we find such confessions as: 'What is patriotism? Let's imagine a German patriot in the period of Hitler's rule' or 'Bertrand Russell accurately wrote that if a human being overvalues his or her own children, family, street, town, country, they also overestimate themselves' (Polański 1980: 15). Although the reasons for rejecting patriotism provided by Russell appear opposite to Gombrowicz (for the English philosopher a patriot is a conceited and arrogant man; for Gombrowicz he suffers an inferiority complex), both authors point out that patriotism is a somehow deformed outlook on the human place in the world.

If the references to Polish and Jewish cultures are relatively infrequent in Polanski's films, so are his allusions to other places and national

Nikola Todorov in *Teethful Smile* (1957)

traditions, and the lack of knowledge of them rarely prevents understanding their narratives and deeper messages. This is also an important reason why Polanski's films 'travel' so well, as opposed to those of many other Polish filmmakers, including Andrzej Wajda and Andrzej Munk (see Chapter 7). Moreover, his films are often made from the perspective of a person who found himself in a particular country or city and adopted it only temporarily, if at all – as would be suggested by the choice of protagonists who are 'not from here' (immigrants, tourists, people on business trips, pensioners who settled far from their original homes).

While the motif of violence reflects Polanski's personal history, the theme of national culture and travel conveys his specific relation to the countries and communities in which his roots lie and which he encountered in his nomadic life, the discourse on voyeurism can be used to decipher Polanski's attitude to the profession he chose: that of director and actor, and his taste as a viewer. Among his favourite films he lists such classics on this theme as Michael Powell's *Peeping Tom* (1960) and Alfred Hitchcock's *Rear Window* (1954) (see Polański 1980: 14–15). The topic of snooping was introduced into Polanski's cinema almost as early as the motif of violence: in the short *Teethful Smile*, made when he was a student at Łódź Film School. Spying is also one of the most enduring narrative and visual motifs in his films, particularly important in such films as *Chinatown*, *Dance of the Vampires*, *Bitter Moon*, *What?*, *Tess* and *The Tenant*. Unlike Powell or Hitchcock, who link voyeurism with mental illness, Polanski perceives it as a universal trait. Among his voyeurs we find men and women, sadists and masochists, oppressors and victims, even animals. More often than not, gazing, observing, snooping does not signify power, but powerlessness. Take, for instance, the horrified Szpilman family in *The Pianist* who from behind the window curtains see an invalid being thrown out of the opposite window by a group of German policemen. Moreover, peeping is often a reciprocal activity – the object of voyeuristic gazing tends to return the gaze. It seems as if nobody is immune either from the temptation of snooping or from the danger of being looked at; the world is a gigantic panopticon. Another specificity of Polanski's attitude to voyeurism is his idea that persistent looking or spying does not guarantee any privileged contact with reality. On the contrary, Polanski's most ardent voyeurs make fundamental mistakes and are punished. The clearest example is Jake 'J.J.' Gittes in *Chinatown*, who despite relentless watching, often through binoculars, as well as using assistants who spy on his behalf, is unable to reach a valid conclusion about any of the issues he investigates. By recognising the universality of the *libido videndi* and demonstrating that seeing or even seeing perfectly does not afford the voyeur any epistemological privileges, in a postmodern fashion Polanski scorns his own profession and himself as a filmmaker.

Polanski likes to depict subjective visions – his camera is often identified with the eye of the protagonist. This is the case in *Repulsion*, *The Tenant* and *Chinatown*. Such a device is conducive to achieving an autobiographical effect. However, as already noted, the director often shows that his protagonist's view of the world is wrong. Thus we experience a distance between the main character's vision and that of the filmmaker, which hinders any identification of the two and weakens the autobiographical effect. Similarly, when voice-over narration is used, as in *Macbeth* or *Bitter Moon*, what is said makes us aware that the narrators do not have authorial authority. For example, Oscar's pompous and kitschy style of describing his relation with Mimi makes us aware that Polanski treats this figure with a fair amount of contempt, mixed with pity. Thus Oscar cannot be his true alter ego, but more likely a repository for the vices attributed to the director by the media.

The autobiographical effect can by facilitated or strengthened by casting choices. I have already mentioned that Polanski often appears

Roman Polanski and Shelley Winters in *The Tenant* (1976)

in his films and suggested that his presence encourages the viewer to seek autobiographical traces in them. However, I will argue that the autobiographical motifs are not concentrated in the characters he plays, but distributed among many characters. For example, although Polanski plays Trelkovsky in *The Tenant*, we can also see the 'real' Polanski in the child who at the end of the film wears Trelkovsky's mask. In particular, this abused child, regarded as monstrous by his neighbours, brings to mind Polanski's dire situation during the war. In *Chinatown* Gittes might be regarded as being closer to Polanski's alter ego than the 'midget' in a white suit Polanski himself plays in the film. Moreover, in some films, especially *What?*, Polanski is so provocative in underlining the resemblance between his character and certain features ascribed to him by the media, such as arrogance and huge appetite for sex, that it is difficult not to regard his method as a means of disguise rather than self-revelation. Finally, in neither of these films does he name his characters after himself, nor refer directly to the episodes from his life (if he alludes to them, they are represented as events in somebody else's life). Similarly, he never shoots in his own house, or represents places which can be identified as his own. Despite his films' interest in voyeurism, they do not feature filmmakers.

On the whole, Polanski's autobiographical discourse comes across as much more subdued and indirect than that of such arguably autobiographical filmmakers as Woody Allen, François Truffaut, Jean-Luc Godard or Nanni Moretti. The difference between Polanski on the one hand and the directors on the other lies in their whole approach to filmmaking. While Allen, Truffaut, Moretti and Godard consciously decide to make films about themselves or about similar people, and in this way say something about the wider world, Polanski's starting point appears to be the external world, as testified by the large proportion of his films which are literary adaptations. Only through reworking stories and characters that Polanski has found in someone else's novels, plays or scripts, or which he himself has invented, does he somehow 'return to himself'. Thus autobiography, rather than being a raw material of Polanski's films, is their final product or by-product. Or, more exactly, this was the case until *The Pianist*. From the perspective of autobiography this film differs on two accounts from earlier films that Polanski directed. Firstly, it combines the various autobiographical motifs that were previously dispersed among a number of Polanski's films. Its protagonist is a Polish Jew, the victim of racial hatred and a Holocaust survivor. He is also an artist and a voyeur (although more due to his isolation than a desire to spy on people), as well as a nomad, looking for a place to live in a hostile world. As a result of these features, all pertaining to Polanski's history and character, the autobiographical effect of this film is stronger than in any other film he has made.

Secondly, off-screen the director openly admitted and even exploited the similarities between Władysław Szpilman's life and his own history. In the process of adaptation certain episodes and aspects of Szpilman's memoirs were changed in order to reflect Polanski's circumstances during the war rather than the pianist's. I will discuss them and their functions in greater detail in Chapter 6. Here I limit myself to suggesting that producing autobiographical effect in this case was Polanski's goal – Szpilman's book was only a means to achieve it.

Some autobiographies, apart from being portraits of unique and highly unusual individuals (their authors), can also be seen as biographies of larger groups of people. I regard these autobiographies as the most successful. A paradigm of such autobiography is for many readers, including myself, *Remembrance of Things Past* by Marcel Proust. This book, despite concentrating on Proust's life and showing the world from his perspective, provides an excellent panorama of French society, an insight into the lives of people in love (both hetero- and homosexual), and a portrayal of many other groups and types of people.

Similarly, if Polanski's oeuvre is autobiographical, it is equally relevant to the experience of many other people. Following Michael Eaton's (2000) (rather marginal) remark in his book about *Chinatown*, which was chosen as a motto for this chapter, I will suggest that Polanski's films and his life (as lived or as popularised by the media) reflect the most important events and cultural changes which took place in the twentieth century. Among them we can list the Second World War and the Holocaust; a shift from stable and settled to nomadic as the dominant lifestyle, and, consequently, a loss of stable identity; also Western sexual liberation and the backlash towards its achievements[3], and the dominance of the visual media over other types of communication. Equally, Polanski's unsentimental take on these events, characteristic of both his films and his off-screen pronouncements (most importantly, his autobiography, *Roman*); can be regarded as paradigmatic to the moral stance of people who lived through a large part of the twentieth century. Perhaps this is also the single most important reason why the public remains fascinated by Polanski's life and his films. In them we see ourselves and the world as it changes in front of our eyes.

2

THE ABSURD AND HOW TO DEAL WITH IT: NARRATIVES AND CHARACTERS IN POLANSKI'S FILMS

Anyone is capable of anything at the given time in history.

Roman Polanski

Polanski's cinema is known for the versatility of its characters and narratives, which is quite an unusual feature of the work of an *auteur*. His characters belong to different nationalities, epochs, classes, occupations, in short, to different cultures – reflecting real and metaphorical journeys undertaken by the director. Similarly varied are the problems they encounter and conflicts in which they are involved. They might suffer because of unfulfilled love, desire for power or intolerant neighbours. Some struggle against particular individuals, others against the system; some are tormented by an inner conflict. Some characters are defeated in the end, others are triumphant; in other cases the overall outcome of their action is ambiguous. At the same time something unifies the characters: they keep at a distance or at least prevent viewers from experiencing any immediate and pleasant character identifications. Identification, if it happens at all, is a source of discomfort, even shame for the viewer.

The purpose of this chapter is to capture the main characteristics of Polanski's narratives and characters and to outline how they changed over the almost half-century that his career spans. Narratives and characters will be treated together, to enable examination of their relationship, namely whether Polanski's characters are the products of particular circumstances (a narrative), or are autonomous agents who shape their world and their story. I will conduct my examination using two categories often evoked in the context of Polanski's cinema, but rarely used systematically. One such category is that of the 'absurd' (see Butler 1970; Liehm and Liehm 1980; Wexman 1987); the second puts forward a dichotomy between tragedy and melodrama. My argument is that Polanski tends to represent the world as absurd, but the type of absurdity he depicts changes and his characters react to it in a variety of ways. Their reactions oscillate between tragic and melodramatic, or, to put it differently, they internalise or externalise the conflict that they encounter. As the terms 'absurd', 'tragedy', 'drama', 'melodrama' are by no means uniformly used, I will begin by clarifying their meanings and discussing the main ideas of some authors who might have influenced Polanski's oeuvre.

THE ABSURD AND ITS PROPONENTS

Every existing thing is born without reason, prolongs itself out of weakness and dies by chance.

Jean-Paul Sartre

'Absurd', a word of Latin origin (*absurdus*), literally means 'dissonant', 'senseless', 'out of harmony'. Out of harmony with what? One is tempted to ask. In its broadest sense, it is out of harmony with everything that constitutes the norm in a certain field: in music, in art, as well as in society and the human soul. In common usage, 'absurd' simply means 'ridiculous' (Esslin 1968: 23). However, when the term is applied to philosophy, literature and to drama in particular, its connotations are more restricted – they concern the human situation. Albert Camus in his essay *Le Mythe de Sisyphe* (*The Myth of Sisyphus*, 1955) regards human life as purposeless and lacking in harmony with its surroundings, and claims that realisation of this predicament produces a state of metaphysical anguish (see Camus 1955; Esslin 1968: 23–4; Hinchliffe 1969: 1).

The movement most strongly associated with the idea of absurdity of human life is the Theatre of the Absurd, represented by such authors as Samuel Beckett, Eugene Ionesco, Arthur Adamov and Harold Pinter, but its literary predecessors include surrealists, Antonin Artaud, Franz Kafka, Lewis Carroll and even William Shakespeare – all of them names very relevant to Polanski's cinema as sources of inspiration or even in providing material adapted for the screen. The philosophical roots of the Theatre of the Absurd lie in existentialist philosophy. Existentialism, in very general terms, is a philosophic doctrine or intellectual movement proclaiming that people have absolute freedom of choice and that the universe is absurd. In the writings of the leaders of this movement, such as Jean-Paul Sartre and Camus, we find themes such as loneliness, the impossibility of communicating with fellow human beings, the absence of God, the strangeness of ordinary objects, the inevitability of death and, consequently, hopelessness and despair. Camus claims that 'at any street corner the feeling of absurdity can strike any man in the face' (Camus 1955: 16), but it was also pointed out that modern man is more prone to absurdity than his ancestors. Theatre of the Absurd and existential philosophy thus constituted the thinkers' and artists' response to modernity, and especially to the horrors of the Second World War (see Esslin 1968: 23).

Absurdist literature also had a strong presence in Poland. Martin Esslin observes that when Samuel Beckett's *Waiting for Godot* was first performed in Poland at the time of the political thaw of 1956, 'the audience there immediately understood it as a portrayal of the frustration of life in a society which habitually explains away the hardships of the present by emphasising that one day the millennium of plenty is bound to come' (Ibid.: 307). More importantly, in Poland in the 1950s and 1960s a number of talented dramatists, such as Sławomir Mrożek and Tadeusz Różewicz, turned to this type of play to articulate their interests and ideas. Again, critics regarded their absurdism as a kind of heightened realism, reflecting life in Poland under communism. In the same vein, Polanski's films made before his emigration to the West, particularly *Knife in the Water*, were interpreted as parables of postwar Poland (see Liehm and Liehm 1980: 782; Alvarez 1965: 22).

I would like to invoke Mrożek's play *Na pełnym morzu* (*Out at Sea*, 1961) as a possible inspiration for Polanski. Depicting three shipwrecked men on a raft, who are faced with the prospect that one of them will be eaten by the others, the play deals with one of the favourite themes of Polanski: that of the victimisation of one person by another. Moreover, its setting and choice of characters bear similarities to Polanski's 'boat films', especially *Knife in the Water* and *Pirates*. The latter begins in a very similar way to *Out at Sea*: two men, one old, one young, are drifting on a raft and the old one tries to eat the young one – until they see a large ship on the horizon. Polanski's link with Różewicz is primarily his interest in the cruelty to be found in everyday, seemingly normal, even decent life, and in people's indifference to horrendous acts committed by others. In both cases critics seek to explain this interest on account of the artists' experience of the horrors of the war. Różewicz's brother, to whom he dedicated *Nasz starszy brat* (*Our Elder Brother*), a collection of stories published in various volumes since the 1950s, was murdered by the Gestapo.

The idea of the absurdity of human existence also pervades the work of Witold Gombrowicz. Both artists, Gombrowicz and Polanski, call attention to social circumstances, as opposed to individual morality, as the main mechanism of human behaviour. Consequently, they attribute to them the main responsibility for the absurdity of human life, as well as the ability to overcome it. For the director of *The Pianist* anyone is capable of anything at a given time in history. The opportunity creates the murderer, the thief, as well as the victim and the hero. In a similar fashion Gombrowicz criticises the work of a fellow absurdist, *L'Homme révolté* by Camus, by stating:

> For me conscience, individual human conscience, does not have the power which it has for [Camus] to save the world. Do we not see at every step that conscience is almost helpless? Does the man kill or torture because he came to the conclusion that he has the right to do so? He kills because others kill. He tortures because others torture... And from that we can derive that it is not in the conscience of an individual that the mechanism of human actions lie, but in the relation between the individual and others. (Gombrowicz 1997: 70)

Esslin argues that, in order to be regarded an 'absurdist writer', it is not enough to depict the human condition as absurd. Equally important is to represent it according to the 'logic of the absurd', which defies ordinary logic. The use of unconventional form, consisting of fragmented narrative, incoherent dialogue and underdeveloped or enigmatic characters, is in Esslin's opinion the main difference between the absurdists on the one hand and the existentialist philosophers and novelists on the other. Absurdist art is also expected to awaken a certain reaction or mood in the audience: distance, alienation, even a desire to laugh (see Esslin 1968: 24–8).

The absurdist movement also shares common ground with romantic art, especially the Polish version of romanticism (which is regarded as a dominant paradigm of Polish culture, including postwar cinema), as both types of art are concerned with people whose situation is dire, even hopeless. However, while absurdist work is meant to distance the audience, romantic art evokes compassion and solidarity. It could be argued that Polish absurdism is a backlash to the saturation of Polish art with romanticism. This view is conveyed in many of Gombrowicz's works, including *Ferdydurke* (1937) and *Dziennik* (*Diary*, 1953–66), where he mocks the Polish desire to 'romanticise' or 'dramatise' life. Similarly, Polanski's films made in Poland can be regarded as a reaction to the excessive romanticism of Polish culture.

The majority of Polanski's films can be classified as absurdist on account of their content and the emotion evoked in the spectator. Their primary concern is the lack of harmony in human life and the consequences of this situation: fear, cruelty, humiliation, sadness, passivity, distaste, madness. It suffices to look at the titles of some of his films, such as *Repulsion* and *Cul-de-Sac*, and compare them with the titles of the leading exemplars of absurd drama: *Waiting for Godot, Endgame, Theatre of Cruelty, The Endless Humiliation, Nausea* and *Deathwatch*. Moreover, Polanski is described as a 'cold' director, who treats his characters with detachment or even malice, like a clinician examining living specimens on a board or a small boy slowly pulling off insects' wings (see Jackiewicz 1977: 144; Stachówna 1995: 143). The typical reaction of a viewer is therefore laughter mixed with embarrassment (see Chapter 7). Furthermore, some aspects of his narratives, such as the similarity between the beginnings and the endings, the sparse use of dialogue, and frequent use of dreams and nightmares are very much in accordance with the absurdist form. At the same time it must be stressed that Polanski, despite being influenced by the works of such authors as Beckett, Pinter and Gombrowicz, never wholeheartedly committed himself to their aesthetics, most probably because he regards film as a much more realistic medium than theatre.

While Polanski reveals an absurdist sensibility in the majority of his films, the causes of the lack of harmony and the circumstances that allow his characters to realise the ultimate absurdity of their lives vary. Three main types of absurd in his films can be identified. The first occurs where there is a conflict between two or three people that cannot be resolved in a satisfactory way. This conflict can be seen as the cause of an absurd situation or as a catalyst allowing the character to realise that his life lacks harmony. The second category, which I call 'inner discord', refers to the characters who appear to be in conflict with themselves. In the most serious cases they are schizophrenics. The third category encompasses the situation in which a protagonist who is healthy in mind cannot reconcile even his most basic interests and rights with the world in which he finds himself. In this case the entire world is absurd.

These categories coincide with the chronology of Polanski's cinema. The first type of absurd prevailed in the early part of his career, marked by films such as *Knife in the Water* and *Cul-de-Sac*; the second type dominates its middle part, renowned for *Rosemary's Baby* and *The Tenant*; the third is typical of Polanski's recent films: *Death and the Maiden, The Pianist* and *Oliver Twist*.

This categorisation can be mapped onto the division of characters into tragic and melodramatic, as proposed by Robert Bechtold Heilman in his book *Tragedy and Melodrama: Versions of Experience*. Heilman maintains that

> the identifying mark of the tragic character is dividedness: he is caught between different imperatives each of which has its own validity, or that he is split between forces or motives or values ... In melodrama, on the other hand, character is viewed as essentially undivided ... the complicating elements are eliminated or made ineffectual; there is an impression of unity of being and singleness of direction. (Heilman 1968: 89)

Heilman describes drama as 'polypathic', as it arouses a multitude of contrasting feelings, while melodrama is 'monopathic' – the emotion it awakens is strong and points in one direction. Not surprisingly, tragedy and melodrama are used for different purposes: the first serves to depict timeless conflicts; the second is topical to a particular period of history (Ibid.: 92–101). From the perspective of the representation of characters we can delineate a particular trajectory in Polanski's films which moves from depicting inner to outer absurdity, and from a proliferation of tragic to melodramatic characters. However, the boundaries between the categories of drama and melodrama and between the characters and situations Polanski depicts are blurred. As Heilman notes, there are virtually no pure dramas and melodramas (Ibid.: 95). The genius of Polanski largely lies in allowing the viewer to decide whether he or she is watching drama masked as melodrama or a melodrama that appears to be a drama.

THE CONFLICT OF STRANGERS

In a number of films Polanski shows characters that are in discord with each other. While this lack of harmony might be grudgingly tolerated in stable circumstances, it usually leads to a conflict with serious consequences when the delicate balance is broken by an intruder, or even by the passage of time (which is regarded by existentialists as a destructive force). The first of Polanski's films in which this scenario is explored is a short feature, *Mammals*, in which two men with one sledge change places several times, using increasingly sophisticated methods to gain the position of mastery, until a third man snatches the sledge. Realising that they have lost their precious possession, the men make up with each other, but soon return to their earlier tricks until a new conflict erupts.[1]

The title of the film invites us to treat the three individuals not as characters in their own right, but as representatives of a larger category:

that of mammals. Polanski suggests, reminding us of Darwin and the many attempts to transplant his theory into social sciences, that fighting and seeking power is embedded in the nature of human beings. Men cooperate with each other only as a means to survive in a hostile environment, in this case in a harsh climate, and when an enemy threatens or weakens them. Yet, even then, they find it very difficult to sustain equality and harmony among themselves. Individual behaviour, as Gombrowicz suggested, depends principally on one's position in relation to other individuals, rather than on one's conscience. The end of the film, which mirrors its beginning, suggests that conflict is eternal; the actors in the game of life might change, but the game remains the same. History has a cyclical nature – the end of one cycle is the beginning of another, similar cycle. However, as will be demonstrated later, the existence of a cycle does not preclude change.

The emphasis on conflict, as well as on force and deception as a means to gain the upper hand, can be regarded as a very bleak diagnosis of the human condition, resembling Beckett's *Waiting for Godot* (1952) and *Endgame* (1957). However, not all is bleak in *Mammals*, as the film's main premise is the social character of humans. Happy or not, people cannot

Henryk Kluba and Michał Żołnierkiewicz in *Mammals* (1962)

live without interacting with fellow beings. The need to communicate and be accepted forces them to mitigate their selfish and cruel instincts. Polanski even draws attention to pity and compassion and hence solidarity as a driver for our actions. His characters might only pretend that they are blind or crippled, but they do that in the knowledge that a partner will not allow them to work hard while in pain. In other words, they might abuse certain values, especially the requirement to help a person who is suffering, but they are well aware of their existence. *Mammals* is shot in black and white, contains no dialogue and its action is artificially speeded up, which makes it look like a silent burlesque comedy. Not surprisingly, it was compared to the films of Laurel and Hardy. Such a technique renders an intolerable and tragic situation humorous, and distances the viewer, producing an effect intended in absurdist art.

The situation when a third person (or a couple) interrupts the interaction of two people also provides a structure for several later films by Polanski, such as *Knife in the Water*, *Cul-de-Sac* and *Bitter Moon*. All these films place at the centre of the narrative a married couple whose very physical appearance invites suspicion of the presence of discord. In each case the wife is much younger and physically more attractive than the husband, who either looks plain like Andrzej in *Knife in the Water*, is bald, short and clumsy like George in *Cul-de-Sac*, or is crippled like Oscar in *Bitter Moon*. Moreover, their lives are full of games and rituals that suggest the married couples to be lacking in emotion – a feature that they share with characters in the absurdist dramas. It seems that in order to communicate something to their partners they cannot say it directly, but must use a highly coded language. In *Knife in the Water* Krystyna plays in the water with an inflated crocodile, which acts as a substitute for her husband and perhaps as a surrogate of the child they do not have. In this way she acknowledges his impotence and redundancy. In *Cul-de-Sac* we see Teresa putting the make-up on George's face and dressing him in her nightdress, thus attesting to his lack of masculinity. He, on the other hand, asks Teresa whether the meagre number of shrimps is everything that she's caught during her expedition to the sea – which can be interpreted as an allusion to her unfaithfulness, which he has no courage to discuss openly. In *Bitter Moon* the game between man and woman is most elaborate and overtly sexual, with the characters putting on special masks and dresses and using sadomasochistic instruments, such as whips and dog collars.

Polanski makes it clear to the viewer that there is little chance that the marriages he depicts can be rescued from inside, so to speak. Not surprisingly, two of the three couples, in which the husband is most unhappy with the situation, Andrzej in *Knife in the Water* and Oscar in *Bitter Moon*, invite a stranger or a couple to assist. Such a device was frequently used in earlier films, most commonly in *film noir*, for example in *The Postman Always Rings Twice* (1946) by Tay Garnett. It was also employed in *The Comfort of Strangers* (1991), directed by Paul Schrader and based on Ian McEwan's novella, which was adapted for the screen by one of the main proponents of the absurd in drama, Harold Pinter. In most cases, the invitation to join a couple forebodes something dramatic, most likely the murder of the host or the guest. Polanski, however, frustrates these expectations. There are deaths in *Bitter Moon*: Oscar kills Mimi and commits suicide, but these deaths appear to have little to do with Nigel or Fiona. Thus, while in most films the role of the strangers is to disrupt the initial equilibrium of the couple's life so dramatically that it cannot be restored, Polanski uses them to demonstrate the difficulty of change. This is perhaps because, unlike in *film noir* and *The Comfort of Strangers*, where the emphasis is on the distance between the hosts and the guests (as implied by the use of the word 'strangers' in the title of Schrader's film), Polanski's guests are similar to their hosts. This phenomenon exemplifies a wider rule concerning Polanski's narratives and characters – the director tends to universalise the situation that he represents, not unlike a biologist examining an individual exemplar to learn about the whole species. Most importantly in this case, the guests, and male guests especially, also lead ritualistic lives. For example, rituals and gadgets connected with sailing, which Andrzej proudly shows off, are balanced by customs and objects associated with the guest's student life (hitchhiking, the flick knife, the jeans, the small rucksack). Each man emphasises the importance of his possessions, using them more than is necessary and in this way teasing his adversary. It almost feels as if the men do not communicate with fellow human beings, but with objects. Not surprisingly, among Polish reviews of *Knife in the Water* we find such titles as 'Sztuczne serca' ('Artificial Hearts') (see Michałek 1962) and 'Statek kabotynów' ('The Ship of Posers') (see Bryll 1962). The artificiality of the characters' behaviour and the use of gadgets to facilitate their communication, regarded as a typical feature of modern life, precludes solving conflicts, and instead obscures and dislocates them.

Some critics suggest that Polanski's males who enter contests with other males are their alter egos or the personification of a hidden or suppressed part of their psyche (see Lawton 1981).[2] The student is thus the double of Andrzej, and Nigel is the double of Oscar. There is, no doubt, a strong similarity between the psychological constitutions of these characters, underlined by visual means, such as their tendency to occupy the same spaces. Nigel at one point even sits in Oscar's wheelchair. In such an interpretation the conflicts observed on screen, for example between Andrzej and Krystyna and Andrzej and the student, are only a substitute or metaphor for an inner conflict, which has to do with male lack of security, recognition and real power. Thus, what looks like a melodrama might in fact be a drama.

However, only Polanski's males in these films need to find their double or counterpart. His women appear to be more wholesome and unified. Consider Krystyna, who does not fit any of the worlds that are inhabited by her male companions. She is the ultimate outsider, superficially fitting in everywhere, but in reality belonging only to herself. Much younger than her husband, but older than the student, she knows about sailing and student life, but is neither a true sailor nor a student. Accordingly, she cannot be impressed by any of the paraphernalia they sport.

Unlike the two men, Krystyna talks little and never says anything that might reveal her social background or her interests, preferring to observe the men. With her glasses in the shape of batwings she enjoys enhanced sight and even the aura of an intellectual (see Eberhardt 1982: 115), while at the same time concealing her true identity. This position perfectly equips her for the role of arbiter in the conflict between the men. She takes advantage of this position by treating both her husband and the student with a mild contempt and making them aware of their shortcomings; she manages to seduce the student and keep her husband, thus demonstrating that she has power over both of them, although she never tried to gain the upper hand. In her dignified, cool detachment and, ultimately, wisdom Krystyna can be regarded as a superior character than the two men with whom she shares the yacht and, temporarily, her life. Nevertheless, her return to her cuckold husband, expecting that they carry on as before, perpetuating their disharmonious existence, puts a question mark over her emotional sincerity. The question arises as to why she ended up in this position. Polanski refuses to give a clear answer, leaving it to the viewer to guess her motives. One can deduce that the position of women in socialist Poland does not allow them to live independently, but forces them to rely on men. Following such a reading we can view her as a woman who attempts to preserve some dignity and independence in a patriarchal society. Treated with less sympathy, she might be regarded as a lazy consumer who is sucked in by the pleasures of the Polish nouveaux riches. Either way, we can regard her as a forerunner to some heroines of Polanski's later films, especially Teresa in *Cul-de-Sac*.

Knife in the Water finishes in a similar way to that in which it begins. The car stops on the open road and Krystyna and Andrzej discuss what to do next. This circular narrative underscores the cyclical character of human existence. Something, however, did change in the situation of the central couple, as after their meeting with the young man they will find it more difficult to play at being a happy couple. They might be able to continue deceiving strangers, but not each other. The narrative of *Bitter Moon* also unfolds as a recurrence of cycles: Oscar living without Mimi, then with her, then without her, and so on. Again, the rhythm of separations and reunions is reflected by a more linear story that leads to the ultimate exhaustion and collapse of their relationship.

The narrative of *Cul-de-Sac* is based on a similar premise to that of *Knife in the Water*. An outsider approaches a rich couple in a remote location. Richard imposes his company on George and Teresa, rather than being invited. Although this encounter leads to a re-evaluation of the couple's relationship, as well as testing their physical, emotional and intellectual strength, it takes place in circumstances that are more difficult for the husband than those in *Knife in the Water*. Unlike the macho Andrzej, who competed with the student on a territory that was the perfect setting to show off his strongest points, George, being an ineffectual, middle-aged man with questionable virility, does not have the slightest desire to compete with anybody. He wants to be left alone, knowing that only at

Zygmunt Malanowicz, Jolanta Umecka and Leon Niemczyk in *Knife in the Water* (1962)

a distance from the 'madding crowd' does he have any chance of keeping his wife for himself. In an early scene we see Teresa lying half-naked with a slim, young man with fair hair, obviously her lover, while George is showing to the young man's parents the charms of Lindisfarne. This juxtaposition of George's and Teresa's pastimes demonstrates that George's recognition of his position within the family is correct, but also that he overestimates his ability to keep his wife close to him. The fact that he associates with the older generation emphasises the age gap between him and Teresa. George is further impaired by the fact that in Lindisfarne he is an outsider himself. He is from a different part of the country and did not inherit his castle, but bought it. Being American, Richard is also an outsider, but he has learned to use this position to his advantage. As an American gangster, he is not expected to have good manners (something which is required of the English 'thieving class' in film), and the unexpectedness of his visit gives him the upper hand in any dealings with George and Teresa, as he catches them completely unprepared for such an encounter.

In common with Krystyna, Teresa is more of an outsider than either of her two male companions. Being French, she does not even share the same language as George and Richard, and does not belong to the refined culture represented by her husband, who chose the remote location as their home partly to enjoy the ancient treasures of their castle. Her difference from George is also suggested by her physical strength and fondness for strong alcohol, in contrast with her husband's abstinence due to having ulcers. At the same time she despises Richard at least as much as she does George and uses every opportunity to annoy and humiliate him. One gets the impression that she disdains everybody, even her own lover. In the same vein, she shows little respect for material possessions, which is surprising in the light of her previous poverty, from which George apparently saved her. Everything appears to her as temporary and lacking in deeper meaning. She acts on impulse, pursuing fun and pleasure, as there will be no tomorrow. For this reason she is less distressed by the gangster's visit than her husband. It could be argued that Teresa has accepted the ultimate absurdity of life, while her husband yearns to overcome it by possessing something permanent: house, family, love. Her lack of concern for other human beings and even herself gives her a certain strength, resilience and clarity of vision, which her two male companions lack. This also assures her ultimate survival. While at the end of the film Richard dies and George is left devastated and yearning for his former wife, Teresa leaves the Holy Island with a handsome man whom she hardly knows.

As in *Knife in the Water*, the end of *Cul-de-Sac* is similar to its beginning. On both occasions we see a car, first approaching, then leaving the castle. This image suggests the repetitiveness, transience and absurdity of human life. Yet, as in *Knife in the Water*, in *Cul-de-Sac* there is no theme without a variation. Between the arrival of one car and departure of another, the roles of the characters change. The person who was earlier the guest, Richard, becomes a permanent resident of the island, so to speak; with his dead body lying next to George's car. Teresa, on the other hand, who was earlier the host, changes into a guest, leaving the castle with a stranger, most likely forever. The type of absurdity they experienced has also changed, at least as far as George is concerned. At the beginning he was in some discord with his wife, later he is in conflict with both her and Richard, and in the end he suffers a mental breakdown and his personality disintegrates, which is signified by his talking to himself. Accordingly, George's trajectory and the road taken by the film lead from melodrama to tragedy. The final stage of George's story is marked by 'inner discord' – which is also a central topic of several of Polanski's later films, including *Repulsion*, *The Tenant* and *Rosemary's Baby*.

The emphasis on rituals as the main principle organising human behaviour, as well as the circular narrative, link Polanski's films discussed above, especially *Mammals, Knife in the Water* and *Cul-de-Sac*, to the cinema of Andrzej Munk, most importantly his *Eroica* and *Bad Luck* (on which Polanski worked as an assistant director). Munk's characters, in common with Polanski's, also try to fit into a certain cultural pattern: each attempts to behave like a proper scout, soldier, patriot or hero, but fails dismally. Moreover, each cycle of adjustment to some cultural norm leads to another cycle. Likewise, cycles for Munk do not preclude dramatic changes; his most famous character, Jan Piszczyk in *Bad Luck*, eventually refuses to play any roles and is happy to be sent to prison where he can at last be himself, even if this means being nobody.

However, there is also an important difference between Munk and Polanski in their approach to rituals and cycles. The former concentrates on national rituals and cycles specific to Polish history; they are consequently the main causes of the absurdity in the lives of his characters. For Polanski the absurd is more common, even universal: it transcends social classes and national borders. Krystyna, Andrzej and the student in *Knife in the Water* might be English, French or Italian and still give the impression of a lack of fulfilment and harmony in their lives. Moreover, as already noted, conflict or discord can be regarded as private, the external contest being only a symptom of what takes place in the human soul. These features protect Polanski's films from ageing and from being seen as 'Polish'. An additional reason for these films maintaining their interest over time is their emotional tone. By presenting characters who are not particularly sympathetic, Polanski distances the viewer from them. One reviewer wrote that there is 'an almost frosty absence of compassion' in *Knife in the Water* (Dyer 1962–3: 23). That may be true, but it does not mean that this film and the others discussed here do not elicit an emotional response in the viewer. Rather, emotional involvement is postponed because the heart is reached through the brain, so to speak, which in Susan Sontag's opinion is the feature of great reflective art in the mode of Bertolt Brecht and Robert Bresson (see Sontag 1994a: 177) or Antonioni (see Dyer 1962–3: 23). Moreover, to use Heilman's term, these films are 'polypathic'. They encourage ambivalent or contrasting responses, rather than a clear-cut judgement. This quality has assured or at least assisted their longevity: they linger in the viewer's mind, encouraging repeated viewings.

INNER DISCORD

The second category of Polanski's absurdist characters consists of those whose personality is irreconcilably and unhealthily divided – the schizophrenics. It is worth mentioning here that, according to Heilman, schizophrenia is the pathological extreme of 'the tragic condition' (see Heilman 1968: 90). Schizophrenics appear in a number of Polanski's films, including *Rosemary's Baby*, *Dance of the Vampires* and *Macbeth*, but my focus here will be on *Repulsion* and *The Tenant*. A schizophrenic remains at a distance from his own perceptions and thoughts, to the point of failing to recognise himself, his physical body, as belonging to him. Similarly, he tends to misrepresent people and objects – taking them for what they are not, ascribing to them non-existent qualities or failing to notice them, which leads to behaviour that from a normal perspective is strange, irrational and often morally unacceptable (see Kępiński 1974: 104; Sass 1997: 210).

Polanski used the scenario of inner discord for the first time in *Repulsion*, in which a young manicurist named Carol Ledoux gradually loses connection with outside reality. The choice of a manicurist is not accidental: a person whose job is to look after somebody else's hands can be seen as particularly prone to mix subject with object (see Maurin 1980: 24). The first clear sign of Carol's mental illness is when she injures the hand of an elderly client. When her sister goes on holiday with her lover, Carol locks herself inside her flat, hallucinates that she is being raped and then kills two men who manage to enter the flat despite her barricading it. In the end, she is found by her sister, lying under the bed in a kind of catatonia, unable to realise what is going on around her.

This short description indicates that *Repulsion* is a pure drama – the conflicts Carol experiences are all in her head. In a sense, this is indeed the case. However, Polanski also suggests that Carol's pathology might result from some external factors. Firstly, as a Belgian immigrant in London Carol feels alienated. She cannot communicate well with the English because she does not fully understand their language or culture. Moreover, she is at the mercy of the landlord, who, as Peter von Bagh observes, 'after doing his sums, arrives at the conclusion that as a house owner he has the right to rape the girl' (von Bagh 1965: 27). Konrad Eberhardt suggests that the condition of immigrant and the banality and ugliness of the world which surrounds her are at least as important factors in her state as her mental constitution. Besides, these two factors are connected: as an immigrant, Carol is condemned to a poorly paid, low-status job and standardised rented accommodation where there is little scope to arrange things according to one's taste (see Eberhardt 1967: 4). To support his assessment of the aetiology of the heroine, Eberhardt draws attention to the fact that she is not the only character in Polanski's narrative who

Catherine Deneuve in *Repulsion* (1965)

feels repulsion towards the surrounding reality, again conforming to the rule that Polanski tends to universalise his character's condition, instead of concentrating on its uniqueness. The other person disgusted with his surroundings is Colin, who has fallen in love with Carol. His reaction to the sexist prattle of his pub pals is similar to that of Carol's: he attacks them with his bare fists and then wipes in disgust his mouth, which one of the men kissed (Ibid.: 4). Both Carol and Colin also have profound problems communicating with others. Charles Barr goes so far as to claim that nobody in this film is able to transmit his or her thoughts effectively: 'The film builds up a terrifying picture of a world where no one, in a crisis, can get outside himself and help, or be helped by, another' (Barr 1965: 26).

It is widely accepted that inability to communicate mostly affects people living in the modern environment, and London in the 1960s was widely regarded as the centre of modern life. This was recognised in the series of films labelled 'Swinging London films', such as *Georgy Girl* (1966), directed by Silvio Narizzano. Ironically, *Repulsion* is sometimes regarded as belonging to this paradigm, although it is difficult to find a film whose mood contrasts more with the careless feeling conveyed by the term 'Swinging London'. Here it is worth quoting Polanski, who said that he could not make *Repulsion* in Poland or, if he were to shoot this film in his country, he would not choose Warsaw where there are few mental pathologies and loneliness is relatively easy to bear. Instead, he would choose the coal-mining region of Silesia, where the conditions of work are difficult (a high proportion of migrant workers living far from their families) and mental breakdown and pathologies are more common (Maurin 1980: 23).

Carol's family and childhood environment are other possible causes of her pathological condition. Polanski hints at this possibility by repeatedly directing the camera to a picture showing a young blonde girl, most likely Carol, surrounded by her family, looking concerned at a man sitting in front of her. Herbert Eagle and Gordana Crnković suggest that he might be a relative or a family friend who raped her when she was a child and who is ultimately responsible for her later illness (see Eagle 1994: 123–4; Crnković 2004). Although this interpretation contradicts Polanski's own explanation of using the photograph as an indication that there was always something impenetrable and sinister in Carol's personality (see Polanski 1984: 182), it is perfectly plausible. If we accept either of these interpretations, then Carol's drama becomes in fact an internalised melodrama.

The causes of schizophrenia are largely unknown. Some scholars situate them in the physical constitution of a patient, such as neurobiological abnormalities; others blame the social and psychological circumstances of the schizophrenic, particularly his family situation (see Jackson 1960). In the opinion of Louis A. Sass, the relatively high number of cases of schizophrenia in the modern industrialised West suggests that modernity (and late modernity in particular) is very conducive to this condition. Sass quotes, among others, the sociologist Anthony Giddens, who stresses the dynamic, rapidly transforming quality of modern institutions and practices, as well as a concomitant disembedding of these institutions and practices from their grounding in custom and tradition (see Sass 1997: 219). It is easy to imagine, according to Sass, 'how transformations such as these might foster schizophrenic forms of pathology – by encouraging social withdrawal and negativism, emotional flatness, intense self-consciousness,…sense of inner division, and feelings of derealisation and ontological insecurity' (Ibid.: 220). It is worth noticing that the link between schizophrenia and modern life, as observed by Sass, parallels the connection between absurdity and modernity, as seen by Camus and several other authors close to existentialism and the art of the absurd.

Repulsion is often compared to Hitchcock's *Psycho* and undoubtedly there are similarities in the way that the respective directors construct their characters. Both directors construe schizophrenics as people who have serious problems with their sexuality and draw attention to the family as a site where mental illness is born. Yet behind these similarities important differences lie. Hitchcock depicts Bates as a man with a deranged mind who kills innocent people. The most sympathetic feeling Bates can get from the audience is pity. In *Psycho* (1960), society constitutes medical and moral norms that are violated by people like Bates. Once he is captured, the moral equilibrium is reinstated and the viewer experiences a sense of relief. *Psycho* provides the viewer with a sense of security that *Repulsion* does not offer. Moreover, the reason that Bates is a dangerous schizophrenic lies solely in his unhealthy relation with his mother, or perhaps with himself – he might have used his mother as an excuse to kill women who attracted him (see Modleski 1988: 15).

By contrast, Polanski depicts Carol with sympathy, as a defenceless, naive and innocent victim. With her blonde, yet modest hair and long fringe, which almost hides her eyes, and in white dresses, she can be regarded as an epitome of moral purity, an angel, or even a Madonna. At the same time, with the exception of the man who falls in love with her and is killed, her victims come across as unpleasant figures. The landlord, who invites Carol to pay her rent with sexual services, is truly obnoxious. Killing him seems an act of self-defence on her part, as well as punishment for sexual harassment. Similarly, her sister's lover, whom

Carol deeply despises, has some serious moral flaws, betraying his wife and treating Carol's sister in a rough way. Moreover, he comes across as a simpleton. Even the lady in the beauty salon, whom Carol injures when doing her nails, is an unsympathetic figure: gossipy, patronising, and in her judgements driven by clichés. People recognise Carol's innocence, subtlety and complexity, so different from the social norm, and become intrigued and charmed by her. Moreover, Polanski uses cinematic devices to facilitate the viewer's identification with Carol, such as frequent close-ups and point-of-view shots thanks to which we see the world her way. By contrast, Bates is typically looked at from a distance. We only see him in action and never find out about the reasoning behind his behaviour. Thus how his mind works remains an enigma.

The main character in *The Tenant*, a Polish immigrant settled in Paris called Trelkovsky, also gradually sinks into schizophrenia. His own identity disintegrates and he appropriates the personality of a woman who lived in his apartment before him, Simone Choule. Like Carol in *Repulsion*, the sicker Trelkovsky gets, the more violent he becomes. He attacks a child playing in the park and tries to strangle a woman who accidentally injured him when he threw himself under her car. However, as with Carol, his violence is represented as an act of self-defence; he attacks people because he is convinced that they are attacking him or would do if he did not assault them first.

Trelkovsky's shy character plays a large part in his own demise, as symbolised by his name which includes the Polish word *trel*, French *trelle* and German *Triller*, all referring to the sound uttered by birds and signifying gentleness, therefore vulnerability to being destroyed (see Balcerzan 1995: 127–8). Yet, to an even greater extent than in *Repulsion* the director draws attention to the social context of the emergence of schizophrenia. A crucial factor is the behaviour of Trelkovsky's landlord Monsieur Zy (and his neighbours), who impose on him a strict code of conduct that forces him to live a solitary life. Trelkovsky is asked not to invite any guests and to detach himself from the only person in the apartment block who has shown him sympathy and solidarity and who is, like him, an immigrant. The bigotry of the wider population of Paris is conveyed by the recurrent motif of enquiries about the origin of Trelkovsky's name. Although nobody tells him directly that being foreign reduces him to the position of a second-class citizen, on each occasion he feels compelled to defend his right to live in France. Thus, he is doubly punished for being foreign: firstly, by being separated from his family and personal past and for being divorced from his indigenous traditions; secondly, by being ghettoised and persecuted for his foreignness.

Trelkovsky can also be regarded as the victim of the French class system. Being a clerk and not having a place of his own, particularly as he is in a situation where, as Monsieur Zy puts it, 'it is difficult to find a good apartment', makes him almost helpless in his relations with capitalists like his landlord.

Both Carol and Trelkovsky are introverts with few friends, but they are not complete loners. They go to work where they share space with fellow workers. Carol lives with her sister; Trelkovsky visits his acquaintances and has an affair with Simone Choule's friend, Stella. It can even be argued that their shyness and modesty attract some people to them. Nevertheless, even those who are closest to them and care about them fail the most to realise the gravity of their problems. This failure to notice their cry for help is a perfect illustration of the existentialist and absurdist idea that people are always lonely: impenetrable, unable to communicate or share their problems with fellow human beings. Polanski himself admitted that an important theme in his film is 'the lack of awareness of those who live with the mentally disturbed' (Polanski 1984: 182). This, Polanski maintained, 'is because familiarity blunted their perception of the abnormal' (Ibid.: 182), and it is accompanied by another principle: those who care about the schizophrenics become their main victims. This rule applies to Colin whom Carol kills in an act of misguided self-defence and to Stella, whose apartment Trelkovsky robs and destroys, being convinced that she is conspiring with his neighbours to force him to take his own life. In the fates of Colin and Stella lies one of the main sources of pessimism in Polanski's films: love and friendship are futile, if those who love and care are punished for their good intentions.

The most recent film of Polanski in which we see people who go mad is *The Pianist*. This time, however, they are not at the centre of the narrative, but provide the background to the actions of the sane character, Władysław Szpilman. We can list here an older, eccentric looking lady, who walks the streets of the ghetto asking everybody if her husband has been seen, the man who eats food from the pavement, the musician who boldly approaches a German policeman for a cigarette, and a young mother who suffocates her child. All these people sank into mental illness as a result of the war and all the calamities it brought with it: hunger, loss of personal space, extreme inequality, lack of security, fear, loss of dignity, death of close relatives and friends, and institutionalised objectification. In such situations madness is a form of escape from reality; it is a way to find inner harmony in a world which has become extremely discordant. However, the hope for harmony is not fulfilled. The mentally ill in *The Pianist* come across as unhappier than those who have remained rational.

We can also assume that all of them went on to die in the ghetto or perish in the gas chambers while Szpilman, who managed to preserve his sanity, survived.

I want to argue here that schizophrenia, as depicted by Polanski, is a person's reaction to extreme alienation and to an assault on his freedom or, to use Heilman's terminology, a tragic reaction to a melodramatic situation. Someone who is unable to lead his life in the way he wants to, starts to 'hide himself' in a different, imaginary person and invent narratives which allows him to lead a parallel life. However, becoming schizophrenic does not bring a new cohesion to the lives of Polanski's characters, but fragments them even further and eventually leads them either to literal death, as in the case of Trelkovsky, or to states similar to death: catatonia or animal-like behaviour. Polanski also shows that the weaker people are – economically, physically, emotionally – the more their selves are prone to fragmentation and displacement, and the easier it is to limit their freedom and further diminish their sense of identity. Accordingly, he comes close to Gombrowicz, who emphasised the relationship between the individual and other people (as opposed to individual conscience) as the driver of that individual's actions and the

Roman Polanski and Isabelle Adjani in *The Tenant* (1976)

determinant of their wellbeing. Polanski also approaches Sartre's notion of absurdity according to which everybody is in danger of leading an absurd life, but it is not what they choose to do. Those who suffer inner discord are those whom society has failed. At the same time, the circular narration Polanski uses points to the difficulty of changing society and individuals in such a way as to avoid suffering 'inner discord'. The absurd might not be inevitable and eternal, but it is omnipresent and infectious.

ALONE IN AN ALIEN WORLD

Between the man who makes himself understood and the one who doesn't there is an abysmal difference: the first saves himself.

Primo Levi

The final category discussed in this chapter comprises films in which a perfectly mentally healthy individual finds himself in a world conforming to rules that seem unacceptable both to him and to the viewer. The structure of these films is melodramatic; a man is pitted against a force outside of himself: a hostile group, historical events such as wars, or an unfortunate coincidence. In this category I would list *When Angels Fall*, *Two Men and a Wardrobe What?*, *Frantic*, *Pirates*, *Death and the Maiden*, *The Pianist* and *Oliver Twist*. Before discussing some of these films it is worth mentioning Camus's assertion that the mind's deepest desire is to understand and familiarise the world; the inability to fulfil this wish is an important source of the absurd, and consequently of pain (see Camus 1955: 21). Such pain is at the centre of the majority of these films.

In *Two Men and a Wardrobe* the two men emerge from the sea, carrying a wardrobe on their shoulders. Such an origin, bearing associations with the birth of Venus, sets them apart from the world they enter. Moreover, as Herbert Eagle observes, their appearance accentuates their difference. They could be taken for a gay couple or Jews (see Eagle 1994: 100).[3] The narrative consists of the pair's encounters with a hostile environment, including meeting a group of young thugs. Eventually they return to the sea, taking the wardrobe with them, pointing to the impossibility of reconciliation between them and the 'normal' human world.

The scenario offered in *Two Men and a Wardrobe*, was largely repeated in *What?* – a film that is treated as one of the lighter pieces in Polanski's portfolio, although in my opinion it conveys some serious meanings.

An outsider like the two men with the wardrobe, Nancy, a young, naive and gentle American, is different to the others in Noblart's house, and everybody acknowledges this by challenging her right to stay there. Her new Italian 'friends' constantly ask her to do something to please them, but when she does so, a new task, typically of a pornographic nature, is imposed on her or it turns out that the old request is no longer valid. It seems as if she is forced to play a certain game, but the rules of the game continually change so that she cannot win. Neither does she understand what is going on. Her childlike observations, recorded in her diary (which is eventually stolen by the people staying in the villa), demonstrate that she is alien to this environment, not unlike Alice in Wonderland, to whom Nancy is compared by some critics (see Elley 1974: 45; Wexman 1987: 37). In the cruellest episode of the film Alex, the man who appears to be her closest friend, puts on a *carabinieri* uniform, chains her up and beats her. It is difficult for Nancy and the viewer to establish whether Alex's behaviour is part of a game or whether he is punishing her for being an intruder. The distinction is insignificant, as Polanski's heroine comes across as frightened and tormented by the experience. In the end she escapes Noblart's house after unwittingly causing his death.

What is significant is that at the end of the film Nancy not only leaves Noblart's house, but, not unlike the two men with the wardrobe, moves to a different ontological order. This transition is indicated by her pronouncement to Alex that she must leave, otherwise the shooting of the film entitled *What?*, in which all of them play, will never be finished. Nancy's abandoning cinematic fiction and entering into authentic reality (or perhaps only a different fiction), similar to the two men's return to the sea, demonstrates the impossibility of a successful escape. After all, in real life people have no opportunity to move to a different planet or to the other side of the mirror. The utopian finale of *What?* and *Two Men and a Wardrobe* can be compared to the ending of *Korczak* by Andrzej Wajda, in which the Jewish orphaned children taken to Auschwitz abandon the train and escape into an idyllic countryside. In all of these cases the fantasy of escape points to the ultimate inescapableness of the situation.

Although Nancy's condition is not dissimilar to the two men in Polanski's short film, the surroundings are different. The industrial waste, overcrowded trams and poorly clad people shown in *Two Men and a Wardrobe* point to the drabness, disorder and lack of prospects characteristic of postwar Poland and the Soviet bloc. In *What?*, the large collection of modern art decorating Noblart's house, the sounds of people playing table tennis, and the ridiculously large hats worn by otherwise naked women epitomise the decadent West. That the inhabitants of both worlds prove selfish, indifferent or cruel can be regarded as a sign that most of the world 'went absurd' and that little hope remains there for gentle creatures. However, the director tries to play down the relevance of his narratives to a particular time and place. Consequently, they can be interpreted both as political metaphors and as representations of archetypal situations.

By contrast, *Frantic, Death and the Maiden, The Pianist* and *Oliver Twist* heavily gravitate towards the topical and time-bound. Moreover, they are realistic films in the sense that their protagonists do not have any imaginary or fantastic routes out of their oppression, but must look for a solution in 'this' world. The causes of their oppression, such as patriarchy, fascism, racism, terrorism and the incompetence or malice of authorities, will be discussed in greater detail in Chapter 5. Here I am more interested in the protagonists' reaction to them. In each case the main character acts very single-mindedly and is oriented towards his future. He might regard the present world as cruel, but hopes that the future will bring something better. This hope helps Paulina (in *Death and the Maiden*) to survive torture and humiliation, Walker (in *Frantic*) to find his wife, Władysław Szpilman to survive the war and Oliver Twist to escape the workhouse and endure

Henryk Kluba and Jakub Goldberg in *Two Men and a Wardrobe* (1958)

the tough world of the criminal underground of nineteenth-century London. They owe their success principally to two factors: their refusal to accept the world as inevitably absurd, and their willingness and ability to 'read' the world correctly and communicate effectively. All of them during the time of their oppression think about their future: Walker about finding his wife and reuniting her with their children, Szpilman about being able to play the piano, Paulina about facing her oppressor and Oliver simply about survival. They quickly learn how to operate in the world into which they have been thrown. In the case of Walker this means giving up on ineffective institutions, looking for clues and using the help of the right people. Władysław's method of survival, which at the beginning is more an intuitive way of behaving than a conscious strategy, is to remain in the background in order to avoid direct contact with the oppressors and to act swiftly, rather than thinking too much about what he has left behind. In his encounter with Wilm Hosenfeld he uses music as a form of communication. It is worth noting that the prime victims in *The Pianist* are those who find themselves at the front and who ask the Germans questions, rather than trying to find the answers by observing their behaviour.

There is a paradox that in *Death and the Maiden*, *The Pianist* and *Oliver Twist* the world is most harsh and cruel, but the characters prove very successful in overcoming problems and finding meaning in their lives. Needless to say, few things awaken greater happiness than winning when the chance of victory is very slim. The optimism of *Death and the Maiden* and *The Pianist* results not only from the personal victories achieved by the protagonists, but also from the recognition that the whole world changed in their lifetimes: after the period when cruelty and absurdity ruled, come more just and gentle times. The new political regime, as shown in *Death and the Maiden*, is not perfect, principally because the old perpetrators walk free, yet the difference between the two orders remains stark and Polanski is keen to point it out. The two films, as did many before them, recognise that absurdity is like a cloud which always hangs over individuals and whole societies, but they focus on the ways to overcome it.

While the challenge for an author of drama is to convey the complexity of the character, in melodrama the emphasis is on depicting the character's external circumstances. According to this rule, the characters in Polanski's melodramas, especially *Death and the Maiden* and *The Pianist*, appear less developed than in his dramas. Detractors of *The Pianist* have even accused the director of constructing Szpilman as nothing more than a man who plays the piano and tries to avoid death (see Sobolewski 2002).

However, Polanski's portrait of Szpilman is not 'reduced' in the sense of neglecting certain important traits of Władysław's psyche, but rather it is a full portrait of a 'reduced man' who stopped thinking about fellow sufferers and yearning for his loved ones, and whose only emotion became a desire to survive. Several authors who have written about the Holocaust, such as Tadeusz Borowski and Primo Levi, have pointed out that the 'reduced man' was the product of the extreme circumstances of the ghetto or the concentration camp, where people were utterly objectified and deprived of their basic rights (see Levi 1988; Borowski 1992). Levi even suggests that this reductionism was an important 'medium-term' objective of Nazism, as it helped the perpetrators to quell any qualms of conscience they might have. Once they reduced their enemies to an animal-like existence and state of mind, they stopped being worried about slaughtering them (see Levi 1988: 101).

As mentioned already, the longevity of Polanski's early films, such as *Knife in the Water* and *Cul-de-Sac*, lies largely in their deploying the structure of drama, which is surprising in the light of the fact that they appear to promise much melodramatic action. The appeal of his films about schizophrenics, on the other hand, lies in their ambiguity: they can be viewed as both dramas and melodramas. The same ambiguity can be found in *Tess* and *Chinatown* (which I shall tackle in greater detail in the

Harrison Ford and Emmanuelle Seigner in *Frantic* (1988)

following chapters). In contrast to all these films, *Frantic, Death and the Maiden, The Pianist* and *Oliver Twist* are melodramas *tout court*, where the viewer can achieve, to use Heilman's term, 'monopathic' satisfaction. The question arises as to whether Polanski's 'real melodramas' will fare as well over the passage of time as his earlier films have done. In most cases we can already provide a negative answer: *Frantic* and *Death and the Maiden* have not achieved recognition to match that of *Knife in the Water, Cul-de-Sac, Chinatown* or *Rosemary's Baby*, although their melodramatic structure is not the only reason that they are placed on a 'lower shelf' of Polanski's films. As for *Oliver Twist*, Polanski somehow downgraded himself by claiming that it is a film for kids, including his own children (see Kemp 2005: 80), hence a film which by definition offers a simplified outlook on life. The one film on which the jury is still out is *The Pianist*. The numerous awards that this film received, including an Academy Award for its director, indicates that it is highly regarded, but its critics claim that this points more to respect for the theme and its author than the way he handles the topic. At this stage I refrain from assessing whether Polanski has approached the Holocaust in a 'right' way as this problem will be discussed in due course (see Chapter 6); but will accede that if *The Pianist* becomes a classic, it will not happen because Polanski managed to universalise a topical issue by discovering in it patterns of reality that give it life beyond its own day (which according to Heilman is the main means of increasing the lifespan of a melodrama), but because of the universal and prolonged interest in certain subjects. The Holocaust is one of them, one of the few historical events that has not lost and might never lose its topicality.

The experience of the absurd has been at the centre of Polanski's cinema throughout his career. However, different kinds of absurdity have dominated narratives of his films at different periods of his career. The artistic route taken by Polanski is approximately a route from drama to melodrama. Some critics regard it as a downward path, as drama is usually held in greater respect than melodrama, but others treat it as a sign of the director's growing willingness and competence to engage with serious issues. For me, what matters more is Polanski's ability to use both forms, often in one film, testifying to his unrelenting curiosity in the motives for and consequences of human behaviour and respect for the complexity of human nature. Both these traits of Polanski's attitude to the represented reality pertain to his position as a cultural traveller. He does not take his circumstances and opinions for granted, but approaches the world with an open mind, assuming that people are more varied than one can imagine.

3

LANDSCAPES AND INNER SCENERIES: RECURRING VISUAL MOTIFS OF POLANSKI'S FILMS

For as far back as I can remember, the line between fantasy and reality has been hopelessly blurred.

Roman Polanski

Few directors have received as much praise for their ability to create and organise the visual dimension of their films as Polanski. He is regarded as a master of the visual, a metteur en scène in the original sense of the word: somebody who is in control of every aspect of the frame and in whose films the image tells the story. The importance Polanski attaches to the mise-en-scène can be explained by two tendencies in his films. The first is his tendency towards the approach of a cultural historian or ethnographer, somebody who tries to reconstruct with the utmost care the physical appearance and the meaning of historic buildings, interior design, clothes, vehicles or old machinery. This is best summarised by Polanski himself, who said in a conversation with David Brandes: 'If you make a film about vampires, it still has to happen somewhere. The worst films or books or plays are those which happen nowhere' (Brandes 1997: 227). The greatest compliment (although it is not devoid of sarcasm) that the director has achieved as an 'ethnographer' is that *Tess* looks very much like a documentary about nineteenth-century dairy farming (see Polanski 1984: 381). Polanski also inclines towards the psychologist or psychoanalyst who believes that in order to learn of a person's most secret thoughts we should consider what surrounds him and how he perceives and uses the objects that he has at his disposal. Accordingly, in the films Polanski directs, the camera angles, the costume, the setting, the props, often tell us more about the characters than do their actions and dialogue.

In this chapter I will examine these two tendencies, which can be roughly equated with the realistic and the psychological, by looking at some recurring motifs of Polanski's mise-en-scène: the fragmented human body, the house, the city and the sea, exploring their narrative and symbolic functions. First, however, I will consider the influence of surrealism, especially the work of René Magritte, on Polanski's cinema.

THE DOUBLE LIFE OF PEOPLE AND OBJECTS AND THE INFLUENCE OF RENÉ MAGRITTE

The mind loves the unknown.

René Magritte

I was developing as an artist being fascinated by surrealism.

Roman Polanski

In *Repulsion* Carol's colleague from work, Bridget, tries to amuse her by describing a film she watched the previous evening: *The Gold Rush* (1925) by Charlie Chaplin. She mentions the funniest scene in the film; in it a hungry Charlie is eating his shoe, imagining that the laces are spaghetti and he is mistaken for a chicken by another starving gold seeker. Bridget even walks like a chicken, making Carol laugh. This scene is symptomatic of Polanski's inclination for quoting other filmmakers in his own films, in the style commonly associated with the creators of the French New Wave, such as Jean-Luc Godard and François Truffaut. More importantly, however, it alludes to the double, or in some cases, multiple lives that material objects have in his own films; examples are houses which are like labyrinths or coffins used as sleighs.

Different critics focus on different reasons for the double life of things in Polanski's films. Some argue that the root of it is ontological. Polanski's universe – and the human world in particular – is full of doppelgangers or doublings, resembling a hall of mirrors, where every person is a reflection of another person, who is similar but not identical, as a mirror both reflects and distorts the rendered object (see Chapter 2). Gordana Crnković, on the other hand, regards an epistemological factor as the main cause of the double life in Polanski's films: the main character's 'double vision'. The main character sees 'normally', as well as having access to the perceptions unavailable to other characters. This statement refers especially to Polanski's victims: Carol in *Repulsion*, Trelkovsky in *The Tenant*, Evelyn Mulwray in *Chinatown* (see Crnković 2004). Although I agree that many of Polanski's victims see something that other characters are unable to notice, I will refrain from claiming that they have double vision. Many see things only their own way, in dreams and hallucinations which they mistake for objective reality. Nevertheless, it is true that Polanski frequently shows objects, including people, from two unreconciled perspectives: one is that of the victimised or insane protagonist and one which appears 'objective' but for some reason comes across as flawed. The viewer must decide for himself which vision is true. Another factor causing the double vision and as a result, the apparent multiplication of objects, is the characters' use of instruments which affect their normal perceptions. One such instrument is spectacles. Polanski probably holds the world record among filmmakers for the high proportion of bespectacled protagonists populating his films. His characters do not wear glasses all the time (which would furnish their vision with consistency), but frequently take them off, lose them or have them destroyed. Polanski uses this narrative device to put a question mark over their perceptions and, consequently, their knowledge. Take, for example, scenes in *The Ninth Gate*, when Corso notices or fails to notice the Girl with Green Eyes according to whether or not he is wearing glasses. We can also list here such optical instruments as binoculars, magnifying glasses and field-glasses. They are meant to enhance vision and in a sense they do, but at the cost of overlooking something important, of getting a distorted image of the object observed. This concept is conveyed most persuasively in *Chinatown*, in which Gittes extensively uses binoculars, but in the end gets a completely false view of the events he investigates. Furthermore, perceptions and therefore the mode of life of objects in Polanski's films are strongly affected by the relation between the object and the subject: their distance from one another, the objects that stand between them and the angle from which they are observed. Often we see a character looking through a misty, dirty or inconveniently situated window, or peeping into a room from a distant corridor or through a keyhole. Thus he must content himself with a partial or obscured image. Even if he sees relatively clearly, he often does not hear what the people he observes are saying. As Philip Strick notes, Polanski specialises in the vision of an outsider, who tries to gain the knowledge of an insider (see Strick 2000: 46). This, however, leads to the proliferation of visions and objects, as every partial image encourages the character (and the viewer) to complete it in the way that assures the coherence of his entire outlook on things.

We can identify more factors leading to objects' multiple lives that are related to the two factors already mentioned. Polanski underlines the fact that the physical and cultural context plays a major role in what the object becomes or how it is perceived. For example, at night ordinary objects become more alive and frightening than in the daylight. Take the potatoes in *Repulsion*, which in the dark look like monsters: dragons with many heads, or the rabbit found by Bridget in Carol's handbag which makes Bridget cry in fear and disgust. Similarly, the dolls in the poorly lit workshop in *The Lamp* give the impression of being injured, and of abandoned babies. The whole archaic workshop looks like a dark parody of a Victorian hospital. To achieve the effect of life in inanimate objects Polanski frequently sets his entire films or their crucial scenes at night.

Furthermore, the director focuses on objects which are heavy with meaning by their very nature, or because they encourage symbolic reading. An example is the eponymous knife in *Knife in the Water*. Paul Coates observes that it 'suggests a variety of crimes or primal confrontations culminating in a Macbethian need to cleanse a blade steeped in blood... The knife can trump Andrzej's many gadgets because it is itself already a multiplicity of objects, something made explicit in the invention known as the Swiss Army knife, of which it is the poorer Polish cousin' (Coates 2004: 79).

Johnny Depp in *The Ninth Gate* (1999)

Polanski also uses visual irony by employing objects in a way that is atypical for them or even contrasts with their normal usage and destination; the miniature Statue of Liberty in *Frantic*, for example, entraps virtually everybody who touches it. Similarly the crown, which is normally a symbol of power, renders Macbeth and his wife virtually powerless: prisoners of their uncontrollable desires and puppets of fate. Furthermore, the director repeats certain images, gestures and movements, but each time furnishing them with a different meaning. One such image is that of the hands of Oscar and Mimi approaching from a distance and eventually touching. We see them first when they are on a merry-go-round. The gesture then testifies to their mad love and desire to be together. Later Oscar, incapacitated in hospital, turns his hand towards Mimi, hoping that she will lend him her helping hand. Mimi, however, mimicking the gesture from the merry-go-round, takes his hand only to push him out of bed, causing severe injuries.

On the whole, Polanski's films excellently illustrate contingency of meaning: a concept that originates in the work of Ferdinand de Saussure and has been developed by such writers as Roland Barthes, Julia Kristeva, Jacques Derrida and Umberto Eco. They all argue that the relationship between signified and signifier is not fixed, but instead arises out of the interaction of signs across the system. Signs live among other signs, texts among other texts; and they influence each other. The relation of system to sign is dynamic, as the culture that produces signs and is their 'home' is in a state of continuous flux. Hence arises the practice of intertextuality, understood as integrating a variety of foreign discourses within a text through such mechanisms as quotation, commentary, pastiche, parody, allusion, imitation or irony, all very relevant to Polanski's oeuvre.

The ideas of contingency of meaning and intertextuality pertain to modernist and, to an even larger extent, postmodern discourse. Some modernist writers, painters and filmmakers who are preoccupied with the idea of contingency of meaning are often listed as artistic predecessors of Polanski. Remaining in the area of visual arts, the names that crop up most often are Luis Buñuel, Alfred Hitchcock and René Magritte, all artists belonging to or having close links with surrealism. Buñuel is evoked in the context of Polanski's cinema principally due to his interest in the unconscious and his abandonment of the 'psychological integrity of character, calling into question the very nature of human integrity through repeated splittings and doublings of a once unitary self' (Williams 1981: 65). Polanski is likened to Hitchcock because he shares with Hitchcock his scepticism about human perceptions and tends to represent psychological and social realities as multi-layered. Martin Sutton claims that 'both men are concerned with undermining our preconceptions, opening up our dark anxieties, and manipulating us with sparsely-scripted, cinematic storytelling' (Sutton 1988: 25).

The affinity between Magritte and Polanski appears to me even greater than that between Polanski, Hitchcock and Buñuel, despite the difference in medium.[1] Not only are both artists interested in the 'logic of dream', but Polanski quotes Magritte directly in some of his films, such as *Mammals* and *The Tenant*, while his references to Buñuel and Hitchcock are more subdued. Therefore it is worth referring to the common traits of Polanski and the Belgian painter before looking in detail at the lives of material objects in Polanski's films. Magritte liked to paint the sea and the sky (which also play a major role in Polanski's films), as well as common objects, many of them constituting an iconography of a bourgeois milieu, such as the figure of a man in a dark coat, a bowler hat, a shoe, an apple, a house, a window, an umbrella. The same objects appear time after time in his paintings, like leitmotifs, but in each painting they look differently as a result of altering their scale and placing them in an unexpected setting. He makes what is giant, small and what is small, giant, as in *La légende des siècles* (*The Legend of Centuries*, 1950) and *La carte postale* (*The Postcard*, 1960). He brings the outside in and takes the inside out, as in *La fin des contemplations* (*An End to Contemplation*, 1927) and *Le musée du roi* (*The King's Museum*, 1966). This practice bears association with the way Polanski treats some objects that are identified with bourgeois lifestyle, particularly the wardrobe, which appears in surprising contexts and behaves in unexpected ways (which will later be discussed in detail). Magritte and Polanski can both be considered as 'critical insiders', as in their art they appear to struggle against bourgeois cultural hegemony (which in Polanski's case means mainly mainstream cinema), yet at the same time show a fascination with what they mock in their work.

Another similarity between Magritte and Polanski is their interest in doublings. Many of Magritte's paintings include two or more similar or identical elements, typically humans, such as *Les deux soeurs* (*The Two Sisters*, 1925), *Le double secret* (*The Secret Double*, 1927) or *An End to Contemplation*. Such a device creates an impression, which Polanski also conveys, of the world being the hall of mirrors in which everybody looks for his reflection or a double. At the same time, both Polanski and Magritte question the verisimilitude of the mirror reflection.

Within his *Word Paintings*, produced between 1927 and 1930, Magritte attached to common objects such as a shoe, an egg, a hammer or a pipe, a description which does not correspond to its usual meaning. In this way he draws attention to the arbitrary character of language and, accordingly, to the contingency of meaning. By attaching to objects words which are different to their normal names, Magritte also points to the possibility of multiple lives of an object, which is a theme Polanski explores effectively in such films as *Repulsion* and *The Tenant*.

Magritte was fascinated by the implications of things hidden in his paintings. He depersonalised the human subject by masking its individualising identifier – the face. Often he hid the subject's face from view, blocking it with a suspended object, a drape, an apple, a hand or a shawl, as in *Les amants* (*The Lovers*, 1928) and *La Grande Guerre* (*The Great War*, 1964), or showing a person from the back, as in *The Postcard*. In this way he drew attention to the fact that everything we see hides another thing and arouses our curiosity. The conviction that if there is no concealment, there is no mystery and no interest on the part of the viewer also summarises Polanski's attitude to filmmaking. In particular, the fear in his films is evoked not by the abundance of fearful objects, but by their scarcity or absence, or to use Pascal Bonitzer's words, horror in Polanski's films 'resides in the blind space' (Bonitzer 1981: 58). The same applies to love – the necessary condition of falling in love and sustaining this feeling is not knowing the loved person. This opinion is expressed by one of Polanski's characters, Oscar in *Bitter Moon* (whom many critics regard as Polanski's alter ego). At some point he compliments Fiona for possessing a subtle and mysterious type of beauty, a face which is full of promise. By contrast, Mimi's face holds no mystery for Oscar any more; their relationship is therefore exhausted and dead.

Mirroring David Hume's claim that our notion of causality and the solidity of objects is based on nothing more than habit, Magritte (in common with another famous surrealist Salvador Dalí) toys with the notion of an object's permanence. Many of his paintings show only part of the human body, with the head missing, such as in *Le chemin de Damas* (*The Road to Damascus*, 1966), or a birdcage replacing the torso and head of a man in *Le thérapeute* (*The Therapeutist*, 1937). Depriving human beings of their faces might also be regarded as Magritte's commentary on the anonymity of modern living and the little value society attaches to people as individuals (see Gablik 1970). The practice of representing the human body as discontinuous or an assemblage of human and non-human parts has its equivalent in Polanski's dismembering and fragmenting the human body, which will be discussed later on.

The last characteristic of Magritte's work which is of great significance to my discussion of Polanski, is his preoccupation with the act of looking, and also with the object as a product of a particular way of viewing it. Many of his pictures are populated with people looking and objects framed by windows, picture frames or theatre curtains, such as *Cinéma bleu* (*Blue Cinema*, 1925), *Hommage à Shakespeare* (*Homage to Shakespeare*, s.d.) and *Les nuages* (*Clouds*, s.d.), making us aware that what we see is not reality as such but the world filtered by somebody's gaze. Similarly, as already stated, Polanski's films are not about reality per se, but about human perceptions of reality. Magritte and Polanski can therefore be regarded not so much as surrealists, as subjectivists. However, in the last part of this chapter I will argue that with the passage of time Polanski seems to adopt a more realist style.

Surrealism is the dominant but not the only influence on the visual style of Polanski's work. Other sources of inspiration include Polish romanticism and symbolism, particularly in *When Angels Fall*, cubism in *Two Men and a Wardrobe*, expressionism in several films, including *Dance of the Vampires*, French impressionism and the work of the Pre-Raphaelites in *Tess*, Art Deco in *Chinatown* and the work of Marc Chagall in *Dance of the Vampires*. Yet, with the possible exception of the Pre-Raphaelites, these influences are limited to the sphere of iconography, rather than to Polanski's whole approach to filmmaking.

THE BODY

Films representing humans of course show their bodies, but a striking feature of Polanski's visual style is his focus on body parts. Many of his films bring to the fore a particular part of the body, such as eyes (*Repulsion*), mouth (*The Tenant, Tess*), legs (*Bitter Moon*), breasts (*Teethful Smile, What?* and *Dance of the Vampires*) and hands (*Death and the Maiden, The Pianist*). Accentuated body parts perform several functions in Polanski's cinema. Firstly, they point to the objectifying male look on a woman that, according to feminist critics, is patriarchal. As Laura Mulvey maintains, the female figure in film connotes her lack of penis, implying a threat of castration and hence displeasure. One way to avoid the castration anxiety is by turning the represented figure into a fetish so that it becomes reassuring rather than dangerous. This fetishistic scopophilia, as Mulvey notices, is typically achieved by close-ups of certain parts of the female body, such as the legs of Marlene Dietrich or the face of Greta Garbo (see Mulvey 1996: 117–19).

According to this scenario, Polanski's male protagonists in their perceptions dismember the female body: they see only breasts or legs, rather than the whole person. However, the director not only acknowledges and allows us to indulge in this activity, but also mocks it, and makes his men take responsibility for such a reductionist attitude to women. Thus in *Teethful Smile* a man looks through a window into the bathroom where a young woman washes herself. She covers her head with a towel so he can see only her breasts. He must, however, pretend that he is not looking when a man (presumably her husband) comes out to collect the milk on the doorstep. When the voyeur looks again through the window, instead of seeing female breasts, he is confronted with the teethful smile of her husband. For a heterosexual voyeuristic male this view can be displeasing on several accounts: firstly, obviously, because the spectacle is no longer that of a naked female body, but of a man, secondly, because the husband directs his own look towards the window, thus arousing shame in the peeping man.

Male fetishistic scopophilia is also mocked in *Dance of the Vampires*, where Alfred, a man on a mission to destroy vampires, is shown continuously looking into female décolletage and being so immersed in this that he becomes oblivious to the task of chasing vampires. His interest in female breasts and willingness to pursue this passion even at the risk of disrespecting a woman's privacy is punished when he spies on Sarah through a keyhole when she has a bath. Instead of enjoying the view of her breasts, he catches sight of a vampire, Count von Krolock, who, with the famous 'teethful smile', snatches Sarah from the bath. In common with the peeping tom in *Teethful Smile*, Alfred is a sheepish voyeur; contrary to the scenario presented by Mulvey, his gaze does not afford him any power over a woman. Instead, it changes him into her blind suitor, unable to think or act rationally. In addition, his preoccupation with the sexy body of Sarah transforms him into a vampire, as she herself now a vampire sucks his blood when kissing him.

Female body parts are also on display for male voyeurism in *What?*. The film calls to attention Nancy's bare breasts and legs. It also shows the naked breasts of other women, who walk topless in Noblart's house; although they are wearing large hats, this adds to the piquancy of their nakedness. This time, however, men have a much easier task than Alfred or the man in *Teethful Smile* because Nancy, whose clothes had either been destroyed in an attempted rape or stolen, struggles to find something to cover her body. Consequently, for a large part of the film she walks semi-naked to the enjoyment of men, hanging about in the villa. Even when she finds clothes, she provides a voyeuristic spectacle for Noblart, as he asks her to bare her breasts and her genitals for him, and she obliges, as if she was a well-behaved girl.

In *What?* Polanski also ridicules Hollywood's attitude to the female body. The voyeuristic men are mostly pathetic old perverts, who indulge in scopophilia as the only type of sexual activity available to them. It is worth mentioning here that the younger male characters are much less interested in Nancy's body than the older men. Moreover, male voyeurism is punished when bed-ridden Noblart dies of a heart attack, overwhelmed by the view of her sexual parts. Polanski is also mocking his own conformity to patriarchal mainstream cinema and his private fame as a 'woman-chaser' when Mosquito tells Nancy that he is not interested in her breasts, which he describes as an American obsession, adding that he prefers female bottoms.

The last film that is worth considering with regard to the male eye transforming the female body into fragmented parts is *Bitter Moon*. Oscar falls in love with Mimi without exchanging a word with her, only admiring her beautiful, mysterious and demure face; her eyes looking modestly down. He also touches her leg, when giving her his own bus ticket and in this way saving her from paying a fine. The face haunts Oscar so much that he spends long hours looking for it on the bus where he saw the beautiful stranger, but in the end it will be her feet in white tennis shoes that will allow him to identify her. However, while for Mimi Oscar remains a whole person body and soul, Oscar tends to see in Mimi only 'sexy bits'. It could be argued that this attitude runs in the male line of his family: his grandfather, whose money allowed Oscar to lead an idle life in Paris, made a fortune pioneering cosmetic surgery, selling implants to increase female sex appeal.

Mimi's legs, especially her feet, have the greatest appeal to her lover. During their first night together when they stay outdoors till the morning, Oscar tenderly massages Mimi's cold feet and later, at his flat, he asks her to dance for him. This request, in fact, is Oscar's reaction to Mimi's asking him to show her his writing, which establishes them as a marriage of intellect and body, reminiscent of such famous couples as Arthur Miller and Marilyn Monroe. Mimi is aware of his interest in her body and seeks Oscar's opinion about various aspects of her physique. Moreover, to please him, she tries to become even sexier by curling and bleaching her hair, wearing very tight dresses and putting on a lot of make-up. In this way, however, she becomes a figure of caricatured excess and her looks deteriorate (see Stachówna 1995: 144). Consequently, Oscar gets bored of her. He becomes particularly dismissive of her legs, mocking her ambition to be a dancer. And yet his reductionist attitude to Mimi is eventually severely punished when she visits him in hospital after he breaks his leg. She pushes him out of bed, causing injuries that paralyse him from the waist down. In this way she commits an act comparable to castration; paralysed Oscar is no longer able to have sex with women, and as a disabled man he has little chance of charming them or even looking at them from above.

Polanski's preoccupation with female parts as an object of male gaze likens his cinema to that of Alfred Hitchcock. However, while in Hitchcock's films women are both recipients of male voyeurism and typically pay for male desire by being raped, killed and mutilated (see Modleski 1988), Polanski's universe is in this respect more balanced: men get the pleasure of looking at women, but women make them pay for it.

Polanski also focuses on specific body parts in order to demonstrate that for his protagonists they are specially important, because they are the main vehicle through which they communicate with the world. For Carol Ledoux in *Repulsion* it is eyes. The film begins with an extreme close-up of Carol's eye. When the camera moves back we see that Carol is at work; she is meant to be looking at the hand of the client she is manicuring, but instead she has forgotten about her task and is looking ahead. Such situations will occur over and over again in this film – instead of doing something, Carol only looks. Compulsive looking is a sign of her passivity and her detachment from the outside world. By contrast, as Gordana Crnković has noted, the energy of Paulina in *Death and the Maiden* and Władysław Szpilman in *The Pianist* is accumulated in their hands, which again is suggested by close-ups of this part of their bodies (see Crnković 2004). The close-up of Szpilman's hands on the piano opens and closes the film, which confirms their importance for the character. While Carol is passive and detached, Paulina and Szpilman are active (Paulina is even neurotically hyperactive) and engaged in what takes place around them (Ibid.), allowing them successfully to 'navigate' and survive in the hostile world.

Tess's mouth is also worth mentioning here. Not only is it beautiful (as men around her notice), but it encapsulates her sensuality, her childlike appetite for life and her honesty. For these reasons her mouth is also the cause of Tess's downfall. Alec seduces her by pampering her mouth first, feeding her with strawberries and entertaining her with polite conversation. Later she loses Angel by telling him the truth about her relationship with Alec. While Carol is a completely passive character and Szpilman an active protagonist, Tess is somewhere in-between. She tries to influence her fate, but eventually succumbs to it.

Last, but not least, Polanski 'dismembers' the human body to illuminate the problem of the fragmented and dislocated identity that is characteristic of schizophrenics. As I argued in the previous chapter, schizophrenics lose the feeling that their own bodies are real. If we assume that, as Freud stated, the ego is not born but must be developed, then schizophrenia can be seen as a psychological regression – returning to the infantile state of not being able to distinguish between the self and the outside world.

Catherine Deneuve in *Repulsion* (1965)

Accordingly, Macbeth's sinking into schizophrenia is rendered, as Virginia Wright Wexman argues, by his anxiety about his physical wholeness, especially the connection between his torso and his head (see Wexman 1987: 84). The next stage of his regression into madness and non-being is that he focuses on his head (as a result of being incapable of identifying himself with his body as a whole) by 'strengthening' it by an attribute of power – the crown. This is not long before his death by decapitation. Macbeth's fear about his physical wholeness is also reflected in the numerous images of dismembered people: enemy soldiers mutilated, traitors hanged, the Thane of Cawdor executed by putting an iron collar around his neck, and the human body parts buried by the witches. Polanski depicts Macbeth, as I will argue in Chapter 6, not as an exception, but as a typical member of medieval society. Accordingly, the images of mutilated bodies, filling the screen, suggest that the director constructs the identity of a medieval man as constantly threatened by fragmentation and, consequently, by madness.

A trajectory of regression similar to that in *Macbeth* takes place in *The Tenant*. Firstly, there is a physical fragmentation. We see the bandaged body of Simone Choule; only her mouth is not covered as if her whole body were already dead and mummified except her mouth. This impression is confirmed when she utters a terrifying, animal-like cry, while remaining unconscious and unrecognisable. At the end of the film we see Trelkovsky looking exactly like Simone and also crying. Secondly, there is a 'verbal' fragmentation. On several occasions characters talk about people who could not come to terms with losing their limbs. For example, in Trelkovsky's office his colleagues quote a newspaper article about a man who lost an arm and wanted it to be buried in the same way as a 'whole' person is buried. Such stories correspond with Trelkovsky's discovery of a tooth buried in the wall of his flat. This perfectly preserved tooth bears associations with the tradition of burying people or their body parts (hands or hearts) in churches and pyramids. Mademoiselle Choule herself was allegedly interested in ancient Egypt, perhaps in order to find out how in this culture the human body was given a chance of prolonged life. One suspects the tooth Trelkovsky found came from Simone Choule's mouth, being a sign of fragmentation and dislocation of her personality, but also, perhaps, her desire not to perish completely but to leave a trace in the place where she lived. Soon after this incident Trelkovsky starts to experience disintegration and dislocation of his self. Through the window in his room he sees himself on a toilet on the other side of the building, as if he is located in two bodies. Moreover, he increasingly feels torn between his old personality of a Polish male immigrant and that of Simone Choule. The last stage of the tenant's road to complete disintegration and dislocation of self is his suicidal death. In the scene where he throws himself from the window we see people playing with a ball which changes into a human head – his head. In the same scene a crippled girl (the daughter of one of Trelkovsky's neighbours who – like him – has been the object of the neighbours' harassment) wears a mask which shows Trelkovsky's face. It gives the impression that Trelkovsky is everywhere and nowhere, and that he does not belong to himself, but is the property of his enemies.

Fragmentation of a human body and mind is also suggested by elements of the setting. An example is a torso, decorating Monsieur Zy's flat, and the wigs in the shop where Trelkovsky buys a wig to look like Mademoiselle Choule. Trelkovsky's wig can be compared to Macbeth's crown: both objects not only cover these men's heads but also change their personalities. Edward Balcerzan suggests that some of these changes show not only disintegration of the character's identity but demonstrate that in the world Trelkovsky occupies (or the world he imagines) individuals and their peculiarities do not matter: one person can easily be exchanged for another. What matters is the place a person occupies in a particular social structure (see Balcerzan 1995: 128). This motif, as mentioned earlier, can be found in the art of René Magritte and in the work of some famous absurdists, such as *La Parodie* by Arthur Adamov and in *Waiting for Godot* by Beckett (see Chapter 2).

The way in which Polanski treats human bodies in his early short, *Mammals*, corroborates the impression that the place where a person is situated is more important than his or her individual features. In one episode we see a character hiding his head inside his coat so that he looks like a living body without a head, completely unidentifiable and anonymous, reminding us of such pictures by Magritte as *The Road to Damascus*. In another scene we see both main characters covering themselves completely in bandages. As a result, we do not know who is who, and it hardly matters – because their behaviour is determined by the position they occupy. The man who is pulling the sledge does everything to get onto it, the one sitting goes to all lengths not to lose his privileged position. In the background in the snow, men covered in white bandages virtually disappear, again – underscoring the theme that the place is more important than its occupant. This image precedes the way in which Simone Choule and Trelkovsky will at the last stage of their lives merge with the white background of sheets and hospital walls, before disappearing into nothingness.

THE HOUSE

The odd thing is that I am not at all prepared to consider myself insane, and indeed I can see quite clearly that I am not: all these changes concern objects. At least, that is what I'd like to be sure about.

Antoine Roquentin in *Nausea* by Jean-Paul Sartre

Philosophers, psychologists and novelists draw attention to the utmost importance of the house in the life of an individual person, and by extension, in society. Gaston Bachelard, whose reflection on the relation between the space that surrounds people and their inner life seems particularly useful in an analysis of Polanski's films, writes in *The Poetics of Space*: 'Our house is our corner of the world...it is our first universe, a real cosmos in every sense of the word... Through dreams, the various dwelling-places in our lives co-penetrate and retain the treasures of former days. And after we are in the new house, when memories of other places we have lived in come back to us, we travel to the land of Motionless Childhood, motionless the way all Immemorial things are. We live fixations, fixations of happiness' (Bachelard 1994: 4–6).

In this and many other fragments of his study, Bachelard acknowledges the connection between the house and the womb. The womb is our first home and in moments of crisis we would like to hide in our house as we were protected inside our mother's body. The importance of the house to a person also means that someone who is deprived of his shelter or whose house is inadequate to his needs suffers immensely.

A typical condition of Polanski's protagonists can be described as 'partial homelessness': they have a roof over their head, but it is not their proper house, either because of the way it looks, or its location, or because of the nature of the relations with co-habitants and neighbours. Moreover, often the house, that at first looked perfectly normal and solid, in due course reveals its hidden character, becoming something opposite to what the protagonist assumed it to be: not a shelter, but an open or fragmented space, a road to another reality or a labyrinth; not an inanimate object, but a living creature, which shrinks, sprouts, changes colour, like a plant or an animal changing from one stage of development to another (see Maurin 1980: 22–3). The characters' suspicion that the chosen house will never be their home and their anxiety about their dwelling is conveyed by Polanski's 'trademark' camera positions and movements. He uses extended crane and pan shots (most famously in *The Tenant*) to give the impression that the character will fail to discover, far less master the house; it will remain a mystery to him. Such an image, especially in *The Tenant*, also allows Polanski to arrange various spatial elements as a premonition of things that will happen in the character's life (see Rosenbaum 1976: 253). Inside his home the camera often encircles the character, as if he were a prisoner inside it (which proves to be the case) and lingers on the objects that surround him, rendering them strange and threatening.

The first inadequate house appears in *Repulsion*. This is a small flat that Carol rents with her sister, Helen. Ted Gershuny describes it as 'shabby-genteel' (Gershuny 1981: 2012); one of thousands of apartments of the sort rented to people who come to London to work and live, it is pervaded by an aura of temporariness and depersonalisation. It is dark, dilapidated, cheaply and basically furnished – in Carol's bedroom there is barely enough space to put a small bedside cupboard next to her bed. The walls are very thin so that Carol can overhear what happens in her sister's bedroom and in the neighbouring apartments. The flat is situated on one of the higher floors, thanks to which Carol can observe from her bedroom window the convent's courtyard where nuns play football – an image inviting associations with both purity and perversion. Many contours in the apartment, especially in the kitchen, are acute and diagonal, like in the interiors of expressionistic films, where the characters seem to be thwarted by the walls – as is Polanski's heroine. From Carol's perspective the worst feature of the house is the constant intrusions: the prolonged visits of her sister's lover, Michael, his wife's and the landlord's telephone calls and the nosiness of the neighbours. Most of the intrusions are by men or are related to male–female affairs; this is particularly painful to Carol, who wants her life to be completely male-free. According to Iwona Kolasińska, visually Carol's flat is constructed as a space of conflict between male/ phallic and female/vaginal elements. Michael's razor, his toothbrush, the picture of the Tower of Pisa sent by Carol and Michael from their holiday belong to the male world; the sprouting potatoes and the rabbit on the plate looking like a human foetus have feminine attributes (see Kolasińska 1995: 78). Obviously, the space's structure reflects the inner conflict that Carol undergoes: she is both repulsed by men and attracted to them.

Carol's apartment is contrasted visually with the cosmetic salon where she works, which is light, spacious and very modern, as demonstrated by the specialist equipment its employees use. However, both interiors lack intimacy and they are already taken over by other people, offering Carol little scope for leaving any personal stamp on them. The flat is dominated by Helen, who not only appropriates more space than Carol (her bedroom is much larger than Carol's and she appears to fill most of the space in the kitchen, pushing the passive Carol into a corner), but also allows her lover to stay there as if it were his own place. The employees in the salon are never alone: they either look after their clients or wait in a communal room for an order from their boss. The owner of the salon is a benevolent older lady; she nevertheless constantly surveys her workers, as if they were in a panopticon, making sure that they earn their wages. Moreover, the salon resembles a hospital: the workers and their clients wear white overgowns, the clients typically lie on beds covered in white sheets like hospital patients. Some of the women with masks on their faces look like mummies, rather than human beings, fighting the passing of time and, ultimately, death. In different ways, both places signify disease and decay. Nevertheless, Carol appears to be healthier in the salon than at home; she is even able to laugh at work. Therefore when the manager, noticing Carol's strange behaviour, sends her home, she unwittingly sends her to her doom.

While we can assume that Carol's perception of the beauty salon does not differ much from that of her colleagues, in her eyes the flat changes into a cross between a living creature and a haunted house. First cracks appear in the walls. They can be a normal feature of an old house, but they also bear associations with the cracks appearing on the body of a chrysalis when it changes into a butterfly or on a plant when it is sprouting. When Helen goes on holiday, Carol locks herself in, believing that she will be safe in her flat, but she is most vulnerable when barricaded against outside reality. The small cracks on the walls and ceilings change into large holes, giving way to hundreds of hands that try to catch her. Carol also imagines that somebody comes through the walls and rapes her. The flat appears to grow longer and narrower, suffocating, like a tunnel or, perhaps, the belly of an animal or a womb – which is a perfect shelter for a foetus, but for an adult person is a prison. The change of the flat into a womb experienced by Carol parallels her regression into childhood, as signified by her childlike singing and compulsive eating of sugar. When Helen returns from holiday, she finds Carol lying under the bed, motionless. Michael carries her from the house as if she were a defenceless child.

In *The Tenant* we witness a similar transformation of the house into an aggressive creature and prison; and in both cases this change is subjective – it takes place largely in characters' minds. The walls of Trelkovsky's apartment peel and become 'elastic' as if it were an animal or plant transforming into a new form. Hands sprout from the walls like branches of a tree.

Another transformation of the house is that into stage. When Trelkovsky attempts to commit suicide by jumping from his window into the inner courtyard of the tenement block, his neighbours stand in the windows and on the balconies, wearing festive costumes and applauding his performance.

The house in *The Tenant* also possesses some characteristics of a labyrinth. In particular, as in a labyrinth, the same place, such as a toilet, can be reached by more than one route; what appears distant is close and vice versa. The labyrinth can be both compared and contrasted with the house. According to the Cretan legend, the Minotaur lived there. However, most people associate the labyrinth with enclosure and exposure to foreign eyes rather than with shelter, with a space that is impossible to domesticate or mould according to one's own needs. To put it differently, the labyrinth belongs to the Other (see Bonitzer 1981).

The motifs of a labyrinth and a stage are developed further in *What?*. Noblart's villa boasts a multitude of entrances and exits, including an entrance from a cable car, as well as several staircases and terraces. Rooms can be accessed from the corridor and from other rooms. Moreover, the house has some additions and extensions, such as a tower where Alex lives. The complicated structure of the villa, combined with the strange behaviour of its inhabitants, causes Nancy's continuous confusion and bewilderment, followed by her sense of déjà vu, which is a sensation a well-designed labyrinth is meant to create. As in a labyrinth, she cannot find somewhere she is looking for and always appears to be in the wrong place at the wrong time, and with the wrong people. Moreover, to a certain extent, the house is also alive, having plastic walls in which objects disappear as into the mouth of a monster.

A certain kind of performance takes place all the time in Noblart's villa. Some inhabitants take part in it voluntarily, largely because they are exhibitionists (Alex and the naked ladies, for example); others are forced to provide entertainment. In this case the performance is ominous and cruel. Here we should list Nancy's performances (already discussed) and the response of Noblart when the guests celebrating his anniversary at one point encircle him and look at him from above as if he were an actor in a theatre. For him (as for Trelkovsky) this is a sign that they wish him dead and he responds by threatening to live for two hundred years.

The houses in *Repulsion*, *The Tenant* and *What?* are subjective or even belong to the realm of the imagination. However, Polanski constructs space in such a way that it is often impossible to establish a boundary between real and surreal. The difficulty derives from the contrast between the concreteness and precision of the depiction of space offered by Polanski (one that we normally associate with a realistic mode of representation), and the improbable events that take place there. It is worth invoking again the words uttered by Polanski: 'If you make a film about vampires, it still has to happen somewhere.' In this respect he acts like Magritte whose pictures strike us as simultaneously realistic and unrealistic.

There is a link between the quality of the dwellings in which characters in Polanski's 'psychological' films live and the way in which they experience their bodies, especially their perception of dislocation and fragmentation. Tom Milne puts it bluntly and very adequately: 'Trelkovsky, having been robbed of a place to rest his body … is also robbed of a body to rest' (Milne 1976: 193). But the connection between the body and the house does not end here, as the dislocated and fragmented body projects its features onto the house, making it even more dislocated, chaotic and fragmented than before. We see it best in *Repulsion* and *The Tenant*, in which the characters become increasingly lost in their untidy, messy and eventually ruined apartments. Moreover, as I will argue later, the wider environment, almost the whole world, becomes a reflection of the tormented body.

In Polanski's more realistic films the house is not as menacing as those depicted above, but it also plays the role of oppressor, making the characters feel unwelcome, almost homeless despite having a roof over their heads. Take, for example, the houses where Tess from the eponymous film and Mimi in *Bitter Moon* live with their partners, respectively Alec and Oscar. In both cases the space is shaped according to the needs and tastes of their male owners. Alec's is a rich and orderly home, which serves more as a sign of the social status of the couple than their family nest. Moreover, Alec expects Tess to behave in a way that confirms their bourgeois status and conceals her lack of warm feelings towards him. For Tess, who is a free spirit, this is unacceptable. Oscar's interior matches the stereotype of a writer's studio. It is rather small and packed with books, photographs and personal mementos. The single object dominating the flat is a computer on which Oscar writes his unpublished novels. At the beginning of his romance with Mimi, Oscar attempts to create some space for her. We can see this in the scene when she dances for him in an almost empty room. Later, however, the space appears to shrink and Mimi has nowhere to dance or even to cook. At this stage Oscar is continuously reproaching her for disturbing him, especially when she tries to clean the house. He appears to regard her desire to put some order into the domestic chaos as a threat to his creativity. On the whole, both Tess and Mimi feel marginalised and oppressed in their homes. However both manage in the end to overcome their predicament: Tess by killing Alec and leaving their house, Mimi by crippling Oscar and making him completely dependent on her. At this stage Mimi dominates their space, forcing Oscar to stay in the least comfortable parts of the flat, such as the bath with cold water, and not allowing him to use the telephone.

George in *Cul-de-Sac* owns the house; and it is one of the largest and most imposing buildings shown in Polanski's films: an eleventh-century castle named Rob Roy, situated on Holy Island. However, he does not feel happy here. The house is too large for his purposes and he constantly loses sight of his wife, Teresa, who disappears in the house or in the surrounding sand dunes. George himself complains about draughts and coldness, which can be understood literally as well as metaphorically as a lack of cosiness and love. Moreover, as a short, bald, myopic and almost effeminate man, George does not fit the stereotype of an owner of a fortress. He looks particularly ridiculous in this role when he and Teresa are terrorised by Richard, to whom he completely succumbs, losing the remains of his dignity. Similarly to George, Macbeth feels unhappy and unsafe in his castle. George's and Macbeth's predicament invites revision of the famous English saying that 'my home is my castle' by adding 'but my castle is not my home'.

Polanski also conveys the partial homelessness of his characters by the scant amount of personal possessions furnishing their houses. The only personal item Carol seems to have is a photo from her childhood. Trelkovsky moves into his rented flat with only a small suitcase, containing the most basic and nondescript items. Moreover, later on burglars steal everything of value from his flat. This event, which leaves him in despair, leads to further unpleasantness and humiliations such as a visit to the police that precipitates his relapse into madness. Nancy, running away from the rapists, enters Noblart's house with virtually nothing. Even her own T-shirt is in such a poor state that she must steal Noblart's pyjamas to cover her naked breasts. There is also very little that Tess carries with her on her numerous journeys from one house to another.

The small amount of luggage carried by Polanski's characters suggests not only and not always their modest economic status, but also how separated they are from their personal past and their homeland. They are literal and cultural travellers, but their trips do not enrich their luggage, so to speak, but impoverish it. In most cases the scarcity of possessions makes Polanski's characters feel themselves to be the inferiors of those whose houses are full of their own things. Often they prefer to stay in the places belonging to their friends rather than to return to their own homes. For example, Trelkovsky is filled with awe when he visits the flats of other people who loudly play their favourite music and fill the space with treasured mementos. Particularly touching is an episode when he looks at Stella's photographic album and smiles on seeing her as a little girl. The episode is sad because we realise that he probably has no pictures from his own childhood.

Some pieces of furniture gain particular prominence across Polanski's narratives. One such is a large wardrobe, usually with a mirror in it. In *The Tenant* it contains a dress belonging to Simone Choule. Trelkovsky's discovery of the dress, which he looks at with a mixture of fascination and disgust, precipitates his transformation into Simone. Rosemary looks in a wardrobe for a glove left by her friend Hatch, but cannot find it. The glove was probably stolen by the Castevets in order to cause Hatch's illness or death. A wardrobe also constitutes a passage to a different ontological order, which usually is less appealing and safe. Therefore when the character moves a wardrobe to protect himself from danger, it releases evil forces. For example, Trelkovsky uses a wardrobe to hide a window and is confronted with a hand in a glove which tries to catch him. Carol barricades the door of her room with a wardrobe and in this way she allows the rapist to attack her, because he is her mind's projection and 'flourishes' when Carol is on her own. Similarly, when Polanski's characters look in the wardrobe mirror, they do not recognise themselves or they even see somebody else.

Lionel Stander and Françoise Dorléac in *Cul-de-Sac* (1966)

When we discuss wardrobes we should not omit the one that gave the title to Polanski's first internationally recognised film, *Two Men and a Wardrobe*. Although here the wardrobe is divorced from its natural context of a house, it performs a similar function to that of wardrobes in *Repulsion*, *The Tenant* and *Rosemary's Baby*: leading the characters from a material, ordinary life to the supernatural, in this film symbolised by the sea. The mirror in the wardrobe shows us a world that does not exist in reality: a fish floating in the sky, although on this occasion the reflection can be explained rationally. Polanski's take on the wardrobe in this film is reminiscent of Magritte's painting *L'homme du large* (*The Man from the Sea*, 1927); it represents a man against the background of the sea with two pieces of wooden floor to which are attached fragments of an interior, most likely pieces of a fireplace. The image of a man in whom critics recognised Fantomas,[2] was regarded as 'the embodiment of forces which menace the stability and order of society' (Whitfield 1992: 17), which is also the role Polanski ascribes to the heroes of his story.

In *The Ninth Gate*, a bookshelf performs a similar function to that of a wardrobe in Polanski's earlier films: a gate to another reality. When the shelf is moved or when a book is taken off the shelf, it reveals a bottomless pit, a print used in a Satanic ritual, or the face of a young woman whose very existence is problematic, possibly a devil. Yet, unlike looking at a wardrobe mirror, looking at a bookshelf does not lead to a change of identity. In contrast to Trelkovsky, Corso in *The Ninth Gate* remains himself.

If a bookshelf behaves like a wardrobe without a mirror, then the mirror, or any object making a reflection, such as a kettle in *Repulsion* or a windowpane, is like a wardrobe without shelves or drawers. It distorts the image, it shows a different reality, but does not allow characters to reach it. They must find another tool to transfer themselves to the 'other side of the mirror'. Mirrors in Polanski's films often reveal something about characters that they want to conceal, therefore looking in the mirror is an act of revelation. Take the scene in *Dance of the Vampires* when Alfred discovers that most of the people who dance in the hall have no reflection in the mirror, and therefore are vampires. Similarly, Fiona's gaze into the mirror that shows her alongside Nigel makes her realise that their marriage is stale. Rosemary's gaze at her reflection in the toaster makes her afraid that she is unwell and that her child is in danger.

Objects of art – paintings, sculptures and old books – are also abundant in Polanski's films and play important roles in their narratives. For example, in *What?* one of the guests in Noblart's villa, to gain his favours, tries to organise the theft of a painting by Theodore Géricault, *The Raft of the Medusa* (1919), and the plot of *The Ninth Gate* revolves around finding the missing copy of a unique ancient book. Interestingly, while Polanski elevates the status of more ordinary furnishings, such as a wardrobe or a mirror, by representing them as mysterious and poetic, objects of art tend to be deprecated in his films as ordinary commodities with only a commercial value (see Wexman 1987: 38). In *What?*, nobody with the exception of Nancy pays any attention to the masterpieces of modern art decorating Noblart's house. Paradoxically, the person most dismissive of art appears to be Noblart himself, to whom one of his guests ascribes the view that 'He would rather eat an apple than look at an apple' (Ibid.: 38). Polanski also shows that the accumulation of objects of art in Noblart's house making it look like a museum leads to the diminution and almost invisibility of any individual masterpiece. Such a view brings him close to Witold Gombrowicz, an ardent enemy of art 'imprisoned' in a museum (see Gombrowicz 1997: 39–40).

In other films the function of art is pragmatic. In *The Ninth Gate* the painting of a horse serves to cover a hole in the wall where something more precious is kept: a book used in Satanic rituals. In *Rosemary's Baby* paintings hide pictures used in Satanic rituals. Even if Polanski's characters genuinely admire artistic objects, it is not for their aesthetic dimension, not, as Susan Sontag put it, that they 'are something', but because they are 'about something'. For example, they represent a mysterious ritual, or a close resemblance to something, they provide information or simply testify to the passage of time. Such a dismissive attitude to art clearly invites the putting of it in the context of Polanski's own distance from cinema as art for art's sake.

THE CITY

A city is a blind courier. It brings nothing. It takes nothing. That is why we grow so fixated on roads.

Walter Benjamin

Polanski can be described as an urban director, as most of his films are set in towns. However, he does not have a predilection for a particular real metropolis, as Eric Rohmer has for Paris or Pedro Almodóvar for Madrid. His films are set in a number of different cities, including Paris, London, Los Angeles, New York, Amsterdam and Warsaw, partly mirroring Polanski's own relocations. Moreover, there are locations which appear to convey his ideas and interests better than a city, such as the sea, which I will discuss later in this chapter. Nevertheless, in some of his films, including those in which no concrete city is foregrounded the idea of the city is still very significant to the film's story and its message. On such occasions it is represented from the perspective of an outsider: somebody who has just arrived for business or recreation, has lived here for only a certain period of time or even looks at it from a distance. Alternatively, as in *The Pianist*, he becomes a foreigner in his own town due to dramatic changes the city undergoes. This has a major influence on the characters' perception of the city – they are unable to have a neutral or balanced view of it, instead they tend to idealise, exoticise or demonise it. Walter Benjamin's words perfectly capture 'Polanski's cities': 'The superficial inducement, the exotic, the picturesque has an effect only on the foreigner. To portray a city, a native must have other, deeper motives – motives of one who travels into the past instead of into the distance' (Benjamin, quoted in Klein 1997: 235).

The first of Polanski's films in which the city plays a major role is the short *The Fat and the Lean*. The lean man (played by Polanski) who lives with his master far from other people's dwellings attempts to escape to

Roman Polanski and André Katelbach in *The Fat and the Lean* (1961)

a large city, which he sees on the horizon. For him it encapsulates modernity, communality and fun, all of which he is deprived of. The city is nameless, although the contours of the Eiffel Tower suggest that it is Paris – European capital of modernity. Viewed from a distance, it looks like a city from a postcard, reduced to clichés and remote in both the geographical sense (people who receive postcards being usually far from the objects pictured) and the ontological, as it is only a representation of a real city. On the whole, as if confirming the truth of Benjamin's words, it feels like a deceptive lure. Yet the lean man has no opportunity to test it – his attempts to run away are aborted by the fat man's intervention. We can assume that it will always remain the city of his dream.

By contrast, Carol in *Repulsion* and Trelkovsky in *The Tenant* have managed to reach large, modern cities, respectively London and Paris. Yet, if they had any dreams about big cities, the cities do not live up to their expectations. Both appear grey, sad and neglected. On the streets, which Carol passes on her way to work, there are always roadworks. We see holes in the asphalt and the pavement. Polanski avoids any London landmarks, anywhere that attracts tourists. The city is full of people, but they are not friendly, only nosy and intruding. On the whole, London increases Carol's sense of alienation rather than diminishing it, not unlike Cathy's experience in Ken Loach's *Cathy Come Home* (1966). In both films the heroines are detached from the city: Carol through her foreignness and schizophrenia, Cathy through her poverty and homelessness.

Initially Trelkovsky, more than Carol, tries to integrate with the city, which can be explained by his desire to be regarded as a proper Frenchman, not just a 'French citizen'. He goes to a café for his breakfast, visits his workmates at home, takes Simone Choule's depressed friend to a pub. However, wherever he goes, he experiences hostility and aggression. A stranger in a pub buys everybody a drink except him and his companion. The reason for this is their sadness, which differentiates them from the merry crowd in the pub. In this way Trelkovsky is doubly marginalised: being identified as different and having his differences exposed and punished. The city itself, although shot in colour, is grey or nocturnal, therefore unwelcoming and mysterious. Moreover, Trelkovsky often walks along the walls that render passers-by entrapped and ghettoised. Even the Seine, usually represented in films as a friendly place, is here a site of alienation. Trelkovsky walks on its banks with nobody in sight, as if confronted by his own complete solitude and nothingness. As mentioned earlier, the protagonist of *The Tenant* moves to a flat with only a small suitcase containing his most basic possessions. Nevertheless, among the things that he brings is a geographical atlas – a sign of his desire to travel and to orientate himself in the world. Even Stella, despite coming across as being happy in Paris and in her apartment, decorates her flat with posters of exotic locations of the sea and desert, as if she dreams of leaving the urban environment.

Critics have noticed a correspondence between the immediate and wider environments of the protagonists of Polanski's films, particularly their houses and the cities where they live (see Maurin 1980). This is not surprising, as both spaces reflect the way they perceive the world and themselves. To put it bluntly, a secure, orderly and happy home is conducive to seeing the city as secure, orderly and friendly, and reflects the inner harmony of the person. And chaos and lack of security experienced in one's home typically causes and later mirrors inner turmoil and is projected onto the wider world. In line with this observation, holes in the streets, roadworks and the refurbishment of the metro station correspond with the cracks that Carol and Trelkovsky see in the walls of their apartments, and these in turn with the 'cracks' and 'wounds' in their personalities and bodies (Ibid.).

If in *Repulsion* and *The Tenant* Polanski conjures up the city of a disappointed emigrant, in *Frantic* he proposes the city (Paris) of an unhappy tourist. Future disenchantment is forecast in the early images of the city, shot from the perspective of the American passengers of a taxi, which takes them from the airport to the centre of town. The nondescript motorway, 'decorated' by huge adverts of products sold in every corner of the world, serves as a metonymy of a 'neutered' European city. Pierre Sorlin, who coined this term, argues that in modernist cinema, towns ceased to be a solid presence, and became instead anonymous. In films such as Narizzano's *Georgy Girl* (1966) and Godard's *Deux ou trois choses que je sais d'elle* (*Two or Three Things I Know About Her*, 1966), London and Paris are almost unrecognisable:

> Instead of being played as a counterpoint, as a supplementary delight, cities were flattened, reduced to prosaic clichés. There was surely a 'message' underlying the pictures, something like: towns become increasingly humdrum expanses crossed by indifferent drivers and damaged by greedy property developers. Spectators either caught these implications or they did not but they could not miss the dullness, the anonymity of the urbanised areas. (Sorlin 1994: 133)

In *From Moscow to Madrid: Postmodern Cities, European Cinema*, Laura Rascaroli and I argued that this description also suits many European cities, represented in the films made in the 1980s and 1990s (see Mazierska and Rascaroli 2003: 236–7). Paris in *Frantic* is one such city, as dullness, anonymity and standardisation are all around it. The airport, the Grand Hotel where Walker and his wife Sondra are staying, the underground parking, the motorway, and almost everywhere Walker finds himself closely resemble airports, hotels and motorways in many different countries. Paris's lack of individuality can partly be explained by Walker's situation as a wealthy foreigner whose hosts try to create conditions for him similar to those he enjoys at home, but also by the homogenisation and loss of individuality of European towns during the period of modernism, mourned by Sorlin. 'It changed so much,' Walker tells his wife on their way to the hotel, when she asks him whether he recognises the locations they pass. The object that plays a crucial role in the film's setting and narrative, the Statue of Liberty, is hardly associated with France, despite the fact that its original was designed by a French sculptor, Frédéric-Auguste Bartholdi, and presented to America as a gift from the French nation. In the final episode of the film the characters meet near the Parisian Statue of Liberty: the small replica that stands on the banks of the Seine. We also see the Eiffel Tower in this scene, but it is pushed into the background, which can be interpreted as a sign of American dominance over French traditions. In most of the film the statue functions as a cheap reproduction: a tacky souvenir from New York, which can be read as Polanski's conviction that the postmodern culture of simulacra has supremacy over modernist culture, of which both the Statue of Liberty in New York and the Eiffel Tower are potent symbols.

Paris in *Frantic* comes across as fragmented. Typically it is difficult to establish the location of a scene because in each shot only the fragments of buildings and streets are revealed. Spatial fragmentation is accompanied by fragmentation of languages, making Paris sound like a contemporary Babylon. Rarely do we see the whole sign describing a particular object, and the names of places are strange or contain directions that are misleading (see Jankun-Dopartowa 2000: 113–14). Moreover, people cannot understand each other because they do not speak each other's language, because telephones do not work properly, or because they simply do not pay attention to what the other person is saying, only pursuing their own agenda. It is worth citing here the episode in the nightclub 'Blue Parrot', in which an American drug dealer sells Walker cocaine because he is looking for a 'white lady', or the frequent telephone calls from a man organising the medical conference who is completely unaware of Walker's personal problems.

When Walker decides to search for his wife on his own, Paris reveals itself to him as a nocturnal space, even an inferno. It is a place lit by flashy lights, populated by people with 'dark faces': Arabs, Afro-Americans, as well as white women who indulge in various sins such as drug dealing and drug taking, prostitution, promiscuity and, most importantly, terrorism. Not knowing Paris's geography, the French language or the motives of the people who kidnapped Sondra, Walker must rely on the help of a young Parisian named Michelle. Together they visit dingy nightclubs, desolate car parks and smoky cafés. Although Michelle appears to be very streetwise, in the end she is defeated by the same forces that she earlier used to her advantage, principally her acquaintance with immigrants. Michelle's death and Sondra's arrival by boat, which can be seen as her return from the dead, both happen at dawn, as if suggesting that nocturnal and daylight Paris, the Paris of white people and of dark immigrants, like earth and hell, cannot be reconciled. Hence, while in *The Tenant* Polanski interrogated and criticised the view that 'immigrants are a problem for Paris', demonstrating that native Parisians are the greater problem in their bigotry and xenophobia, in *Frantic* he wholeheartedly embraces this position (see Chapter 5).

Harrison Ford and Emmanuelle Seigner in *Frantic* (1988)

For Oscar in *Bitter Moon*, Paris is a symbol of modernity as perceived by Americans: a place where Ernest Hemingway, Henry Miller and Scott Fitzgerald[3] used to live, and the place which – as Oscar believes – made them distinguished writers. He came to Paris dreaming of following in their footsteps, but as he frankly admits, was too fascinated by their lifestyles and writings to be able to conjure up anything original or even to look at his environment in a new way. Yet looking into Oscar's lifestyle we get an opposite idea: unlike his famous compatriots, Oscar makes little effort to become a Parisian. Obsessed by the idea of writing a novel, he rarely leaves his flat, has no interest in Parisian culture or art, and has no real friends there. His only acquaintances, at least prior to meeting Mimi and after abandoning her, are women whom he meets for casual sex. Not surprisingly, he speaks only basic French. Photographs of the famous American writers hanging above his desk complete the image of a man who has remained an outsider in a double sense: as a foreigner and as somebody fascinated by a Paris which belongs to the past. His enchantment with the Paris of (classical) modernity is conveyed by the first image of the city from the window of his apartment. With the Eiffel Tower dominating the cityscape and shot in sepia, gradually changing colour, it looks more like a postcard from the turn of the century than the real Paris of the 1980s. Oscar's sexual exploits and his clichéd descriptions of his erotic experiences do not make him look 'in vogue', but rather old-fashioned, more in tune with the Paris of the beginning of the twentieth century, as immortalised by Toulouse-Lautrec and Degas, or of the 1960s, than of the 1980s when the film was made.

Thanks to Mimi, Oscar's boundaries within Paris expand, both metaphorically and literally. She takes him to places that symbolise Paris, such as Notre Dame and those that are important to her personally, such as the dancing school. Together they go to funfairs and shops, where they can observe the everyday lives of Parisians and tourists. However, this period does not last long. After a short infatuation with Mimi, this unfulfilled writer returns to his sedentary and enclosed lifestyle, and even transforms his lover into a person bound to home, a couch potato. In this way not only does he fail to immerse himself in Paris but he alienates a true Parisian from her town. Eventually, when he disposes of Mimi by sending her to Martinique, his relationship with the city becomes even more tenuous, as he goes out only at night, to look for women, as a vampire looking for victims.

To capture the specificity of Los Angeles in *Chinatown*, it is worth returning to the observation of Walter Benjamin that in order to portray a city a native must travel into the past, because in this case the memory of the native, the scriptwriter Robert Towne, had a crucial influence on the town's representation. As Norman Klein notes, the film recreates and compresses several myths of Los Angeles, each dominating a different period of the city's history (see Klein 1997: 27–72). One of them is the myth of climate, of rural paradise, which prevailed from the 1880s until the 1930s. It is encapsulated by the images of horses and sheep, and the fields and orchards that Jake Gittes visits when trying to find out what happens to Los Angeles' water resources. Hollis Mulwray's estate looks like a rustic paradise, with ponds, porches and gazebos. However, the fact that it belongs to one of the richest families in the town makes us realise that only the minority of the town's population enjoys this paradise. Virtually all rural pleasures are closely guarded by their owners. Wherever Gittes goes, he sees signs reading 'Private territory' or 'No trespassing', and eventually he is beaten up when he enters somebody's orchard.

Another myth of Los Angeles, referred to in *Chinatown*, is of a *noir* city, full of illegal enterprises controlled by the Mafia and dingy streets where numerous crimes are committed – crimes which the LA police are unable or unwilling to investigate; they are therefore left to private detectives to explore. To this myth is linked the myth of downtown renewal, specific to the years 1936–49, when the city's authorities embarked on the programme of improving Los Angeles, largely at the expense of uprooting, dislocating or destroying the immigrant population. Robert Towne explained that he learned about Chinatown from a retired Hungarian vice cop who said that 'police were better off in Chinatown doing nothing, because you could never tell what went on there' (Ibid.: 61). Thus Chinatown became a metaphor for the ambiguity of modern life and for 'the futility of good intentions' (Ibid.). The myth of Los Angeles as *noir* city and the rural paradise contradict each other. Mike Davis suggests that the reason for this contradiction is the city itself. It is heaven and hell, utopia and dystopia in one (see Davis 1998: 18).

Polanski and Towne not only present Los Angeles myths, but also subvert them by using a story containing a moral lesson. At the outset of the film Gittes holds the opinion (which in reality was the basis of the policy of 'downtown renewal') that Chinatown is the blight on the healthy tissue of Los Angeles, and regards his move to the richer part of the city as social and moral advancement. However, eventually he learns that the source of the disease is hidden in the white and affluent part of the town, encapsulated by unscrupulous Noah Cross, who is also a sexual pervert. By contrast, the inhabitants of Chinatown prove decent and loyal. The Mulwrays, who in the narrative are contrasted both with the corrupt Cross and with the racist and ultimately naive Gittes, employ exclusively

Chinese servants. Their entire residence, as Michael Eaton describes it, 'is a mini-Chinatown' (Eaton 2000: 37). The last fragment of the film, shot in Chinatown, in which Evelyn Mulwray is shot by the police in front of the bewildered Chinese people, excellently illustrates the fact that the crime and corruption associated with this district was predominantly the consequence of white policies (see Klein 1997: 58–9). Although the scene is short, there is enough time to notice that the space in which the Chinese people live is very cramped and dark – like a ghetto.

Although Warsaw is geographically, culturally, even climatically very distant from Los Angeles, in *The Pianist* it reveals important similarities to the Los Angeles of *Chinatown*, partly because both films are set in a similar period: the end of the 1930s in *Chinatown*, 1939–45 in *The Pianist*. Crucially, after the Nazis captured Warsaw, it was also divided into two distinctive parts: the Aryan one and the Jewish one, and this partition reflected the project of the 'town's renewal', albeit one more extreme than has ever been imposed on Chinese or Mexican populations in America. It must be mentioned that even before the break-up of the war, Warsaw was a somehow divided city, in the sense that the Jews tended to live in certain areas, such as Muranów, where the ghetto was raised in 1940. They

Jack Nicholson and Faye Dunaway in *Chinatown* (1974)

did so partly to be among themselves and have easy access to Jewish institutions and facilities such as shops and synagogues and partly to avoid anti-Semitic attacks from Poles. However, while before the war the division along ethnic lines was largely voluntary and the difference between Jews and Poles was blurred, during the war it became imposed by the law and military force and was extremely rigid.

In the short part of the film preceding the Szpilmans' imprisonment in the ghetto, and in the brief moments when we have an opportunity to glimpse beyond the ghetto walls, we receive an almost utopian image of the harmonious existence of Warsaw's Poles and Jews prior to German occupation. Szpilman works in a very Polish institution, the radio, where he plays Chopin's music and becomes romantically involved with a young Polish woman, Dorota, who is a cellist. In a scene where the ghetto is open so that the trams carrying Poles can pass, we see a signboard reading *Bar dla wszystkich* (Bar for Everybody) – a remnant from the times when there was one Warsaw for Jews and Aryans. It is poignantly contrasted with the numerous signs, such as 'Not for Jews' or 'Jews not allowed', hanging in cafés and shop windows during the war.

I have established that Chinatown was a cancer on the body of Los Angeles because the white authorities decided to treat it as a repository of the sins and misdemeanours of the predominantly white population.

The road to the Warsaw ghetto in *The Pianist* (2002)

A similar situation can be observed in the Jewish ghetto, as represented by Polanski. The official reason for creating the ghetto was to protect the non-Jewish population from the diseases supposedly transmitted by Jews. Although before the war the state of health of Jews was not worse than that of Poles, after the walls were erected and the links severed between the inhabitants of the ghetto and the outside world, the ghetto indeed became a locus of disease and chaos due to the extreme loss of space suffered by the Jews. Thus the Nazis could demonstrate that their policy was rational, although it was this very policy that created the situation it was meant to tackle.

In *Chinatown* we could only guess where the policy of the 'town's renewal' might lead. In *The Pianist* the ultimate consequence of dividing and ethnically cleansing Warsaw was its total destruction, which affected all of its inhabitants: Jews, Poles and Germans. After the war Warsaw had fewer than twenty thousand inhabitants, and although it arose like a Phoenix from the ashes, it never regained its cultural richness.

On the whole, city in Polanski's film is typically represented in negative terms: as a deceptive lure, a site of alienation, a paradise hiding a disease, an ultimate hell created by one group of people for another. Not surprisingly, most of his characters leave it. Growing roots in the city is

Nicole Karen in *A River of Diamonds* (1964)

never a viable option. The only exception to this rule is the French heroine of *A River of Diamonds*, who genuinely enjoys Amsterdam. Although, like Carol, Trelkovsky, Doctor Walker and Oscar, she is foreign to the city, her position does not lie heavy on her soul, but liberates her. Not only is she able to fulfil her plan by conning a Dutchman into acquiring a diamond necklace for her, she also takes no responsibility for her actions and receives no punishment. Her position as a foreigner in this case does not dispose the natives negatively towards her, but on the contrary grants her the privileges of a guest. Her final decision to exchange the precious item of jewellery for a parrot stresses her position as a careless *flâneur*. Joanna Guze in her review of the film anthology *The World's Most Beautiful Swindlers* (for which Polanski wrote the episode entitled *A River of Diamonds*) praises Polanski's novella claiming that *A River of Diamonds* 'proves that one does not need to come from Amsterdam to capture the aura of this town and convey its particular beauty' (Guze 1966: 4). While I agree with Guze's opinion, I would argue that Polanski's film betrays the attitude of a tourist who had neither the time nor the opportunity to learn about the darker side of the city.

WATER

The sea and other large areas of water, such as lakes and rivers, are probably the most distinctive element of Polanski's mise-en-scène. His characters come from water (*Two Men and a Wardrobe*), live on or near the water (*Pirates, Death and the Maiden, Tess*), travel on water (*Bitter Moon, Knife in the Water, Pirates*), dream about water (*Rosemary's Baby*), fight, kill and die for water (*Chinatown*), even have 'water names' (Noah Cross in *Chinatown*). Sea is also one of the most potent symbols. In many cultural discourses (myths, religions, literatures), it signifies a different ontological order than that of the stable land; it can be eternity or nothingness. Sea is a space where miracles and unusual things can happen. It suffices to mention the biblical story of Jesus walking on the sea and Venus being born out of sea waves. Cultural representations are also full of images and descriptions of tragedies that took place on the sea: ships being flooded by the menacing waves or taken hostage by pirates. In Homer's *The Odyssey* we find the statement that no force is able to break a man, even the strongest, as the sea. Accordingly, boarding a ship signifies a rite of passage, entering a different reality that is both exciting and dangerous, and which includes the risk of losing one's life. The protagonists of *The Odyssey* and *The Iliad* travelled by the sea to fulfil a particular quest and to test themselves, to escape from home and to return to it in glory. Sea also promises, or brings the risk of, crossing the boundaries of oneself, changing one's identity (see Eleftheriotis 2000: 99–100). Therefore water is used in the rituals of baptism. Similarly, the land near the sea, comprising beaches and seaside resorts, is a liminal or carnivalesque space where normal behaviour is suspended and the rules of 'decency' no longer apply (see Rojek 1995: 85–8). From its beginnings cinema has used sea as a milieu extensively, largely drawing on the meanings it had in earlier cultural texts. Testimony of its importance is the fact that we can identify two genres in which the sea plays a crucial role: the pirate genre (see Chapter 7) and the ship disaster film of which a model is James Cameron's *Titanic* (1997).

Polanski alludes to the meanings the sea acquired in earlier representations and subverts them. In one of his earlier films, *Two Men and a Wardrobe*, the sea constitutes a better reality than that existing on land. The two men who come from the sea are gentle and altruistic, while the people whom they encounter on land are aggressive and selfish. There is no communication between the sea and the land, however. The men's eventual return to the sea, which Anna Lawton describes as a 'cowardly return to the womb' (Lawton 1981: 128), demonstrates that the promise of renegotiation of identity is not fulfilled. The 'sea men' did not change due to being on terra firma, the 'earth people' did not become any different as a result of meeting the people from the sea.

In *Knife in the Water*, which depicts a sailing trip on the Mazurian Lakes, the student – with his outstretched arms, a halo of coiled rope and appearing to walk on water – is visually compared to Jesus Christ (see Thompson 1964: 61). The iconography suggests that the young man will prove morally and physically superior to the older, decadent couple and even become, as Virginia Wright Wexman puts it, 'the virile Messiah of the new Poland' (Wexman 1987: 27). Yet the development of the narrative, and other elements of iconography, including the knife, prove the opposite. The student is not a selfless and mighty Jesus, but a younger version of Andrzej: conceited, selfish and aggressive. Moreover water is for him a frightening and menacing element. The lake scares him when it is rough and annoys him when it is silent.

The film's setting of the Mazurian Lakes had a special meaning for the Polish postwar intelligentsia, especially the generation born in the 1920s and 1930s, including writers, actors, filmmakers and composers such as Jerzy Markuszewski, Olga Lipińska, Alina Janowska, Stanisław Tym and, most importantly, the poet and songwriter Agnieszka Osiecka – who arguably inaugurated the fashion for spending holidays and weekends at the Mazurian Lakes (see Turowska 2000: 118–23; Michalak 2001: 60–8). The lakes acted as a liminal zone in a political and cultural sense. Travelling to the Mazurian Lakes from towns such as Warsaw or Kraków signified a mental escape from socialist ideology into long philosophical and literary discussions, and promised unleashed creativity. Here famous cabaret pieces, plays, poems and songs were written, including Osiecka's *Na całych jeziorach ty* (*You on All the Lakes*). Life on the lakes was more natural because this was one of the least industrialised and populated parts of the country, therefore less important for the communist authorities than Warsaw, Łódź or Silesia. Not unlike the Lake District in the North of England, the Mazurian Lakes were also regarded as 'romantic' space, conducive to falling in love.

In *Knife in the Water* Polanski shows awareness of the significance of the Mazurian Lakes as a site of intelligentsia's rebellion against socialism and as one of romanticism. The clearest sign of that is his inclusion in the film of Osiecka's love song – sung by Krystyna. However, he uses the 'Mazurian legend' in an ambiguous or even subversive way. Firstly, although Andrzej's profession of a sport journalist links him to the 'Warsaw bohemian society' of those in love with the lakes, his other attributes suggest that he will not comfortably fit into this milieu. His ostentatious affluence, signified by his Western car, his yacht and its anglicised name ('Christine'), contrasts with the more modest lifestyles of people like Osiecka (who possessed only a motor boat) and their affinity to Polish culture. More importantly, Andrzej comes across as a propagator of socialist values, such as obedience, humility and blind trust in authority, which were scorned by the free spirits belonging to Osiecka's circle. The student, on the other hand, comes across as somebody who is still too immature to embody any particular system of values and lifestyle.

Yet, in comparison with the sea in *Two Men and a Wardrobe*, the lakes in *Knife in the Water* show a greater power to transform people from the land. After the journey the men are not the same – Andrzej's control over his yacht, the people around him and over himself as a 'sea man' was challenged and diminished, while the student started to learn to use the water to his own advantage.

The characters in *Bitter Moon*, like those in *Knife in the Water*, also travel by water. This time, however, it is not a small private yacht, but a large and luxurious ship, used for cruises lasting weeks if not months. Such a vessel bears an association with ship disasters, especially the maiden voyage of the *Titanic*, as represented in novels and movies. Kenneth Womack, discussing the recent literary representations of the loss of the *Titanic*, such as Beryl Bainbridge's *Every Man for Himself* (1996) and Cynthia Bass's

Maiden Voyage (1996), argues that in these novels the disaster of the ship's sinking parallels the more personal tragedy experienced by the protagonist who has managed physically to survive the catastrophe. This tragedy can be equated with one's loss of faith in human solidarity and honesty (as conveyed by the title *Every Man for Himself*) and hence innocence, leading perhaps to questioning the very meaning of human life (see Womack 2004: 85–94). Similarly, Susan Sydney-Smith in her discussion of James Cameron's *Titanic*, situates it in the tradition of 'rites of passage films' (see Sydney-Smith 2004: 185). The passage in question primarily concerns the transition from one century to the next, from prehistory to modernity, but also entails personal passage understood as psychical journey (Ibid.: 186).

In *Bitter Moon* Polanski plays on these associations by partially fulfilling and partially frustrating them. In many scenes the focus is on the porthole from which the characters look at the sea and their own reflection. The contrast between the immense area of water and one's own smallness is conducive to contemplating one's place in the world – an important precondition for fulfilling a successful personal transition or reconciling oneself with one's demise. The ship is also often depicted from the outside in a long shot that allows the viewer to appreciate its

Jolanta Umecka and Leon Niemczyk in *Knife in the Water* (1962)

magnitude and majesty (rendering the subsequent disaster even more catastrophic), in a way that brings to mind the earlier ship disaster films and anticipates Cameron's *Titanic*. At one point Oscar even says jokingly that he hopes that the ship will sink and a moment comes when the cruiser starts to shake precariously. This happens during a New Year's ball, which is reminiscent of the sinking of the *Titanic* while the guests were enjoying themselves. Yet, the cruiser does not sink after all. The disaster Polanski depicts is limited to personal tragedy, and the psychological passage experienced by the characters is not facilitated by their direct encounter with the forces of nature. Nevertheless, the sea plays its part in the chain of events. Thanks to the long journey in a spacious vessel, which is conducive to boredom and the befriending of fellow passengers, Oscar manages to find a perfect audience for his unfinished *Bildungsroman* – Nigel. Being relatively young, upper class and English (which promises sexual innocence), Nigel is the type of man that can be impressed by the older man's erotic antics, and indeed he is. More importantly, he allows Oscar to act as his mentor. The failed writer, therefore having fulfilled his dream of telling his story to somebody who might benefit from it, feels free to end his life. Thus to him the cruiser is not a vehicle for change, but the vessel of his last journey – a grand coffin. Perhaps the same is true of Mimi. The answer, 'Much further', that she gives to Fiona on her question where they are going, after Fiona informs her that she and Nigel are travelling to India, suggests that, Mimi like Oscar, perceives their journey as final. For the English couple the situation is different; they change profoundly during the trip, first by acknowledging the crisis in their marriage and looking for a solution in extra-marital affairs, and in the end by ascertaining their importance for each other. Julian Graffy sums it up: 'At the film's close, the couple stand huddled together on deck, their Passage to India no longer necessary' (Graffy 1992: 54).

In the part of this chapter devoted to the house I mentioned that the flat where Mimi and Oscar live is first totally dominated by Oscar, then by Mimi. The cruiser is also a kind of house, as people spend many nights there before they reach a stable land. Unlike an ordinary dwelling, it also possesses a large public space filled with restaurants, bars, clubs and the walking areas. As a house, for Oscar and Mimi it feels more comfortable and gender-balanced than their Paris flat. Oscar informs Nigel that he and Mimi have separate cabins and we never see them disputing the living arrangements. On the contrary, it feels as if they cooperate with each other to maximise each other's comfort and pleasure. Moreover, the cruiser offers them space that they lacked when living in Paris – space to observe and meet other people and to perform for them, and proves less claustrophobic than their proper home.

As already mentioned, places near the water, such as beaches, rocks, seaside houses and roads, in common with water itself, signify liminality. In Polanski's films they stand between nature and civilisation, often having the worst features of both worlds: being decadent and barbaric. Such is Noblart's seaside villa in *What?*, and also a nearby beach where Alex performs a 'theatre of cruelty', chaining and beating Nancy in a military uniform. The house near the sea is particularly vulnerable to the visits of unwelcome, even barbaric strangers, as shown in *Cul-de-Sac* and *Death and the Maiden*, leading to revenge and murder. At the same time the sea can act as a tool of catharsis. When Paulina in *Death and the Maiden* pushes Miranda's car into the sea, it seems as if she started to conquer the nightmares of her past and her rites of passage will soon be completed.

As with many elements of Polanski's mise-en-scène, the sea has its double – the sky. Their resemblance is perfectly captured in *Two Men and a Wardrobe* when a fish appears to fly through the sky. The mirror on the wardrobe where the fish is flying produces this illusion. Similarly, in the first scene of *Macbeth*, we are not certain whether the land touches the sea or the sky. After a while the whole landscape is covered with a mist, a kind of *materia prima* from which everything emerges and to which it eventually returns. The similarity between the sea and the sky is also suggested by the behaviour of many of Polanski's characters who in the moment of crisis tend to look at both as if expecting some help from them – usually in vain. One feels as if they are surrounded by two eternities or two types of emptiness, which render their struggle against absurdity particularly difficult.

FROM SUBJECTIVISM TO REALISM

The sentence that opens Roman Polanski's autobiography, *Roman*, and which was used as a motto for this chapter, can be regarded as a summary of much of his life and cinema. However, the closer we approach the present day, the easier it is to say what in Polanski's cinema belongs to the realm of objective events and what constitutes purely subjective visions. Ontological and epistemological ambiguity, which was Polanski's trademark, gradually evaporates from his films and the kingdom of fantasy shrinks. The dividing line, in my opinion, is constituted by *Tess*. Many critics were taken aback by this film's realistic style, which was surprising both in the context of Polanski's earlier work, and given Hardy's novel, which offered much opportunity for creating subjective and even surreal visions.

The overall shift from subjectivism to realism in Polanski's cinema takes place on several levels. Firstly, by Polanski's growing affinity to genres regarded as realistic – melodrama (*Tess*), war film (*The Pianist*) – at the expense of psychological horror which was his favourite genre in the earlier part of his career and of which *Repulsion* and *Rosemary's Baby* are the seminal examples. Secondly, unrealistic, expressionistic effects, when they appear in later films, are explained in a rational way, such as the power cut in *Death and the Maiden* which forces Paulina to use candles and results in the ominous atmosphere.

Furthermore, later films, which because of their subject matter should encourage ambiguous readings, do not come across as ambiguous. From this perspective it is worth comparing *Rosemary's Baby* with *The Ninth Gate*, as both films deal with the presence of the devil in human life. As Beverle Houston and Marsha Kinder note, through the use of colour, textures, make-up, costumes, camera focus and angle, as well as acting style, Polanski demonstrates in *Rosemary's Baby* 'how difficult it is to choose among various and sometimes conflicting perceptions' (Houston and Kinder 1968–9: 18). By contrast, in *The Ninth Gate* such multiple meanings are avoided. We are rarely, if ever, forced to choose between conflicting perceptions or conflicting realities. The reality which Polanski creates might be strange, even fantastical, but it is internally coherent. In particular, the 'devil' of this film, the Girl with Green Eyes, feels very concrete and she features in the perceptions of a number of characters. Moreover, the dominant vision is that of the objective camera, rather than of any of the film's characters. In *The Ninth Gate* the focus is not on epistemological issues, such as whose perception is truthful, but on fulfilling a certain quest, achieving something. To put it differently, *Rosemary's Baby* is about the internal world, *The Ninth Gate* the external. Moreover, this external world, as Zygmunt Kałużyński argues, is shaped according to the conventions of the action film, rather than the horror film (see Kałużyński 2001: 70).

Another sign of the shift from surrealism to realism can be observed in *The Pianist*. Although the film focuses on a single, isolated character who hardly leaves the frame and through whose eyes we see the gradual annihilation of the Jewish community and Warsaw, the character's vision feels far from unique. Prewar Warsaw is presented through the form of a documentary, in black and white footage. Warsaw during the war also strikes us as familiar, and is reminiscent of many well-known images and literary descriptions of life during the Second World War, particularly those present in Polish culture. We could list such probable sources of inspiration as the pictures and engravings of Bronisław Linke, and many Polish films depicting the Warsaw ghetto and Warsaw after the uprising, including, Andrzej Wajda's *Korczak* and *Wielki tydzień* (*Holy Week*, 1995) and even Jerzy Zarzycki's *Miasto nieujarzmione* (*Unsubjugated City*, 1949) which was the first attempt to adapt Szpilman's memoirs for the screen. Interestingly, in *The Pianist* Polanski hardly draws on those Polish films which attempted to provide a highly subjective vision of the war, such as Wajda's *Kanał* (*Kanal*, 1956).

This impersonal vision of the war, if tackled in the reviews at all, was usually evaluated negatively. Tadeusz Sobolewski accused it of being built of clichés, which left him indifferent towards the protagonist and his fate (see Sobolewski 2002). Similarly, Jean-Michel Frodon criticised Polanski for his traditional representation of the war and compared *The Pianist* to Atom Egoyan's *Ararat* (2002), suggesting that the latter film is much more personal despite Polanski's personal experience of the war while Egoyan knew only representations (see Frodon 2002).

The shift in visual representation from subjectivism to realism coincides with other changes in Polanski's cinema, which comprise his approach to characters and narratives. As mentioned in the previous chapter, his characters are increasingly ordinary and normal, therefore easier to identify with. Consequently, I would argue that nowadays Polanski, while still remaining an advocate of outsiders and the dispossessed, is more interested in the common ground between their perceptions and experiences and those of the rest of the world. Such a shift goes against the trends set by postmodernism, and which Polanski himself pioneered in the 1960s. For this reason his recent films, especially *The Pianist*, are regarded by some critics as well intended but old-fashioned, a sign of the artistic ageing of a filmmaker who for so many decades was associated with youthfulness. On the other hand, this transition testifies to the growing optimism on the part of the director, especially to his faith in the possibility of human communication, which is a prerequisite for overcoming or alleviating the absurd which clouds every human existence.

4

ALL THAT JAZZ AND NOISE:
MUSIC IN POLANSKI'S FILMS

There are at least two reasons for granting special attention to the music in Polanski's films. Firstly, some of the scores are innovative, particularly in the context of the music used in Polish films at the time he started his career as a director. One might say that Polanski 'discovered' Krzysztof Komeda for film music. Before his untimely death Komeda was widely regarded as the best Polish jazz musician and one of the most outstanding Polish film composers. The second reason is that some of Polanski's films are about music as the object of someone's passion.

This chapter will trace what influenced Polanski's approach and choice of music in his early productions, as certain tendencies survived in his films even after he changed his composers. I will begin by describing the use of music in Polish films of the 1950s and 1960s, and Polanski's own approach to it. Then I will proceed to one of the main functions fufilled by music in Polanski's movies: representing madness. I will finish this chapter by referring to the films about people for whom music is particularly important. Consequently, I will omit from my discussion some films for which the scores were widely praised by critics, such as *Chinatown*,[1] but which do not fit the above criteria.

FROM THE POLISH SCHOOL TO JAZZ FILMS

His music was cool and modern, but there was a hot heart inside it. Komeda was a film composer *par excellence*. He gave truth to my films. Without his music they would be meaningless.

Roman Polanski

Polanski started to direct short films several years after the Polish School replaced socialist realism in Polish cinema. Apart from offering new types of characters, particularly young men who fought and died in the Second World War, and introducing new visual styles, such as expressionism, the Polish School brought a new approach to film music. The authors of scores for films directed by Andrzej Wajda, Andrzej Munk and Wojciech Jerzy Has – such as Andrzej Markowski, Jan Krenz and Tadeusz Baird, all famous composers in their own right – specialised in avant-garde music. They also used this type of music in films, often blending it with other styles. Consequently, rather than illustrating the film's explicit content, which was typically the case in socialist realist movies, as well as in Polish films made before the war, music in the Polish School films became somehow autonomous or counterpointed the narrative, drawing attention to the film's hidden meanings. The composers also broke with the tradition of employing the whole symphony orchestra and opted for a more selective use of instruments (a single piano, drum, clarinet or xylophone, often applied in an unexpected way) or for an ensemble of only two or three instruments (see Kułakowska 1961: 42). In this way the changes in Polish film music preceded those in Hollywood, where symphonic scores did not decline until the 1960s (see Prendergast 1992; Ross 1998).

In the late 1950s and early 1960s some of the creators of the Polish School, as well as directors just beginning their careers, realised that the subject of war had somehow become exhausted. New plots and characters, relevant to contemporary reality, and new ways to convey their problems were needed. As a consequence, they turned to jazz, or, more precisely, to modern jazz.[2] It should be mentioned here that after the Second World War the communist authorities denounced jazz as music which was foreign to the Polish national character and which promoted imperialist values, not unlike Coca-Cola or blue jeans. The official slogan proclaimed: 'Today you play jazz, tomorrow you will betray your country' (see Tomasik 2004: 179). Such accusations towards jazz and jazzmen might be regarded as paradoxical, taking into account the origins of jazz in the culture of black slaves. However, jazz was also, as George McKay argues, 'a culture of the great hegemon of late modernity, the United States of America' (McKay 2005), and on many occasions it indeed served as a tool of American propaganda, as the communists claimed (Ibid.). As a result of a negative attitude to jazz on the part of communist authorities till the mid-1950s, jazz in Poland went 'semi-underground', being performed largely in private houses and students' clubs, which led to the name 'catacomb period' (see Kowal 1995).[3] However, the hostile attitude of the political authorities helped Polish jazz, rather than thwarting it, by giving it the aura of a forbidden fruit and an antidote to the stale pseudo-art produced according to the rules of socialist realism (see Tomasik 2004). Theodor Adorno, who was an ardent critic of jazz, regarding it as a purely commercial product of unfounded avant-gardist pretentions, claimed that 'in Europe, where jazz has not yet become an everyday phenomenon, there is the tendency, especially among those devotees who have adopted it as *Weltanschauung*, to regard it…as a triumph over the musty museum-culture' (Adorno 1981: 122), and this perfectly reflects the status jazz enjoyed in Poland at this time. The position of jazz changed with the political thaw that followed the death of Stalin in 1953 and that of the leader of the Polish communist party, Bolesław Bierut in 1956. Jazz began to be played legally, even at specially organised jazz festivals in Sopot and Warsaw. However, even at this 'legal' stage, jazz was associated with rebelliousness and freedom, or at least restlessness, escapism and the 'alternative' lifestyles of urban youth. It should be added that the associations of jazz in Polish postwar culture were not very different to those in America, where jazz was also linked with youth and urban subcultures. For example, in Toni Morrison's novel *Jazz*, as Jan Furman argues, jazz is the music of the city which sends competing messages; its excitement 'masks a "complicated anger" of wronged lovers…and of a generally disillusioned existence' (Furman 1996: 97).

The first Polish postwar feature film that used jazz was *Koniec nocy* (*The End of the Night*, 1955–7); this was a joint project by students and graduates of the Łódź Film School, including Julian Dziedzina and Paweł Komorowski, and was based on a script co-written by Marek Hłasko, one of the most popular writers of the period and one of the leaders of the Polish 'jazz generation'. In this film, as in several others made about the same time, such as the short feature film *Uwaga, chuligani!* (*Attention, Hooligans!*, 1955) directed by Jerzy Hoffman and Edward Skórzewski, and *Lunatycy* (*Sleepwalkers*, 1959) by Bohdan Poręba, jazz is used predominantly as an element of diegesis. It is music listened to by young hooligans and misfits who in this way express their distance from 'decent society' (see Sowińska work in progress). It is worth adding that in

The End of the Night one such jazz-loving delinquent is played by Roman Polanski.

Polanski was also in the vanguard of those who appreciated the opportunities offered to cinema by jazz, especially its potential to provide a film with an aura of contemporaneity and 'cool', and endow its director with an authorial signature. Firstly he used it in his short films, made in the late 1950s. The musician who composed the scores for many of them and for all of Polanski's subsequent full-length feature films up to *Rosemary's Baby*, with the exception of *Repulsion*, was Krzysztof Komeda. Komeda (1931–1968), real name Krzysztof Trzciński, was not only a first-class film composer, but also the leading force of developing modern jazz in Poland as composer, pianist and the leader of the Komeda Sextet. He achieved this position despite dying young, at the age of thirty-seven, as a result of an injury suffered while skiing in California. His individual style resulted from an ability to intertwine various sources of inspiration, such as Polish classical music and folklore, and the sound of the popular jazz combos of that time: The Modern Jazz Quartet and the Gerry Mulligan Quartet (see Kowal 1995). Komeda's collaboration with Polanski is reminiscent of another long lasting and fruitful partnership between director and composer, that of Alfred Hitchcock and Bernard Herrmann, as both pairs were based on the principle of 'opposites attract' (see Brown 1994: 148). While Polanski, like Herrmann, was extroverted, vehement and raucous, Komeda, like Hitchcock, or even more so, was introverted and shy (see Batura 2001: 91–2).

As Roman Kowal argues, the specificity of Komeda's style as a composer of film music was a clash between the lyricism of the leading musical motif and the aggressive sound of jazz (see Kowal 1995: 120). This lyricism, which assured him the label of the greatest 'poet' of Polish jazz, is conveyed in the titles of his compositions, containing words such as 'ballad' or 'lullaby'.[4] As an author of film music scores he was also not afraid to look for ways to reach beyond jazz, for example by venturing into pop music (see Sowińska work in progress). Komeda's fondness for lyrical themes wrapped in prickly and dangerous packaging paralleled Polanski's filmic interests, an example being the theme of unfulfilled love or love that leads to a crime. Critics also draw attention to the elusive and mysterious quality of Komeda's music and his innovative use of individual instruments that often mimic natural sounds (see Kowal 1995: 120). No doubt both these traits attracted Polanski, who from the beginning of his career revealed a predilection to ambiguity and irony and favoured 'rich', multi-layered sound.

Komeda himself, in an interview given in 1961, identified two types of film music. In the first type a leitmotif reappears in various episodes of the film, although possibly in different instrumentations. The second type is more varied, with different musical motifs being used in different parts of the film. Although the composer did not state clearly which approach he favours, he suggested that the first type is more effective. The viewer remembers such scores better, while the nuances of the second type are typically overlooked (see Komeda-Trzciński 1961: 37). It can also be added that in the film with a leitmotif there is a stronger link between the music and the individual character – a feature that proved very important for Polanski. Of course, jazz music, which consists of improvisations on a theme, particularly lends itself to be used as film music of the first type. In the same interview Komeda warned against overusing music in film, arguing that it is most effective when employed sparingly (Ibid.: 36), and he emphasised the link between music and other sounds used in a film, such as city noises (Ibid.: 35). Furthermore, he declared himself to be an adherent of film music that is functional and subservient to the narrative, rather than autonomous, as was the case in *Anatomy of a Murder* (1959) by Otto Preminger (Ibid.: 37), or the Polish *Pociąg* (*Night Train*, 1959), directed by Jerzy Kawalerowicz (see Sowińska work in progress).

Komeda's preferences laid the foundations for the use of music in the vast majority of Polanski's films, including those whose scores Komeda did not compose. Accordingly, music in Polanski's films is typically dominated by a single motif or two contrasting motifs, which reflect the drastic change in the protagonist's situation. Moreover, music is strongly related to other elements of the soundtrack; it is often just one of many noises heard by the characters. Furthermore, one remembers the scores from Polanski's films well, largely because the director uses music in modest proportions, juxtaposing it, for example, with long periods of silence. Komeda believed that jazz is not equally suitable to all film genres, but best serves psychological films and thrillers – in other words, films with a mystery, a hidden meaning which music helps to unleash. He focused on these types of films in his career (see Kowal 1995: 120). It is worth adding that historically jazz was most often used in the types of films Komeda described, especially in *film noir*. This particular suitability might be accounted to such factors as jazz's association with urban life, sensuality or even illicit pleasures of the body, and the strong narrative drive of some types of jazz.

In Polanski's shorts we usually find a simple musical motif or a small number of themes, which are repeated throughout the film with only small variations. Such music reflects Polanski's narratives, which underline the repetititive character of human actions and the characters' returning to the same position in which they started. In *Two Men and a Wardrobe* – Komeda's debut in the role of film composer – there are two main motifs. One, written by Komeda earlier and dedicated to his wife, who described it as a 'lullaby' (see Kowal 1995: 120), is in a minor key and very lyrical. It begins the film, accompanying the two men when they emerge from the sea, recurs four times, each time in a slightly different variation, and finally closes the story, when the men return to the water, carrying their wardrobe with them. The lullaby creates an atmosphere of yearning, conveyed by the sound of a single saxophone. The second theme, which appears only once, when the characters pass through the town, is a fast, bebop motif. Eventually, when the two men encounter a gang of thugs, the motif changes again, into a sinister theme, played by double-bass and vibraphone. The score of *The Fat and the Lean* is even less versatile (despite the film being much longer than *Two Men and a Wardrobe*), with one motif dominating the entire film. This is not surprising, as on this occasion the music conveys the boredom of the lean man and his abortive attempts to free himself from his master. The tenor saxophone, which is also the most important instrument in modern jazz, provides the main theme while the piano establishes the rhythm. Music in Polanski's short films also often imitates natural sounds, such as the jingle of bells attached to the sleigh in *Mammals*.

Already in his early films Polanski uses diegetic music extensively. It appears for the first time in *Let's Break the Ball*, where a group of musicians are playing jazz at a fancy-dress party, attended by young people (who were in reality students of the Łódź Film School). Jazz used in this way points to the modernity of the dancers, communicated by their funny and sophisticated costumes, cool behaviour and the setting. Diegetic music is also used in *The Fat and the Lean*. The lean man plays a drum, a flute and a violin, to entertain his master. He finds playing difficult – it feels like torture to him, particularly when he has to play two instruments at once. Moreover, the master is unhappy with his playing and at some point repossesses the servant's drum to show him how it should be used. Hence, Polanski introduces the theme of music as an element of cruel performance which he will later develop in films such as *What?*, *Death and the Maiden* and *The Pianist*.

The music in Polanski's short films was given particular prominence because the films contain no dialogue. The director explained in one of his interviews that he regards words as unsuitable to the medium of short film – it makes it look like a fragment of a full-length film, instead of being an artistic form in its own right (see Gelmis 1971: 145). In the absence of words, music must not only convey the overall atmosphere of the film, but play a large part in depicting the situation and the feelings of the characters.

Many of the features of Komeda's scores for Polanski's short films can also be attributed to *Knife in the Water*. First of all, the music, again in the style of modern jazz, is very functional, one can even say engaged in the narrative, both in its content and structure. The plot is marked by a recurrent play of tension and the release of tension; so is the music, 'which alternates between the energetic bebop and the "lazy" cool' (Sowińska work in progress). Four motifs are used only once and two more than once. The most important is *Ballad for Bernt*, named after the Swedish tenor saxophone player, Bernt Rosengren, whom Komeda invited to record the music for *Knife in the Water*. It appears four times in the film, including at the beginning and at the end of the film, accentuating the circularity of the narrative. This non-diegetic music, which accompanies Andrzej and Krystyna on their way to the Mazurian Lakes and back, is juxtaposed with the banal piano chords from a radio serving as background to morning exercises. Krzysztof Bukowski argues that the clash of these two types of music in the first scene forecasts the discord between the couple, experienced in full force when they find themselves on the yacht, while in the last scene it confirms that the discord was not overcome (see Bukowski 1980: 9). On two other occasions, *Ballad for Bernt* marks the moments of rest. In the first, the characters are sunbathing, in the second they hide below deck to avoid the rain. The second recurrent theme, built of two parts of contrasting mood, accompanies the yacht when it begins its journey and, later, when it runs aground in shallow water. As Iwona Sowińska argues, it both promises the pleasure of sailing and conveys its danger (see Sowińska work in progress). On the whole, the recurrent themes stress the symmetrical construction of the film and convey its mood, suggesting that behind the appearance of the central couple's happy, bourgeois lifestyle there lurk sinister feelings of exasperation, disappointment, suspicion and cruelty. Some critics went so far as to suggest that the music helps to give *Knife in the Water* the form of a thriller (see Stachówna 1987: 26). It is worth adding that, for the viewers who remember Polish television of the 1960s, this impression is strengthened by the frequent use of saxophone in the score of the television crime plays known as *Kobra* (*Cobra*). In the same vein, Marek Hendrykowski argues that the metaphor of a modern jazz composition is the key to capturing the specificity of the film's theme. He describes *Knife in the Water* as a set of 'improvisatory variations on a theme' – the theme being power (see Hendrykowski 1997: 91–6). Paul Coates seizes upon Hendrykowski's metaphor, arguing that the film has a jazz-like rhythm, largely thanks to 'confrontations sizzling then fizzling, usually whenever Krystyna intervenes to discharge a tension of which she is to some extent the unacknowledged catalyst' (Coates 2004: 81).

Another function of Komeda's score is to individualise the three 'anti-heroes'. At some moments, in an onomatopoeic way it mimics the voices of the characters or imitates their movements, such as the student's ascending the yacht's mast (see Kowal 1995: 120). Furthermore, it conveys the bonds that are built and dissolved during the trip. Krystyna often hums a sad melody suggesting that she harbours some yearnings and unfulfilment. This impression is made explicit when she sings a song about love that went wrong. The melody is seized on by the student, who whistles it; Andrzej, annoyed, forbids him to do so, claiming that whistling on a yacht is against sailing etiquette. In reality he disapproves of his whistling because the student's sharing music with his wife signifies the possibility of them sharing something more: taste, sensibility, even love. Later Andrzej himself starts to whistle the melody, as if trying to appropriate the song, changing it into his and Krystyna's shared experience and in this way regaining his wife.

Knife in the Water was not the first full-length feature film for which Komeda wrote the score. A year before Polanski's debut film, three other films with his music had their premieres. They were *Do widzenia, do jutra* (*Good Bye, See You Tomorrow*, 1960) by Janusz Morgenstern, *Niewinni czarodzieje* (*Innocent Sorcerers*, 1960) by Andrzej Wajda and *Szklana góra* (*The Glass Mountain*, 1960) by Paweł Komorowski. The first of these two films, linked to *Knife in the Water* by the participation in their scripts of Jerzy Skolimowski, a friend of Komeda, were regarded by a number of Polish film critics as the natural context for discussing Polanski's debut feature (see Eberhardt 1982: 112–31; Hendrykowski 1997: 88). All these films can be described as 'jazz films' not because they use jazz music in a soundtrack but because they portray a 'jazz generation' (see Helman 1967: 138). Their protagonists are people in their twenties who have only recently started to look for their own systems of values, ways of expression and life goals. They do not know yet how to live, but are adamant that they will not follow in the footsteps of an older generation who were either physically and emotionally injured by the war (if they survived it at all), or 'sold out' to the communist regime. They largely model themselves on Western or even American youth. They want to be individuals and enjoy everything that life has on offer: sex, cars, fashionable clothes and holidays abroad, but do not know yet how to get it and whether it is everything that they want to achieve. They hide and at the same time betray their disorientation and insecurity by donning masks and playing games. For example, the protagonists of Wajda's film, a young man and woman who meet for the first time in a jazz club, use invented names. Jazz music perfectly encapsulates their sense of freedom and disorientation, as well as a certain distance towards Polish politics and culture, expressed by their clothes and hairstyles, which are inspired by Western fashions, and their unwillingness to talk about anything that is Polish. The function of jazz in Polish 'jazz films' is not very different to its function in French New Wave films, such as À bout de souffle (Breathless, 1960) by Jean-Luc Godard with music by Martial Solal. Jazz scores also reflect the 'freewheeling' structure of these films, where little happens, and the point of arrival is similar to the point of departure.

Even those critics who failed to recognise Knife in the Water's jazzy rhythm or jazz-like structure noted that its music is impossible to ignore and that it creates the mood of the film (see Stachówna 1987: 26; Dondziłło 1984: 15). One reviewer even complained about the music being too importunate, drawing attention to itself rather than to the narrative (see Toeplitz 1962: 12). The jazz qualities of Knife in the Water, as with Wajda's Innocent Sorcerers and Morgenstern's Good Bye, See You Tomorrow, contributed to the relatively poor opinion of this film among a large section of Polish critics and, more importantly, politicians. Knife in the Water and Innocent Sorcerers constituted the core of films condemned in 1963 by the then party leader, Władysław Gomułka, for being contrived, vacuous, alien to the Polish national character (and by extension imitating the Western/American character), and lacking in optimism – all features that were considered dangerous for the young generation (see Stachówna 1987: 24). There then followed the accusation (or compliment) that Knife in the Water was similar to the films of the French New Wave. Although Polanski himself resolutely denied this claim, as did many Polish advocates of the film, eager to demonstrate that Polanski's feature debut had essentially Polish roots, I would support it. This does not mean that the Polish director was influenced by Godard, Lelouch or Malle (I believe he was not); rather, that the French New Wave reflected a similar sensibility, pertaining to the first generation of young people who had no memory of the Second World War and who, for values and models of behaviour, looked outside their national culture, especially to the USA.

In Polanski's subsequent films for which Komeda wrote scores, music is used in a similar way to that in Knife in the Water. The closest to this model is Cul-de-Sac, not least because the film is thematically and structurally similar, focusing on the relationships between two men and one woman. However, in terms of melody, the music is less versatile, as the score is dominated by one simple theme, repeatedly played by different combinations of instruments. Its main function seems to be that of mimicking and foretelling events. Take the first scene of the film, when Richard and Alfie approach the Holy Island by car. First we hear a repetitive theme, played on drums, double-bass and piano, used by Komeda largely to provide a rhythm. Then a variation of this theme is introduced by a trumpet, while the previous music is still heard in the background. It gives the impression of two musical motifs fighting with each other to dominate the 'aural landscape' of the film. This struggle announces the main topic of the film: the conflict or, more exactly, the multitude of conflicts between three characters that are never resolved, only pushed to the background. Such use of music also underlines the repetitiveness and circularity of action, mocking the characters' efforts to resolve the conundrum.

Music also helps to individualise the characters, separating the female from her two male screen partners. Against the background of George and Richard, who are both rather serious and focused on their tasks, Teresa comes across as playful and whimsical. She acts on impulse and likes cruel jokes. Her rebellious and moody personality is reflected in her love of jazz. She possesses a large collection of jazz records, which (not unlike her flock of hens, mentioned in other chapters of this book) constitute a challenge to the ancient ambience of the castle, which George wants everybody to respect. George disdains his wife's taste, but at the same time succumbs to it, as shown by him whistling Teresa's favourite tune. In this respect he is very similar to Andrzej in *Knife in the Water* who shuns Krystyna, but cannot avoid her attractiveness. Teresa's fondness for jazz also contrasts with the coarse taste of Richard, who at some point sings in a horribly hoarse, drunken voice something which sounds like an army song.

Teresa's love of jazz is excellently portrayed in the scene where the son of George's visitors scratches one of her jazz records – which can be interpreted as a metaphor for the growing frictions between the characters. She is so outraged by this act that she pulls the child's ear, making him scream and shout. When the boy's parents arrive, the polite (although tense) atmosphere is ruined. In this episode the music not only reflects the mood but produces it in a literal sense. The boundaries between diegetic and non-diegetic music are blurred in *Cul-de-Sac*, as the theme introduced at the beginning of the film is played later on Teresa's record player. The female character can therefore be seen as the ultimate creator of the atmosphere of the film. By associating women with jazz Polanski also detached himself from the common view of jazz as the ultimate male music, thereby demonstrating, as I will argue at length later (see Chapter 5), that his views on women are not as stereotyped as critics suggest.

MUSIC AND MADNESS

While in Polanski's early films the style of music typically reflects nonconformist and antagonistic, although normal, behaviour, in some later films, especially *Repulsion*, *Rosemary's Baby* and *The Tenant*, the score tends to communicate the mental state of a sick person. Again, the music is predominantly jazz, written specially for the film, although by then Polanski had started to introduce classical themes, usually as an element of the diegesis.

Repulsion starts with an extreme close-up of Carol's eye and the sound of a slow, monotonous drumbeat, which feels like blows on one's head. When the camera pulls out to reveal Carol's face and the hand of an old woman that she is manicuring, it feels as if Carol has interrupted her work because she is overwhelmed by inner turmoil. The drum is followed by a lyrical jazzy motif on the saxophone, suggesting that the beautician is a delicate, romantic and introverted creature, prone to daydreaming. This impression is reinforced by the movement of the camera, which pulls away from the body of the older customer, showing Carol retreating further and further away from reality into her own thoughts. This 'inner journey' is abruptly ended by the old lady poignantly asking Carol: 'Have you fallen asleep?'

The next time we hear jazz is when Carol is walking the streets of London and meets Colin, a man who would like to be her boyfriend. At this point the rather cheerful and relaxed music, paired with the images of workers, resting during their lunch break, bears stronger associations with the mood of the city than with Carol's inner world. For the viewers familiar with the films of 'Swinging London' this association is even stronger, as directors who set their films in London in a similar period also turned to jazz, for example in *Alfie* (1966), directed by Lewis Gilbert, *Georgy Girl* (1966), directed by Silvio Narizzano and *Kaleidoscope* (1966), directed by Jack Smight. This is the last time the music is so light-hearted, however; on later occasions it signifies either terror, as when Carol is kissed by Colin and rushes home to wash her face, or an autistic detachment, as when left alone in the flat, she looks at the ceiling and starts to imagine things. The music in *Repulsion* often produces a kind of echo, which serves as a metaphor of a tormented mind that cannot rid itself of inner voices. The soundtrack is dominated by drum, saxophone and double-bass – the drum to evoke terror, the double-bass the melancholy of the heroine.

The boundaries between non-diegetic and diegetic music, and between music and other diegetic sounds, are blurred in *Repulsion*. Colin McArthur observes that Polanski 'frequently cuts to objects emitting sudden and startling sounds (telephones, doorbells, lift-buttons)' (McArthur 1968–9: 16). The sound is typically so unexpected and loud that it does not seem like a real sound, but a noise amplified by Carol's auditory hyper-sensitivity. Often extra-diegetic music, which can be equated with Carol's 'inner melody', is ended by the introduction of a diegetic sound. Yet after a while it becomes so exaggerated and sinister that we lose certainty as to whether it exists in reality or plays only in Carol's head. Consequently, sounds fulfil a significant role in the viewer's disorientation about the status of represented events. One example is the scene in which Carol

John Fraser and Catherine Deneuve in *Repulsion* (1965)

is lying in bed accompanied by a non-diegetic jazz tune. The tune is gradually replaced by the sound of the chandelier rattling and cracks appearing in the ceiling. Initially it seems as if the music in Carol's head is being replaced by real sound, but after a while we realise that the cracking ceiling also emanates from her imagination. Similarly, the sound of a piano playing in the flat upstairs is so persistent and repetitive that it arouses the suspicion that it only exists in Carol's head. This suspicion is reinforced by the fact that most of the sounds which antagonise or even hurt the ear are only heard when the heroine is alone. Even the sound of the telephone seems to be less violent when Carol's sister is around. The sensation of the suddenness of a sound partly results from the long periods of silence. In the context of silence every sound, even the most innocuous, such as a clock's ticking, becomes menacing. Sounds in *Repulsion* become frightening also by their relation to image. For example, the jangling tune produced by a banjo and some spoons can be regarded as innocent, if not pleasant. However, the crab-like movements of the buskers, whom Carol and Colin encounter on their way to her flat, seem aggressive, as if they want to thwart the person they are approaching. On another occasion we hear Carol singing to herself in a childlike voice. Again, this is not an unusual event, but the fact that Carol sings when ironing a dress with an iron that is not switched on, herself dressed like a child, makes her utterance grotesque, even scary. In this way she is a predecessor to Rosemary who also will sing in a childlike voice.

As previously mentioned, Komeda did not write the score for *Repulsion*.[5] Its author is an even more famous jazzman – composer and drummer from Los Angeles, Foreststorn 'Chico' Hamilton (b. 1921). What strikes me is how similar the music in *Repulsion* seems in its sound, atmosphere and function within the narrative to that composed by Komeda. This resemblance can partly be explained by the closeness between the styles of Komeda and Hamilton, whose work Komeda listed as an important strand in modern jazz (see Komeda-Trzciński 1961: 36). Ultimately, however, it points to Polanski's overall control of the scores – the composers write the music, but the director decides what style it should have and how to use it. It is worth mentioning here that Komeda himself contrasted Polanski's approach to film music to that of his older colleague Andrzej Wajda. The former always told him how he imagined the score and gave precise suggestions, the latter gave him a completely free hand (Ibid.: 35).

Komeda's opinion that film music with a dominant motif is better remembered than a more elaborate and versatile score is validated by the popularity and longevity of the score of *Rosemary's Baby*. The main musical theme in this film, known as *Rosemary's Lullaby*, is the single best-known tune of all Polanski's films and all the scores written by Komeda. The song opens and closes the film and in-between we hear several times its instrumental version, typically illustrating activities associated with the arrival of a new baby, such as receiving a call from the doctor announcing Rosemary's pregnancy or decorating the nursery. Although we do not see Rosemary singing, we ascribe the song to her, not only because it is Mia Farrow's voice in reality, but also because the childlike voice uttering the melody reflects Rosemary's warm personality of a perfect mother. Or it could be argued that the singing, as in Carol's case, signals Rosemary's own regression to childhood and mental illness.

Rosemary's Lullaby is not the only piece of music associated with the heroine. Similarly to Teresa in *Cul-de-Sac*, she possesses a large collection of jazz records. However, in her case it signifies not her rebelliousness, but rather her desire to find peace (which is paradoxical, taking into account that jazz was often considered the soundtrack to urban pollution) and, perhaps, her ambition to become a true New Yorker. Yet she has few

Mia Farrow and John Cassavetes in *Rosemary's Baby* (1968)

opportunities to listen to her favourite music. When she is on her own in the apartment and puts a record on, she is disturbed by Minnie Castevet and her equally noisy female friend Laura-Louise; when she is with Guy, they watch loud advertisements for Yamaha motorcycles in which Rosemary's husband stars. Moreover, somebody in the building is practising the piano and the Castevets' guests often play instruments and sing. Hence, Rosemary and Guy's flat is rendered as an area of continual invasion of unwelcome sounds and aural conflict, almost an open space. Unsurprisingly, in Rosemary's dream her bedroom changes into an ocean, on which her bed floats away. Unpleasant sounds also attack Rosemary when she is outdoors. When she visits the city centre before Christmas, the air is filled with the loud and discordant sounds of jingles and degraded versions of religious chants and hymns. The function of this 'music', in common with religious symbols displayed in the windows of a department store, is purely commercial – to encourage customers to come inside and spend money.

The theme of invasion of sounds and the person's control over noise returns and is even given special prominence in *The Tenant*, the score for which was composed by Philippe Sarde (who also wrote the music for *Tess* and *Pirates*). Non-diegetic music is used in a similar way to that in *Repulsion*: it accompanies the main character, Trelkovsky, when he is on his own, typically in his rented flat. Usually we hear a melancholic theme, which occasionally changes into a more dynamic tune when he becomes worried or frightened, as in the scene when he looks through his window at the inner courtyard where Simone Choule threw herself to her death. Its melancholia reflects the dark and sorrowful ambience of the flat that gradually overwhelms the tenant. Trelkovsky is a quiet man but he is not a loner. Neither is he immune to life's little pleasures as signified by the cheerful Latino music (also a sign of his cultural nomadism) that he listens to in his flat – until his stereo is stolen by burglars or by his neighbours, who in this way punish him for daring to disturb their sleep. Having no music to amuse him when he is on his own, he becomes ultra-sensitive to the sounds around him. As Jonathan Rosenbaum observes, 'The water dripping from Trelkovsky's kitchen tap, the rattle of pipes, the squeak of his cupboard door, the repetitive piano exercises heard from the stairway, the faint cooing of pigeons in the courtyard and the angry pounding of the neighbour upstairs all outline the space of a constricted consciousness' (Rosenbaum 1976: 253). Eventually, like Carol, he starts to hear sounds that do not exist in reality.

Trelkovsky's sensitivity to sounds is not inborn, but acquired – a result of living in a 'quiet neighbourhood' of the apartment block where the tenants continually eavesdrop in order to chastise anybody who does not conform to their social code. Ironically, their punishment of Trelkovsky for being noisy is to produce even more noise: knocking on his door, beating on the floor with sticks and shouting. The right to produce noise and the necessity to endure it is a measure of a person's power and status. Those who are able to be noisy and force others to be quiet are the powerful; those who are exposed to the loud sounds but must remain silent are the powerless. Trelkovsky is contrasted with his workmate, who in his apartment listens to records of marching tunes; when asked politely by his neighbour to turn down the music, the workmate insults the man and turns up the music to its maximum. In such a context music loses its aesthetic distinctiveness and becomes just one of many noises used in the aggressive battle for dominance, as acknowledged in newspaper articles about people singing arias to get on their neighbours' nerves, and subsequently being killed for their behaviour. This repositioning of music to the level of (ordinary) sounds is signified by the transition in the non-diegetic music used in the film. The melancholic melody at the beginning, accompanying Trelkovsky, gradually changes into a cacophony of sounds reminiscent of scratching and drilling.

Polanski provides some clues to help us understand why Parisians are so obsessed with noise. One reason seems to be the shortage of accommodation, forcing people to live in high-density apartment blocks where everybody hears what everybody else is doing. Secondly, he represents Paris as a very noisy city, where cars pass under people's windows twenty-four hours a day, and roadworks and building renovation take place all the time. Even in Trelkovsky's office, workers have little privacy, with desks cramped into a small area with the reception as part of the office. In such circumstances a private apartment can be a refuge, or a prison cell, or even a coffin, in which one is not allowed to show any sign of life.

On the whole, Trelkovsky oscillates between an utter conformity to the 'vow of silence' forced on him by his neighbours, and rebellion against it. As noted earlier in Chapter 2 his noisy suicide which attracts the attention of all inhabitants of the apartment block, and the scream which he utters in the hospital, signify his rebellion. However, his is a 'swan song' – after the scream comes the complete deathly silence.

MUSIC, CIVILISATION AND BARBARITY

In his two recent films, *Death and the Maiden* and *The Pianist*, Polanski not only uses music as an element of diegesis and features people for whom music is very important, but also encourages us to think about the role of music in the life of the individual, as well as in society and culture as a whole. This tendency coincides with an inclination to use classical music or a score which is contemporary but reminiscent of music from earlier times.

The title of the first film is borrowed from the title given to Schubert's string quartet no. 14 in D minor; music from the quartet is repeated in the film several times and is discussed by the characters. The concept of 'Death and the Maiden', however, comes from older cultural traditions and artistic representations, its roots being found in Greek and Roman mythologies. The young goddess, Persephone (Proserpine in Roman myth), was gathering flowers in the company of carefree nymphs when she saw a pretty narcissus and plucked it. At that moment, the ground opened. Hades, god of hell (Roman Pluto), came out of the underworld and abducted her. In subsequent representations of the myth the abduction stands as a prefiguration of the clash, as well as link, between Eros and Thanatos, love and death. The story also has a moral – it points out that life is as short as the beauty of a woman: her body will one day feed the worms.

The theme of 'Death and the Maiden' has also been used by painters as a pretext to represent female nudity. Schubert's music fulfilled this function in one of Polanski's earlier films, *What?*, in which the naked Nancy runs away from Noblart's villa accompanied by the sounds of the romantic masterpiece. Not surprisingly, Polanski himself was later unhappy about having used this motif in *What?*, claiming that the film would have gained from a less melancholic soundtrack (see Thompson 1995: 11). Equally, it can be argued that there is some meaningful similarity in the way that this musical motif is employed in *What?* and *Death and the Maiden* – both films depict cruel and contemptuous behaviour towards a young woman by older men who regard themselves as connoisseurs of music and art in a wider sense.

In Polanski's *Death and the Maiden* Schubert's string quartet is the favourite piece of music of the two main characters: Paulina Escobar and Doctor Roberto Miranda. Miranda, who was Paulina's torturer during the military regime, raped her while the music played from a tape recorder, although he also claimed that the music soothed her. As a result of the association of the *Death and the Maiden* quartet with pain, oppression and death, after regaining her freedom Paulina was unable to listen to it. She 'retrieved' her favourite music, however, by forcing Miranda to confess his crimes. Her repossession of Schubert's masterpiece is conveyed by the contrast between the first and the last scenes of the film. In both scenes Paulina listens to *Death and the Maiden* sitting next to her husband in a concert hall. However, in the first scene she is very edgy, as is suggested by her pressing her husband's hand as if the music is causing her pain. In the last scene she looks relaxed, clearly enjoying the music. Moreover, she looks at her oppressor Doctor Miranda without a trace of fear, on the contrary – triumphantly.

The story of music being using as an accompaniment to torture is a familiar one. There are many tales about German soldiers and policemen (who constitute the archetype of political oppressor in postwar literature and cinema) who amused themselves by forcing concentration camp prisoners to play their favourite compositions. There are also stories of the Nazis themselves playing music while their colleagues shot the Jews. The Nazis were very keen on music, favouring Romantic composers, such as Wagner, Bruckner and Strauss. As a result, as Alex Ross argues, classical music, especially the work of the aforementioned composers, is now strongly associated with spiritual corruption. 'Where musicians were once the noble, fragile heroes of high-class studio pictures,' writes Ross, 'after the war they acquired a hint of sadism, of cultivated malice. Now when any self-respecting Hollywood arch-criminal sets out to annihilate mankind he listens to a little opera to get in the mood. Even Hannibal Lecter, moving his bloodstained fingers in time to the "Goldberg Variations", might be distantly echoing the Nazis' twin enthusiasms for music and death' (Ross 2003). Ross also suggests that after 1945 a new morality of music evolved (from which, however, he distances himself), based on two syllogisms: '(1) if Hitler liked it, it must be bad; (2) if Hitler hated it, it must be good' (Ibid.). Moreover, some of the greatest writers of the twentieth century, such as Vladimir Nabokov and George Orwell, as Richard Rorty put it, helped us 'to see the way in which the private pursuit of aesthetic bliss produces cruelty' (Rorty 1989: 146).

Although in his film Polanski revives the cliché of a musically cultivated oppressor, constructing Doctor Miranda as a South American version of Doctor Mengele, he refrains from using as a criterion of music's value the moral qualities of its admirers. Schubert's quartet is neither morally nor aesthetically belittled by its connection with Miranda. Paulina herself does not condemn the work, only regrets that listening to it after her experience with Miranda does not give her pleasure. Thus Schubert's *Death and the Maiden* and music in general, as represented by Polanski, remains neutral ground which essentially does not belong to anybody, although it can be used by people of different moral qualities.

We can find a similar motif in *The Pianist* with its whole spectrum of people who love music. Among them are Władysław Szpilman, widely admired as an excellent performer of Chopin, his flame Dorota, the

Christian Polish cellist whose affection for Szpilman is largely based on her admiration of his musical talent, and the Jewish policeman who saves Szpilman's life because of respect for his talent, while at the same beating fellow Jews to death. There is also a German policeman who treats a Jewish street performer with some leniency, even giving him a cigarette, and another who cruelly forces Jews to dance to the music played by a street band of buskers. Eventually, Polanski shows us the German officer, Wilm Hosenfeld, who not only spares Szpilman's life, but brings him food and clothing after hearing him playing. On the whole, music in this film is associated more with civilised than with barbaric behaviour. The privileges enjoyed by Szpilman due to his musical talents even strike me as a form of extreme (determining a person's life or death) class

Ben Kingsley and Sigourney Weaver in *Death and the Maiden* (1994)

segregation, parallelling the ethnic segregation of Poles into Christian Poles and Jews.[6]

By depicting Szpilman as a man who played music before, during and after the war Polanski also partakes in a debate as to whether, to paraphrase Theodor Adorno, one is morally entitled to play music 'after Auschwitz'. Szpilman's interpretation of Chopin's piano concerto at the end of the film, which in reality began the broadcast of Polish radio after the war, suggests an affirmative answer to this question. In Polanski's film Chopin's music, as indeed any other music, is not tainted by its association with the Holocaust. Nor is Szpilman for his willingness to exploit his talent and fame for survival. On the contrary, he is depicted as a man of integrity and courage. Władysław's final performance signifies his personal victory over extremely adverse circumstances and a return to normality in which pianists play music, instead of carrying bricks and mixing cement. If Polanski criticises anybody in the film for his attitude to music, it is Władysław's brother, Henryk, who attacks the pianist for playing in the café for rich Jews, but at the same time enjoys the privileges attached to his brother's position, such as better food and even preserving his life.

Szpilman's attitude to music, as rendered in *The Pianist*, parallels Polanski's war and postwar experiences of cinema. On many occasions he admitted to being mesmerised by films during the war, which were largely German propaganda films. This does not mean, however, that he accepted their propagandist message, but rather that he was enchanted by the medium itself. Moreover, his later decision to make films, and particularly to make a film about Szpilman, perfectly testifies to the view, espoused also by Szpilman, that one is morally entitled to engage in art 'after Auschwitz'.

The original scores for *Death and the Maiden* and *The Pianist* were written by Wojciech Kilar. One of the best Polish composers of the twentieth century, he is the author of such works as *Exodus*, *Kościelec*, *Bogurodzica*, *Krzesany*, *Riff 62*, as well as about a hundred film scores which he started to write in the 1950s. Kilar's music is inspired by such heterogenous sources as Polish folklore of the Tatra region, romanticism, the minimalism of Philip Glass and, in his own words, by his love of God (see Podobińska and Polony 1997: 44). In the West Kilar is best known for the music for *Dracula* (1992), directed by Francis Ford Coppola and Jane Campion's *The Portrait of a Lady* (1996), whose soundtrack also included Schubert's *Death and the Maiden* quartet. In Poland he is known for scores written for films directed by Andrzej Wajda, Krzysztof Kieslowski, Kazimierz Kutz and Krzysztof Zanussi. The last director seems to be able to use Kilar's talent with the greatest effect. Kilar also wrote the music to Polanski's *The Ninth Gate*.

Polanski claims that he invited Kilar to work with him not for patriotic reasons, but because his style of music was a perfect match for his recent movies (see Malatyńska and Malatyńska-Stankiewicz 2002: 12–13). One can understand the director of *Death and the Maiden* regarding Kilar's music as being suitable for his later films – these films are full of passion and even pathos, which are the qualities one also finds in Kilar's scores for the films directed by Zanussi and Wajda. Kilar's scores tend to amplify the emotions conveyed by image and dialogue. Take, for example, the 'glass-like', fragmented sounds in *Struktura kryształu* (*The Structure of Crystals*, 1969), directed by Krzysztof Zanussi, reflecting the characters' disquiet, the kitschy, 'holiday' music accompanying characters in *Rejs* (*The Cruise*, 1970), directed by Marek Piwowski, or the persistent string music in *The Portrait of a Lady*, betraying the dreams of the heroine. Kilar presents himself as an advocate of film music that is purely functional, quoting Stravinsky who said that music is 'like a wallpaper: it is cut according to the size of the walls and serves as a background to the action unfolded on screen' (Żukowska-Sypniewska 1999: 24). For this reason his melodies are sometimes criticised as being merely illustrative and predictable (see

Adrien Brody in *The Pianist* (2002)

Cyz 2002: 16), although his adherents, including directors with whom he has worked, regard this predictability as the strength of his compositions (see Malatyńska and Malatyńska-Stankiewicz 2002). Moreover, both Kilar's scores and concert music are admired for their simplicity, even their reductionism (see Widłak 1998).

Kilar's task in *Death and the Maiden* and *The Pianist* was by no means easy, as both films required him to accept a place in the 'second row', behind Schubert and Chopin, so that his music would not compete for the audience's attention. Kilar fulfilled this assignment, composing a score that remains in the background but manages to convey the personalities and moods of the protagonists, who (albeit for different reasons) have difficulties in unburdening their souls. In *Death and the Maiden* the score reflects and amplifies Paulina's grief and yearning for the things she has lost as a result of being imprisoned and tortured, as well as her edginess, panicking at the sound of an approaching car or a stranger coming to her house. In the first part of *The Pianist* the score, dominated by the piano, echoes Władysław's profound sadness when he witnesses the death of his compatriots, as well as his fear. In the second part the soundtrack is saturated with natural sounds: jingles of tramways, shooting, fires burning, objects falling, glass breaking, shoes tapping, the people living in the neighbouring flats shouting. Music here is often used onomato-poeically, for example mimicking and amplifying the dramatic sounds of sirens. In the 'quiet moments', when Władysław stops hearing the sounds of dying Warsaw, he either imagines himself playing classical music or we hear Kilar's non-diegetic music. At such times the music is more fragmented than in the first part of the film and at the same time more monotonous, as if echoing the increasingly muffled consciousness of the hungry, cold and, in the end, also sick Władysław. The composer avoids dramatic tunes and usually uses only a single instrument. David Thompson in his review praised this asceticism, writing: 'Even a soaring crane shot over the devastated city of Warsaw is denied a swelling John Williams score of Spielbergian dimensions, but simply comes to rest with a plaintive clarinet solo' (Thompson 2003: 58). An attentive listener can identify in Kilar's score some traces of Polish music, particularly romantic and folkloric traditions, as well as Jewish tunes, but they can easily be overlooked, not unlike the references to Polish and Jewish cultures in most of Polanski's films (see Chapter 1). Consequently, Szpilman's own national background is also 'underplayed' – music allows us to see him as a human being struggling against adverse circumstances, rather than a Pole or a Jew pondering on his national heritage.

The Pianist is not the first of Kilar's films to tackle the problem of the musician's reaction to the tragedy of the Holocaust. In 1992 he wrote the score to a film, directed by Krzysztof Zanussi, entitled *Dotknięcie ręki* (*The Silent Touch*). It casts as the main character a Polish student of musicology, named Stefan Bugajski, who hears in his dreams a musical theme that he thinks belongs to a larger piece. Stefan does not feel able to write it, so he travels to Denmark to see a reclusive composer, Henri Kesdi, who stopped writing music over forty years earlier. Kesdi's silence is a reaction to the Holocaust; in his opinion this event rendered all art inadequate or immoral. Stefan nevertheless persuades the ageing composer to write the music, which turns out to be a reworking of a Jewish theme. In reality, this work is Kilar's *Exodus*: one of his most famous works. Thanks to resuming his composing, Kesdi regains not only his talent but also his vitality (he even impregnates his new secretary). Hence, Zanussi comes to the same conclusion as Polanski – it is neither necessary nor desirable for an artist to abandon his art 'after Auschwitz'. Kesdi's prolonged silence did not make him a paragon of morality inspiring a younger generation, but changed him into a bitter, frustrated, capricious and sick man who put people off him, including those closest to him.

The music that Kesdi creates, inspired by Stefan, resurrects Polish Jewish culture which was practically wiped out by the Holocaust. Although the music is based on a popular theme, in its final incarnation it comes across as an elitist composition. In Polanski's film, on the other hand, the Jewish heritage of Szpilman's music is neglected. After the war Szpilman is shown playing Chopin, whose music is cherished in his motherland as a perfect expression of the Polish soul, but which also signifies the universalism of Polish culture. We also see him perform a popular Polish prewar song, *Umówiłem się z nił na dziewiętą* (*I will meet her at nine o'clock*), in the ghetto café.

In both respects Polanski is faithful to the historical truth. After the war Szpilman continued to play Chopin. During his long career he also wrote popular songs. Out of about five hundred songs he composed, more than a hundred topped the Polish charts. Some, including *Piosenka mariensztacka* (*Marienstadt Song*), *Pójdę na Stare Miasto* (*I Will Go to the Old Town*) testify the artist's love of Warsaw, but neither was regarded as an expression of Jewish patriotism or even as conveying Jewish musical tradition. Wojciech Kilar depicted Szpilman as a Polish Cole Porter, Gershwin and McCartney (see Szwarcman 2000: 122), an opinion that alludes both to Szpilman's Polishness and to his cosmopolitanism. Moreover, although Szpilman was not engaged in frontline politics, he was always loyal to the communist authorities, as shown by his joining some official organisations of musicians and engaging in promoting popular Polish songs abroad. In particular, in the 1960s he initiated the International Song Contest in Sopot, in which foreign performers were required to sing Polish songs. He even became a pillar of the socialist version of the 'culture industry', so despised by Theodor Adorno and his followers. On the whole, while Szpilman's postwar career (not unlike Polanski's) testifies to his vitality and excellent adaptation skills, it also demonstrates his relative indifference towards Jewish cultural inheritance. Hence, if we regard Szpilman as emblematic of Polish survivors of the Holocaust, it does not come as a surprise that the project of reviving Polish Jewish musical heritage and, by extension, Jewish culture at large, as proposed by Zanussi in *Silent Touch*, remains largely unfulfilled.

In conclusion, I want to draw attention to the versatility of the types of music in Polanski's films. He uses modern jazz, popular songs, the work of Schubert and Chopin, as well as compositions inspired by the folklore of countries where his films are set. As with his other artistic choices, Polanski proves to be a 'man of the world', travelling widely in search of the appropriate music and not shy to test new possibilities for its use. We can also detect a distinctive trajectory in his films: from jazz scores to soundtracks containing largely classical music. This trajectory connects with other changes in his work which are discussed elsewhere in this book – moves towards realism, a classical narrative structure and less ambiguous moral messages. While jazz music perfectly suited his less realistic films and those which underscored a character's mystery and moral ambiguity, classical scores better convey those films that contain clearly defined moral conflicts and employ realistic mode. Moreover, as far as music in his films is concerned, Polanski is not only a cultural (and cultured) traveller, but also one who increasingly returns to his 'home': Polish composers and tunes.

Music in Polanski's films not only serves as a background to or an illustration of the activities of the characters, but is often, one might say, the content and purpose of their actions. They express themselves through music and they live for music. Although the link between the characters and music in Polanski's cinema is very strong, it does not affect the moral judgement of music by the filmmaker. From a moral perspective, music remains for Polanski neutral matter which can be moulded to serve various ideological and political purposes.

5

TRUST YOURSELF: POLANSKI'S IDEOLOGY

'Ideology' is not a word commonly used in discussions of Polanski's cinema. Similarly, off-screen the director plays down any suggestions of an ideological dimension to his work, claiming that his only purpose is to entertain the audience. He is equally critical of filmmakers, such as Jean-Luc Godard, who use the camera as a political tool (see Leaming 1981: 62). Polanski's assertions are sincere enough but at the same time I adhere to the view that all films are unavoidably ideological, and in this chapter I intend to investigate the ideological dimension of Polanski's films. Before doing so, however, it is worth explaining the crucial term.

THE MEANINGS OF IDEOLOGY

In its widest sense ideology means a collection of ideas or the study of ideas. In practice, however, the ideas comprising ideologies are of a particular nature: they refer to people's most fundamental beliefs and are meant to constitute a comprehensive and coherent vision. Stuart Hall argues that 'ideologies do not operate through single ideas, they operate in discursive chains, in clusters, in semantic fields, in discursive formations. As you enter an ideological field and pick out any one nodal representation or idea, you immediately trigger off a whole chain of connotative associations' (Hall, quoted in Thompson 1986: 33).

Secondly, an ideology is normally assigned to a group, rather than to a single person, and it exists in the public sphere, alongside other ideologies.

For example, a large number of people subscribe to communist, capitalist, religious or atheist ideologies but at the same time none of these ideologies has had a monopoly on human thinking at any time. The world of ideologies is pluralistic and in a state of flux. Ideologies compete with one another, often drawing on a common, shared repertoire of concepts, 'rearticulating and disarticulating them within different systems of difference or equivalence' (Ibid.).

Thirdly, ideologies are constructed and proposed primarily for a political reason: they are supposed to influence people's thinking and behaviour, and in this way allow or help a certain group to seize and retain power (Ibid.: 66–97). Antonio Gramsci, Louis Althusser and many of their followers, including Stuart Hall, argue that language plays an important part in persuading people to accept a certain vision of the world, although for most people this role is obscured. Althusser maintains that 'Ideologies are perceived-accepted-suffered cultural objects, which work fundamentally on men by a process they do not understand' (Althusser, quoted in Comolli and Narboni 1992: 685). Similarly, by shifting signification of language, by talking about something 'well enough, effectively and persuasively enough, you can touch people's understanding of how they live and work, and make a new kind of sense about what's wrong with society and what to do about it' (Hall 1988: 188). When most people in a society think alike about certain matters, or even forget that there are alternatives to the current state of affairs, those in authority achieve political hegemony.

Art is always produced in certain ideological circumstances which affect all its dimensions, including its aesthetic form. However, many critics, particularly in the 1970s, argued that the link between ideology and cinema was especially close. For instance, for Comolli and Narboni 'Cinema is all the more thoroughly and completely determined [by the dominant ideology] because unlike other arts or ideological systems its very manufacture mobilises powerful economic forces in a way that the production of literature (which becomes the commodity "books"), does not – though once we reach the level of distribution, publicity and sale, the two are in rather the same position' (Comolli and Narboni 1992: 684). Film is also a very effective ideological tool. Its power lies in the ability to address large numbers of people, to use a multitude of discourses, pitched at various levels of complexity, and thus influence people in more subtle and therefore often more effective ways than does a political speech or pamphlet. It is not an accident that the leaders of two of the most radical, sinister and, for a considerable period of time, successful political regimes, Lenin and Hitler, attached great importance to the development of cinema in their countries. Equally, it is not surprising that filmmakers working under these regimes, such as Dziga Vertov, Sergei Eisenstein and Leni Riefenstahl, developed new understandings of cinema and created new cinematic languages.

Ideologies are divided into various categories according to the areas of human life that they cover. For this reason we can talk about, for instance, epistemological, political and moral ideologies or about epistemological, political and moral aspects of a particular ideology. These aspects are related: a particular moral choice typically influences an epistemological choice and vice versa. Accordingly, my discussion of the ideological dimension of Polanski's films will refer to several ideas he tackles in them: his epistemological position, his attitude to power and authority and his opinion about women and ethnic minorities. These issues by no means exhaust the ideology (or ideologies) that Polanski conveys in his films. However, as it is impossible to distil and analyse every element of them in one chapter, I will concentrate on problems that recur in his films, often constituting their dominant discourse. Polanski's choices in the area of epistemology, politics and morality influence each other, but by treating them separately we can better see their mutual connections.

RELIGION

– Do you believe in the supernatural, Mr Corso?

– I believe in my percentage.

Dialogue from *The Ninth Gate*

When discussing Polanski's attitude to religion, two issues should be taken into account: firstly, how he represents supernatural powers and, secondly, how he portrays institutions facilitating contact with them. Magical and inexplicable elements abound in Polanski's films – the devils and witches in *Macbeth*, *Rosemary's Baby* and *The Ninth Gate*, vampires in *Dance of the Vampires*, 'living walls' and doppelgangers in *Repulsion* and *The Tenant*. However, at the same time as saturating his films with the supernatural, Polanski undermines its power and even questions its very existence. He renders the ontological status of unnatural events ambiguous or utterly subjective by showing them from the perspective of a neurotic character rather than through the impersonal camera or a character, whose judgement we can trust. For example, the Castevets and their circle in *Rosemary's Baby* might be witches and warlocks or simply a group of old friends to whom Rosemary attaches in her mind supernatural powers. Moreover, supernatural creatures and fantastical events often have a comical nature (see Tarratt 1969: 95; Owczarek 1995: 100) and therefore cannot be taken seriously or at least do not allow the viewer a consistent reaction of horror. The comical effect is achieved, among other means, by the choice of actors playing the parts of vicious monsters. This refers especially to Ruth Gordon and Sidney Blackmer, who play Minnie and Roman Castevets. As Barbara Leaming argues, 'With them, [Polanski] thwarted any assumption on the part of the audience that evil characters would appear grim and sinister. Instead, his witch and warlock are jovial, even zany types, difficult to take seriously as emissaries of Satan' (Leaming 1981: 85). This might also be said of some of the actors cast as vampires in *Dance of the Vampires*, whose acting is on the verge of camp. Comedy is also evoked by representing supernatural creatures as very ordinary in their tastes and habits, even more down-to-earth than the people whom they try to corrupt. Margaret Tarratt observes that 'Minnie Castevet…in both aspects of her role as garrulous neighbour and adherent of witchcraft, retains a concern for the wellbeing of her new carpet at the most inappropriate moments' (Tarratt 1969: 95).

Dance of the Vampires, which is Polanski's closest encounter with horror, plays on the viewer's familiarity with the conventions of this genre and knowledge of individual horror films. Ferdy Mayne as Count von Krolock physically resembles Christopher Lee who was cast as Dracula in the film *Dracula* by Terence Fisher (1958) and the name Krolock is reminiscent of Count Orlock from Murnau's horror masterpiece *Nosferatu – eine Symphonie des Grauens* (*Nosferatu*, 1922). There are also similarities between Professor Abronsius and the demonic Doctor from Dreyer's *Vampyr* (*Vampire*, 1932). With these references we are invited to regard the characters and events portrayed not as representations of the real world, but as representations of representations, 'shadows of the shadows'. Thanks to the use of comedy and the citations from earlier films, including references to Polanski's own films, supernatural reality is also put in parentheses in *The Ninth Gate*. Philip Strick in his review mentions such details as the picture of a mansion in flames, borrowed from *Rosemary's Baby* and the presence of Emmanuelle Seigner as an 'undeclared agent for some malevolent conspiracy' (Strick 2000: 46) – which is the role she also played in *Frantic*.

Polanski's scepticism towards the power of religion is also conveyed by the characters' fate. Faith in supernatural forces, be it devil or God, is punished, while religious scepticism is rewarded. The case of the main characters in *The Ninth Gate* is very instructive here. All the devil worshippers perish, either as a result of competing with each other for the guide to the 'kingdom of the shadows' or by placing too much trust in the magical volumes. By contrast, Dean Corso, whose motivation is not esoteric but materialistic, or more precisely pecuniary, not only survives but obtains the infamous key to the supernatural universe. Similarly, in *Dance of the Vampires* the attempt to disarm a (Jewish) vampire with a crucifix is met with the scornful remark that 'this is the wrong type of vampire'.

Along with scepticism about supernatural forces and creatures, we can detect in Polanski's work hostility towards institutional religion. The director furnishes religious figures and, by extension, the institutions they represent, with a fair measure of unpleasant features. The priests and ministers tend to be greedy, vain, intolerant, even cruel and cowardly. A good example is the bishop in *Pirates* who is interested only in his own security and welfare. We always see him hiding when there is any sign of danger, and reappearing when there is something to be gained. Moreover, he gravitates towards those who have money, flattering them even if they deserve criticism, and scorns poor people. He thwarts the qualms of conscience of the dying ship's captain who feels guilty for having killed many innocent people by telling him that as long as his acts strengthened the position of the Catholic Church, he need not feel any remorse. Such an attitude reminds us of one of the darkest chapters in the history of the Church – the Inquisition. Another typical trait of Polanski's priests is hypocrisy. Take Pietro, the priest in *What?*, who as Virginia Wright Wexman observes, 'condemns the behaviour of others by invoking anachronistic slogans while himself enjoying the largesse of the villa' (Wexman 1987: 40). The people who run the workshop for orphaned children in *Oliver Twist* are also hypocritical. The workshop is a room decorated with the inscriptions 'God is Holy', 'God is Truth' and those that run it give themselves large quantities of luxurious food, while the children get meagre portions of gruel and are punished if they ask for more.

The vices and sins of 'God's lieutenants' are reinforced by visual means – the priests tend to be either overweight with round faces, conveying indulgence in worldly pleasures that they deny to others, or very thin, pale and morbid. The latter is the case of the priest in *The Tenant* who physically resembles the sour and severe Monsieur Zy – Trelkovsky's principal tormentor. The long, dark surplice that priests wear serves as a means to hide something, be it a large belly or jewellery. It also makes them look feminine, clumsy and comical.

We also find in Polanski's films criticism of religious ceremonies. In *Rosemary's Baby*, for example, they are associated with modern consumerism and proliferation of the media. As Margaret Tarratt observes, 'An incongruous Santa Claus collecting money in the street shakes his bell challengingly at the audience. The Pope's appearance at a massed rally at Yankee Stadium is relayed as high drama on television. The windows of commercial buildings display an idealised model of a crib with Virgin, manger and sheep' (Tarratt 1969: 93). Consequently, religion in the twentieth century is rendered as lacking spirituality – an empty vessel.

Religious figures, institutions and cultures dominated by religions also play an important, if not crucial part, in the disquiet and demise of Polanski's characters, especially Tess. Thus, if Parson Tringham had not addressed Jack Durbyfield as 'Sir' and revealed to him his noble roots, he would not have sent Tess to her rich cousins to claim kinship and be seduced by Alec. Paul Niemeyer maintains that the attack on the institution of religion in Polanski's *Tess* is far more general and uncompromising than in Hardy's novel. An example is failing to show in the film Reverend Clare's willingness to risk his own skin to save somebody else's and instead depicting him as a stiff representative of religious authority (see Niemeyer 2003: 138). Moreover, Polanski frequently presents Tess praying and attributing what happens to her as God's will. In this way he suggests that either God ignores those who put their trust in him or, as Niemeyer argues, that the most devoted adherents of religion have faith in a dangerous lie (Ibid.: 138–9). It could also be argued that Rosemary's Catholic upbringing, underscoring the link between sexuality and guilt, plays a significant part in her fear of losing her baby to dark forces.

The religion which Polanski treats most sympathetically is paganism, as featured in *Tess* (see Wexman 1987: 115, Stachówna 1994: 215). Less hierarchical than Christianity, it allows its believers to make sense of the world without the assistance of an intermediary and signifies the harmony of people with nature. Moreover, it is effective, providing their adherents with the right answers about their situation and their future. For example, the Dairyman Crick's wife correctly explains why the butter fails to turn by saying that someone is in love. However, Polanski also points to the marginal status of paganism – as a result of the industrial revolution which dramatically transforms not only towns but also the countryside, pagan beliefs will disappear.

Unlike theologians who stress the difference between other faiths and their own, Polanski, like an ethnographer (a profession requiring both physical journeys as well as travelling through cultures with an open mind), focuses on the similarities between religious doctrines and between official religions and black magic. In *Rosemary's Baby* the Satanic worshippers scorn Christianity and the Pope but model themselves on Christian believers. Their behaviour is very ritualistic, even theatrical, involving the wearing of ornate clothes, charms and amulets, chanting aloud and singing. Moreover, they appropriate Christian myths, including that about a pure, innocent woman being impregnated by a supernatural entity (in their case – Satan) and giving birth to the future Messiah who will change the destiny of humanity. The way Polanski represents Satan and the Satan worshippers' attitude to Rosemary (whose very name alludes to Christ's mother) draws attention to the objectification of women by Christianity (see Eagle 1994: 131; Humphries 2002: 88–9) and bears some similarity to feminist criticism of this religion (see Hamington 1995). In particular, both Christianity and Satanism in *Rosemary's Baby* reserve for a woman, at best, the place of a mediatrix with divine male power. Holy Mary and Rosemary have an inferior position even in relation to their sons; they are allowed physically to nurture their offspring, but the sons hardly belong to them: their values and destiny are decided by someone else, namely (male) God and Satan respectively. Even their names are decided by their fathers. Rosemary, who wanted to name her son Andy, is informed by Roman Castevet that his name on Satan's order is Adrian.

The Girl in *The Ninth Gate* is given the role of the female devil or witch who knows how to access the 'land of shadows' and helps Corso to get there. Her belonging to the kingdom of Satan is also suggested by her green, cat-like eyes, which is a reference to the affinity between witches and cats, and an allusion to the eyes of Rosemary's son. However, her protective behaviour towards Corso, even preventing him from committing crimes, likens her to the figure of a guardian angel, and at some point Corso asks her whether she is his holy guardian. This ambiguity leads to the conclusion that the difference between angels and devils is insignificant. When discussing the similarity between 'respected' and 'disrespected' religions it is also worth mentioning Noah Cross, who in the last episode of *Chinatown* wails 'Oh Lord, Oh Lord' when repossessing his daughter and granddaughter, most likely with incestuous intentions. As Donald Lyons observes, it is fitting to the overall message of the film and, I will argue, to Polanski's overall outlook on life, as presented in his films, that the 'Devil should cite Scripture' (Lyons 1993: 53).

Religions, particularly in Polanski's films set in contemporary times, appear to be in a state of decline. The clearest indication of that is the meagreness of religious gatherings and their dominance by old people. Take the 'witches' coven' in *Rosemary's Baby*, the mass attended by

Trelkovsky and the meeting of the circle of devil worshippers in *The Ninth Gate*. It is almost as if both adoration of God and black magic are reduced to being the innocuous pastime of well-off people with plenty of time on their hands (see Chappetta 1969: 38). The 'seduction' of a mediocre actor, Guy Woodhouse, by the Castevets by promising him a career in theatre and cinema is the clearest indication of how devoid of fresh blood (in both a metaphorical and literal sense) the Satanic worshippers became. Moreover, as several critics noticed, the depravity and cruelty of people in Polanski's films matches or even exceeds that of Satan. Guy is a good case in point. Margaret Tarratt observes that 'the rape [of Rosemary] is a literal expression of her introjection of the social evil which surrounds her. There is no conflict between believing in the "rational" explanation that Guy himself raped her or in Roman's assertion that Satan is the child's father. In a metaphysical sense Guy is identical with Satan. His act is not merely that of the casual "necrophile". It is literally Satanic and we are prepared for such an interpretation by the variety of roles he adopts with ease' (Tarratt 1969: 93). In a similar vein Iwona Kolasińska notes: 'When Rosemary at the end of the film spits in his mendacious face...she expresses in this way much greater contempt than she has for any of Guy's Satanic friends. In comparison with him even the appearance of Satan in the cradle proves less off-putting' (Kolasińska 1995: 85).

The crisis of religion in modern times is also testified by the fact that even in the moments of deepest crisis Polanski's characters rarely turn to God, but either expect help from fellow human beings or concentrate on preserving what is most important in their lives and what can be described as their private religion. An example of the first behaviour is Richard awaiting his boss, Mr Katelbach, in *Cul-de-Sac*; of the second is Władysław Szpilman's resolve not to lose his ability to play music in *The Pianist*. The measure of the contemporary crisis in Western religions is also there in the fashion, ridiculed in *Bitter Moon*, to search for spirituality in the East.

Is there then anything that, in Polanski's opinion, has a chance to fill the void that appeared after God's (and the devil's) departure or demotion to the role of provider of Sunday entertainment? Perhaps he gives such a role to the bearing and rearing of children. While in *Tess* the large number of offspring begot by the Durbyfields was presented as proof of their recklessness, backwardness and – ultimately – poverty and decline, in Polanski's films set in the twentieth century there are never families with too many children and it is the lack of children which makes characters impoverished. This idea is most clearly promoted in *Bitter Moon* where the widowed Indian father of a small girl suggests that children make their parents happy, give them purpose to live and assure some kind of eternity. He is living proof of his words: despite losing his wife, there is no sign of bitterness or despair in his behaviour. The hope that an adopted child will heal the wounds of the past and allow some kind of normality to be achieved is also expressed by Paulina in *Death and the Maiden*, who became infertile as a result of torture. The importance of children is also demonstrated by the emptiness and decadence of the lives of childless couples in *Bitter Moon*. Moreover, loving a child gives an opportunity to defeat or disarm the devil. This conviction, in my opinion, is conveyed by the last scene of *Rosemary's Baby*, in which Rosemary reclaims and accepts her monstrous child, rather than leaving it to the mercy of Satanists. Knowing her selflessness and gentle nature, one believes that she will be able to overcome her son's devilish paternity, bringing him up to be a decent man.

Polanski's antipathetic portrayal of priests and religious institutions brings to mind Luis Buñuel, who, like Polanski, declared himself an atheist. However, it seems to me more fruitful to compare Polanski's attitude to religion with that of his compatriot, Krzysztof Kieslowski. Although the filmmakers share a number of narrative and visual motifs suggesting religious interests, such as ample reference to religious symbols, they testify to different ideological positions. Unlike Polanski, who puts supernatural events in humorous parentheses or suggests that they take place only in the character's mind, Kieslowski represents them as part of objectively observed life and treats them with utmost seriousness. Secondly, in contrast to Polanski, who places angels and devils on an equal footing, there is no risk of mistaking an angel for the devil in Kieslowski's films. Moreover, unlike Polanski, who uses religious imagery in an ironic way, an example being the Christian symbols in *Knife in the Water*, or to stress the oppressing influence of a religious upbringing on the life of an individual, as in the case of Rosemary, Kieslowski uses symbols from the Christian tradition to evoke religious feelings in the viewer (see Przylipiak 2004: 231). Although, as many critics noticed, Kieslowski was not very fond of organised religion, his films nevertheless show respect for priests and religious people, and represent churches and cemeteries as places of reflection and spirituality, for example in *Dekalog, Jeden* (*Decalogue 1*, 1988). If there is any conflict between a religious person and an atheist, or between a religious and atheist outlook on life, the former proves right. Finally, in his films, at least the earlier ones, such as *Przypadek* (*Blind Chance*, 1987), Kieslowski links a discourse on religion with discourse on nation and current politics, representing the Catholic Church as a bastion of Polishness and a centre of resistance against communism (see Haltof 2004: 59). Polanski, by contrast, completely avoids such connotations of religion. In summary, he looks at religion not as a Pole for whom it is a refuge from the totalitarianism of the communist state and from Western decadence, but as a secular Westerner, content that the French Revolution and modernity freed his body and mind from its shackles.

POWER AND AUTHORITY

> She had learned her lesson with Dr. Hill. This time she would turn to no one, would expect no one to believe her and be her saviour... This time she would do it alone, would go in there and get him herself, with her longest sharpest kitchen knife to fend away those maniacs.

Ira Levin, *Rosemary's Baby*

The terms 'power' and 'authority' are often used interchangeably, although their connotations differ. Authority involves possessing power to control, judge or prohibit the actions of others but it is a legitimised power. Those who lay claim to authority argue that they deserve respect and obedience, having some noble qualities, such as knowledge or experience, royal heritage, or close relations with God. Moreover, they act to serve not their own interests but those of their followers or the common good. Power, by contrast, can be 'naked': undeserved, selfish and based solely on physical advantages: strong muscles, knives and guns. What interests me here is the relation between power and authority as represented in Polanski's films. *Knife in the Water* is the first film that openly deals with the problem of authority as opposed to 'naked' power, which was the subject of some of Polanski's shorts, such as *Mammals* and *The Fat and the Lean*. In it, Andrzej is represented as a man who strives for authority. This might have much to do with the fact that his wife, although she obeys his orders, does so without any enthusiasm, as if silently questioning his superior position. To become a figure of authority for another person, and to assert his power over Krystyna, Andrzej invites a student to accompany them on a sailing expedition. The student is ascribed the role of a surrogate son to Andrzej but he appropriates the role of an Oedipus, seducing his 'mother' and disposing of his father (see Wexman 1987: 28). Polanski shows, however, that this unfortunate scenario is of Andrzej's own making. Contrary to the impression he tries to give, he does not want to teach the student sailing or patience but to gain control of him and humiliate him in front of his wife. Andrzej himself does not even have some of the virtues that he seemingly wants to instil in the younger man, such as humility and patience. On the contrary, he is conceited and bad-tempered. If he can be compared to a father at all, it can only be as an abusive parent who takes revenge on his children for the wounds inflicted on him by the world.[1] This idea is presented in an episode in which Andrzej, after requesting that the student fulfil a number of tasks which he finds idiotic, tells him that his sailing teacher once asked him to go to the top of the mast and to imitate a cuckoo. The student reacts by asking Andrzej in a mocking voice whether he indeed cuckooed as his master requested, thus implying that a blind respect for authority contradicts common sense and human dignity. *Knife in the Water* was interpreted as a metaphor for a young Polish citizen's rejection of a socialist authority that is paternalistic, hypocritical and inept, in short of a political system that pretends to have authority but in reality possesses only power.

The effects of possessing both political and physical power and moral authority in a totalitarian state is at the centre of the discourse in *Death and the Maiden*. Doctor Miranda, whom Paulina recognises as her torturer during the time of a military regime, as he himself admits at one point, used to be a good doctor and a decent man. For this very reason he was chosen by the fascist authorities to assist the process of torture by making sure the victims did not die during interrogations and passed the required information to their oppressors. Miranda's humanity and decency is also shown in a situation at the beginning of the film when he helps a stranger, Paulina's husband, by giving him a lift home, when his car breaks down. As Nick James observes: 'Miranda arrives twice as an apparent Good Samaritan: in the present as a helpful motorist and in the past as the doctor whose job it was to prevent any death by torture – to clean up wounds and play soothing music – before the invitation to join in became intoxicating' (James 1995: 40). Indeed, Polanski makes the point about the special 'licence to abuse' enjoyed by people in whom society puts special trust, such as doctors, which results precisely from the expectation that they would behave more decently than most people. He also draws attention to their hypocrisy and even self-deception regarding the true nature of their acts. It seems as if until the very end Doctor Miranda is unable to face up to the crimes he committed – even after fifteen years he perceives himself not so much as a rapist and torturer, as Paulina's physician, therapist and friend.

Miranda's perspective, and the whole situation depicted by Polanski, is reminiscent of Andrzej Munk's unfinished film, *Pasażerka* (*Passenger*, 1961–3). Polanski himself encourages us to relate his films to other examples of political abuse and their aftermath by saying: 'In *Death and the Maiden* I never mention any political leader or a concrete dictatorship that's fallen. I'm talking about an unspecified country in South America. And it's more universal than that, because this sort of situation occurs all around the globe, where former victims are faced with their former oppressors or torturers. They have to live through these kinds of encounters and deal with them' (Thompson 1995: 8).

Passenger, like *Death and the Maiden*, has two main characters. One is Liza, a German who during the war worked in Auschwitz as overseer of a female division; the other is Marta, a Polish prisoner, who was sent to the camp as punishment for an anti-Nazi conspiracy. The film takes the form of a retrospective, triggered by Liza's unexpected meeting with Marta more than a decade after the war on a cruise liner travelling to South America. Worried that Marta will approach her husband and reveal to him her Nazi past, and in need of self-exoneration, Liza tells him how miserable her own position was during the war and how much she tried to help Marta. Later, however, tormented by her conscience, she provides us with a second and more truthful version of events. We learn that she did not really want to save Marta but to change her into an accomplice in her crimes as her grateful and obedient slave. Both Munk in *Passenger* and Polanski in *Death and the Maiden* suggest that the category of 'compassionate victimiser', into which Doctor Miranda and Liza both fit, is in fact more devious and dangerous than that of the 'ordinary' torturers because the dubious acts of good they perform on their victims blind them to the weight of their crimes and thus prevent any true remorse in future.

In her review of *Death and the Maiden* Gordana Crnković, mirroring Gramsci and Hall's views of the importance of language for gaining and sustaining authority, draws attention to its function in the power struggle between Paulina on the one hand, and Miranda and her husband, Gerardo Escobar, on the other. Miranda uses medical discourse, and Gerardo legal discourse, to question and ridicule Paulina's version of events.

> In a clear voice, attempting a rational medical discourse in the midst of this unleashed female frenzy, he [Miranda] tells Escobar, 'Obviously, she's insane, she's not responsible for what she does, but you are a lawyer, if you don't stop it right now you're an accomplice, you're gonna have to pay the price.' A highly educated and professional man is addressing himself to one of his kind. An assumed and required male association between Miranda and Escobar is asserted by the positioning of both men in a single frame, with Paulina outside of it. We are thus reminded of the previous

evening's bonding between Escobar and Miranda, and of Miranda's quoting Nietzsche's dictum…on the irreconcilable female difference: 'We can never entirely possess a female soul.' (Crnković 1997: 41)

Yet, Polanski, as Crnković argues, succeeds in convincing the viewers that Paulina, not Miranda, is telling the truth. In this way he questions the link between truth and professional authority (which is usually masculine).

Authority rooted in professional expertise and scientific knowledge is called into question in several other films, including *Rosemary's Baby* and *Dance of the Vampires*. Rosemary is failed by both the obstetricians she approaches: Doctor Sapirstein and Doctor Hill. This harsh diagnosis is true irrespective of whether we regard Sapirstein as a Satan worshipper or not. If he conspires with the Castevets to procure Rosemary's child to be used in their vicious plans, his role as the devil's assistant is irreconcilable with that of an obstetrician helping women to be in control of birth and looking after their babies. If, on the other hand, his connection with dark forces is solely Rosemary's delusion, still he lets her down by arrogantly ignoring her pain and her worries. Moreover, if her baby had died during the birth, then Rosemary would have been right that something was wrong with her pregnancy and Sapirstein proved wrong by dismissing her concerns. The fault of Doctor Hill is lesser by comparison, as he encounters Rosemary very late, when she comes across as insane, but he also shows no respect for her as a patient and, instead, deceives her, blindly trusting his superior, Doctor Sapirstein and Rosemary's husband. In short, doctors in *Rosemary's Baby* are either abusive or incompetent.

In *Frantic* the emphasis is on the incompetence, arrogance and selfishness of state institutions and public services, such as the police and the American embassy, which Doctor Walker approaches for help in finding his wife. Wherever he turns, he is asked first to wait and then to provide numerous personal data, of which much has little relevance to his case. The policemen and clerks do not listen to his story, they follow their own agenda as if observing appropriate procedures is their ultimate goal. Moreover, when Walker tries to make them aware that it is their duty to help him, they behave arrogantly. The impression of a distance between the institutions and their clients is confirmed by the glass and iron bars separating the policemen from their customers. While an individual has no direct access to those who possess authority, such people can invade an individual's privacy whenever they wish. Polanski also shows that the authorities only start treating Walker seriously when they discover that he is in possession of a missile detonator, in other words, when he gains significant power. Yet even at this stage, or especially at this stage, they remain insensitive to his plight of finding his wife. They want him to pass them the deadly weapon even though (as Walker puts it) its price is his wife's life. In such circumstances the only right course of action is to disregard the authorities and to rely on oneself. This is what Walker eventually does and this attitude brings him victory: he regains his wife and then he destroys the detonator.

Walker's trouble with the public services and his eventual success also prove that physical power (or power resulting from possessing tools able to maim and kill) without authority is much more powerful than authority devoid of physical power. This is also a message we find in films such as *Knife in the Water, Death and the Maiden* and *The Pianist*. Polanski shows that people who have knives and guns can be regarded as immoral and insane, but they are able to elicit from others the required reactions. Hence, as long as Walker possesses a detonator, he is hopeful that he will find his wife. Similarly, having a gun gives Paulina the courage to confront her oppressor and to convince her husband that Miranda was indeed her torturer (see Crnković 1997: 44–5). Similarly, as Grażyna Stachówna argues, the knife that the student carries in *Knife in the Water* outweighs all the gadgets Andrzej possesses (see Stachówna 1987: 24–5). The power of the gun, the knife or a fist derives from the simple fact that for the vast majority of people preserving one's life is more important than winning an argument. Furthermore, being alive and in a position of power is the way to convince others of one's righteousness.

At the same time, power not supported by trust, respect and the sympathy of those who are subjected to it is very shaky. Polanski demonstrates this in *Macbeth*, whose protagonist grows more and more insecure and lonely, the more power he amasses. In the end he remains completely alone on his (useless) throne, waiting for a hostile army to take his castle. Macbeth's downfall also proves that it is better to protect one's sword than one's crown, both in the literal and metaphorical sense. By doing the opposite – fighting for and guarding the symbol of his power – Macbeth loses everything, including his life.

To conclude, Polanski shows deep distrust of institutions and people in authority. In his films agents of authority are never altruistic – their main objective is not the benefit of others but their own gain. The author often dismisses authority as incompetent and even as an obstacle to achieving the goal that it is meant to serve and promote. Furthermore, he shows that possessing some kind of authority leads to universalising or even totalitarian attitudes. A person who has authority in one area often tries to impose his will in other areas as well; a man who has authority over one person strives to extend his pool of subjects or faithful followers. In short, power and authority corrupt. If there is a moral lesson to be learned from Polanski's films, it is to put trust only in oneself, rather than in others, and to carry the means of protecting oneself against the menacing forces one can encounter in one's life.

PATRIARCHY AND RACISM

Polanski's attitude to women and to the ideologies addressing women's place in society is one of the thorniest issues in his work. Many critics regard him as a misogynist director *tout court*. For Grażyna Stachówna the proof of his alleged contempt for and fear of women is the multitude of negative stereotypes of women present in his films, often verging on caricature (see Stachówna 1994: 123). Molly Haskell points to the passivity of his female characters and even actresses, who come across as lobotomised or sleepwalking (see Haskell 1987: 346–7). Others draw attention to his unrelenting interest in crimes inflicted on women, such as sexual violence. Also a sign of Polanski's misogyny is the voyeuristic and sadistic gaze at the female body performed by both characters and camera in his films (see Chapter 3). Polanski is also wary of feminism, or at least of its caricatured version, which in his films nevertheless stands for all strands of feminism. We can observe it first in *The Tenant* where, according to Edward Balcerzan, feminist values and lifestyle are encapsulated by Stella, depicted as a 'new woman' who takes the initiative in sex. Although she is totally sympathetic to Trelkovsky, Balcerzan claims that by feminising him, trying to change him into a 'new man', matching her 'new womanness', she accelerates his transformation into Simone Choule and his madness (see Balcerzan 1995: 128). Moreover, Stella is represented as an uncritical follower of fashion; her personality is overshadowed by clichés to which she conforms. Feminism, as portrayed by Polanski, is one of the fashions she has adopted at the expense of losing part of her individuality. Some of Polanski's female protagonists suffer because men take advantage of what is regarded as one of the greatest feminist achievements: women's right to control their reproductive function. In *Bitter Moon* both Oscar and Nigel use women's right to abortion and the availability of the contraceptive pill to free themselves from paternal responsibilities and thus deprive their partners of the children for which they yearn. Hence, feminism, as represented by Polanski, has an infantilising effect on men while at the same time failing to empower women.

Polanski's reputation as a misogynist director is corroborated by his off-screen notoriety, particularly his alleged seduction or rape of a thirteen-year-old girl, and by his own pronouncements about women. For example, a reader (or at least a female reader) of his autobiography, *Roman*, is taken aback by the extent to which this book is devoted to describing Polanski's sexual exploits, his 'laddish' attitude to women which reduces them to attractive or unattractive bodies and the cruelty with which Polanski describes certain women. I feel that Polanski's dubious fame as a womaniser/rapist and misogynist plays a large part in the critics' readiness to search for those traces in his work which confirm this sexist reputation and to overlook those aspects of his films which reveal an opposite attitude. Furthermore, Polanski's comments about his own films confirm his misogynist intentions. For instance, he described *Cul-de-Sac* as a film born out of his and Gérard Brach's loathing of their ex-wives and their need for revenge on women (see Polanski 1984: 165).

On the other hand, we can find in his films a strong fascination and identification with femininity: both in women and in the feminine side of men. The majority of his films are psychologically centred on women, or on a man who appropriates a female identity (as in *The Tenant* in which the man is, meaningfully, played by Polanski himself). I will argue that irrespective of whether the viewer is a man or a woman, the viewer tends to be addressed by Polanski as a woman; this adopting of a woman's point of view, according to Teresa de Lauretis, is an important characteristic of feminist art (see de Lauretis 1987).[2] His fascination with and understanding of women is the more striking because it is not balanced by his interest in men. Polanski's men tend to be underplayed and unsympathetic. Moreover, although his films are about sexual violence towards women, I would refrain from claiming that he chooses this motif solely for the pornographic thrills of the male audience. This happens too, most openly in *What?*, but does not prevail in his cinema. In the majority of cases he does not represent sexual violence as an event, which takes place 'here and now' (we do not see Noah Cross forcing himself on his daughter or Miranda raping Paulina), but concentrates on its legacy for women. In particular, in *Repulsion*, *Rosemary's Baby*, *Chinatown*, *Tess* and *Death and the Maiden*, Polanski allows his heroines to let us know what happened to their psychological health and their position within society as a result of being sexually abused, something which rarely happens in mainstream cinema. Rape is a problem of utmost interest to feminists, largely because its occurrence as a crime primarily committed by a man on a woman and its negative significance for a woman's wellbeing tend to be denied in patriarchal discourses. In many of these discourses, indeed, the woman is made guilty for being raped. By making the viewer sympathise with his abused heroines who try to avenge the harm done to them by men and are subsequently punished by society, Polanski's films allow a critique of patriarchal structures in which his female protagonists are imprisoned.

Readers might find it problematic that the word 'rape' is used to describe the sexual experience of women in some or all of the afore-mentioned films. In many cases the precise nature of the event is obscured, either literally, as in *Tess*, where the fog envelops Alec and Tess, preventing the audience from witnessing what actually happens, or metaphorically, as in *Rosemary's Baby* and *Repulsion*, by suggesting that the rape might only have taken place in the woman's imagination. Polanski himself was wary about calling Alec's sexual encounter with Tess a 'rape', claiming that in their times there was not much difference between rape and seduction; woman's resistance to man's power was part of the erotic game (see Kennedy 1979: 67). Such pronouncements evoke Polanski's own difficulty in differentiating between rape and seduction (which cost him exile from the USA) and are reminiscent of Hitchcock's attitude to one of his female characters who was a victim of sexual violence: Alice in *Blackmail* (1929). As Tania Modleski observes, 'Hitchcock himself uses the word "rape" on one occasion and "seduction" on another, suggesting that for him, as for many men, there's not much difference between the two' (Modleski 1988: 22). This is only one of many similarities between Polanski and Hitchcock's representation of women and patriarchy. Another concerns the fact that sexual oppression of women in the films of both directors is linked to other forms of patriarchal domination. Nowhere is it conveyed more clearly in Polanski's films than in *Tess* and *Chinatown*. Tess's downfall is not only the result of her sexual encounter with Alec, but also a consequence of the patriarchal values and behaviour of almost everyone around her. This includes her mother who sends her to her rich 'cousin' hoping that he will marry her, Angel who refuses to treat her as his wife after finding out about her affair with Alec, and the police and the court who ignore any extenuating circumstances in her killing of Alec. Tess herself, in common with Alice in *Blackmail*, internalised the guilt for being raped or seduced by Alec, as testified by her confession to Angel in which she admits that God condemned her, taking away her child. We also find in this film the idea that patriarchy not only destroys women but cripples men. In particular, by rejecting Tess on the grounds of her lack of purity and decadence, Angel has denied himself life with the woman he loves.

Not unlike Tess, Evelyn Mulwray in *Chinatown* is depicted as a victim of patriarchy in many senses. Firstly, she is victimised by being sexually abused by her father, Noah Cross, by whom she has a daughter. Secondly, his position as one of the most powerful people in Los Angeles (he has the police on his payroll) prevents her from seeking help in the legal system. Thirdly, the taboo surrounding incest and, consequently, her shame about her past make her unwilling to disclose her secret to the private detective Gittes. Ultimately, it assures her death and the loss of her daughter to her repulsive father. By depicting Cross as a monstrous patriarch in the sense of being a bad father to his real children and to the inhabitants of Los Angeles, Polanski calls into question the whole institution of patriarchy. His denouncement of patriarchy is strengthened by contrasting Cross with Hollis Mulwray. While Cross seeks total power and control over his children (who are also his women) and the citizens of LA, Mulwray tries to set them free, protecting Evelyn's daughter and regarding the water resources of the city as public property. Patriarchy and misogyny in this film are also harmful to Gittes. Polanski constructs him as a typical misogynist hero of hard-boiled fiction and *film noir*, who assumes that women must be guilty. Yet, unlike his counterparts in the earlier films of this genre, Gittes is proved wrong. His misogyny, therefore, not only contributes to Evelyn's death, but also leads to his own defeat as detective, man and moral subject (see Wexman 1987: 99).

Forms of patriarchy also act as circles of oppression for Rosemary (see Humphries 2002: 86–9). She is trapped in her marriage to Guy, who treats her as a child and exercises control over almost all aspects of her life. She is also, as was previously mentioned, used and abused by religion and overpowered and humiliated by the medical profession. Rosemary's entrapment is conveyed visually by showing her as smaller and more fragile than the men surrounding her. Polanski also frequently places her between men representing patriarchal institutions or the women who serve them, such as Minnie Castevet and her friend, Laura-Louise. Most importantly, such a triangular composition is used in the taxi scene where Guy and Doctor Sapirstein, sitting on either side of heavily pregnant Rosemary, have her driven back to her apartment. The tight space of the taxi and her pregnancy render her suffocated and powerless. The triangular composition can be regarded as a metaphor of the multi-faceted character of patriarchy. Rosemary's subjugation to sexist systems is the more meaningful because she came to New York and married Guy to escape patriarchy.

Polanski not only shows in his films how patriarchy oppresses women and, in some measure, men, but also how women resist this oppression. In his earlier films, such women appropriate the power to laugh at men. Take, for example, Krystyna in *Knife in the Water*, whose sceptical look and slight smile, which never leaves her lips, drive her husband crazy.[3] The heroine of *A River of Diamonds* steals a precious necklace, conning two older men on the way, the owner of a jewellery shop and her rich suitor, simply for the pleasure of making a joke; she thus exposes their naivety, which is masked as seriousness. Teresa in *Cul-de-Sac* perpetually teases and ridicules both her husband and Richard. The peak of her playfulness is putting strips of paper between Richard's toes as he sleeps and lighting them, making him thrash his legs about as if riding a bike. After this incident, which renders Richard not only funny but also as powerless as a child, he beats Teresa, pointing to the risks that women run in trying to subvert the patriarchal status quo. Even Teresa's predilection for hens, which leads to overflowing the ancient castle with eggs, can be treated as a way to subvert male authority (her husband wants the castle to remain 'pure') and is also her joke on George whose bald head looks like an egg. Furthermore, the composition of some shots points to the heroine's desire and her ability to break free from the male world. For example, in an episode outside the castle first we see Richard, George and Teresa in a triangle with George and Richard on both sides of Teresa, as if they were prison guards, and she their prisoner. However, soon Teresa goes to swim, leaving the men to talk about women. This scene is particularly interesting from a feminist perspective as it reverses the stereotypical situation of idle housewives gossiping about a man who is too busy or aloof to take part in their silly conversations. Again, in granting women the power to ridicule and abandon men for their own solitary pleasures Polanski is reminiscent of Hitchcock (see Modleski 1988: 54). Teresa, in particular, can be viewed as the 'younger sister' of Hitchcock's Rebecca, a woman who does not allow men to contain her and who can even mould a grand house to suit her personality.

Polanski's women might be lobotomised or sleepwalking, as Haskell (1997) argues, but their state does not prevent them from seeking revenge on the men who harmed them. *Repulsion, Chinatown, Tess* and *Death and the Maiden* can be viewed as stories of female revenge and even their triumph, however delayed. The impression that Polanski's female characters are strong and capable of winning is also demonstrated by his casting decisions, such as offering the role of Paulina in *Death and the Maiden* to Sigourney Weaver, whose appearance and manner of acting, underscoring the character's neurosis, vulnerability, as well as physical and mental strength, evokes her role as the feminist icon Ripley in the *Alien* saga.

Polanski's women also resist patriarchy by rejecting heterosexual romance in favour of different sexual and living arrangements. Teresa in *Cul-de-Sac* in her relationships with men adopts a position taken by men described as 'womanisers': she goes to bed with many men but does not commit herself to any of them. Yet she cannot easily be described as a 'whore' or a 'slut', because such descriptions convey women's subservience to men, while Polanski's heroine is a domineering figure, as shown in an early scene where she is on top of her young lover. Similarly, putting make-up on George demonstrates that she is able to force a man to conform to her ideas, rather than the other way round, which is the norm in patriarchy. In *Dance of the Vampires* Alfred, convinced that he is saving Sarah from a miserable life among vampires, abducts her from Count von Krolock's castle and takes her on his sleigh into a more civilised (therefore, we might guess, more patriarchal) world. On the way, however, Sarah plunges her vampire teeth into Alfred's neck, proving that she will not be subjugated to the patriarchal order, but will mould a man to her own image – that of a vampire. It is therefore a woman who has the last laugh in this film. This is a remarkable achievement taking into account how passive and conventionally feminine Sarah appears.

Another case of a woman scorning life with a man is in *Bitter Moon*, where against Oscar's and the audience's expectations Mimi does not seduce Nigel but Fiona. If she went to bed with Nigel, the damage inflicted on her husband's ego would be minor, if any at all, because Nigel functions in the film as Oscar's double (see Chapter 2), and by choosing Nigel, Mimi would in a sense be choosing Oscar. Moreover, she would be submitting to his narrative control – Oscar being a writer, or a storyteller, who not only uses Mimi's life as material for a novel but manipulates it in a way that suits his literary purposes. By seducing Fiona, Mimi denies Oscar the pleasure of identification with her lover (being a macho man he cannot identify with a woman) and proves that she, not Oscar, is in control of her biography. Not surprisingly, Oscar shoots her before committing suicide. His act is accompanied by the words: 'We were just too greedy, baby.' Obviously, from the patriarchal perspective Mimi was too greedy, she went too far by rejecting the place that patriarchal order had assigned to her, and received a just punishment. The director seems to endorse this view. After her fling with Mimi, Fiona returns to her husband and they, embracing each other, look in horror as the caretakers carry out the bodies of Oscar and Mimi, poignantly showing what happens to people and women in particular, who go 'too far', thus undermining the social order.

To sum up my discussion of Polanski's attitude to patriarchy, I will refrain from labelling him a misogynist or a feminist director.[4] Instead, I will argue that, in common with Hitchcock, he is alternately neither and both because he uses a variety of discourses on gender which allow for conflicting readings of his films. However, I will also argue that Polanski's feminism dominates over his misogyny, as it typically affects the way he represents the main heroine and is embedded in the overall message of his films.

Polanski's representation of ethnic minorities and his take on ideologies concerning them has much in common with his approach to patriarchy and feminism. He rejects such ideologies as unjust and degrading to individuals placed in a particular category, as well as misleading those who follow ethnic and racial stereotypes. As was stated earlier (see Chapter 2), his narratives often revolve around the persecution of ethnic minorities; *The Tenant* and *The Pianist* are the clearest examples. The victimisation experienced by Trelkovsky, a Pole (or perhaps a Polish Jew, as suggested by Polanski's casting of himself in this role) living in Paris, and by Warsaw Jews during the Second World War, is depicted as unjust and barbaric. In the longer term, it brings nobody, including the perpetrators, any good, only shame, pain and destruction. The scenery after an act of ethnic persecution, be it on a small scale, as in *The Tenant*, or on a grand scale, as in *The Pianist*, is always the 'landscape after the battle': full of blood, broken glass, rubble. It can be said that the consequence of ethnic cleansing is the opposite to what was intended: plenty of literal and metaphorical dirt which needs to be removed. Narrating the films from the perspective of those who are victimised, strengthens the moral outrage conveyed by the plots because in this way Polanski forces us to identify with many dimensions of their suffering, including those the perpetrators might not envisage. Furthermore, it makes us realise that irrespective of ethnicity we all have similar basic needs and therefore should enjoy the same rights – which is something that racists tend to deny.

In contrast to Trelkovsky and Szpilman, Chinese people remain nameless and silent in *Chinatown*. For a large part of the film they are only a topic of Gittes's conversations. As Virginia Wexman observes, Gittes's approach to the Chinese people mirrors his attitude to women – it is racist (see Wexman 1987: 97–8). He despises and distrusts the inhabitants of Chinatown. But again, he is wrong. It is to her Chinese friends that Evelyn turns to escape her father and save her daughter. Gittes's racism, as does his misogyny, leads to his professional and human failure.

However, Polanski's approach to ethnic minorities is not consistent. While he identifies with the Polish immigrant in *The Tenant* and the Jews in *The Pianist*, he follows racist stereotypes in representing Arabs and black people in *Frantic*. In this film they are anonymous terrorists and kidnappers whose vicious, but never explained, plans are responsible for the disappearance of Doctor Walker's wife, his anguish, Michelle's eventual death and possibly the suffering of many innocent people all over the world. They are also promiscuous and drug dealers, as episodes set in the Paris nightclubs demonstrate, and they corrupt the white French youth. The death of Michelle, although mourned by Walker and his wife, is presented as just punishment for a white girl who mixes with various dark men. Although not malignant as such, another feature of ethnic minorities in *Frantic* – their love of music and dancing – belongs to the racist stereotype of portraying black people as sensual and natural but lacking intellectual strength. As in Gittes's racist discourse on Los Angeles, Walker's Paris is rendered a city blighted by the influx of coloured people. However, Gittes is proved wrong in regarding the people of colour as the cancer of Los Angeles, while Walker's perception that immigrants are the root of his own and Paris's problems is vindicated.

In *Bitter Moon* Polanski simultaneously ridicules ethnic and racial stereotypes and embraces them. The first happens when Nigel and Fiona disclose that the main reason for their trip to India is to find spirituality and inner peace – only to be ridiculed by their Hindu interlocutor who tells them that India is the noisiest country in the world. The second takes place when Mimi invites to the flat she shares with the crippled Oscar a black dancer with whom she also has sex. For Oscar, who lost his physical power but not his intelligence, and for the viewer the black guest epitomises 'brainless virility', which black men used to represent in Western cinema, beginning with *The Birth of a Nation* (1915) by D.W. Griffith.

To conclude, I will reiterate that the values which most strongly permeate Polanski's narratives are rationalism and individualism. 'Trust yourself, rather than putting your faith in God, the law, the state and ideologies they embody, or indeed, other people, and do not follow stereotypes' is the message we can find in most of his films. Polanski's anti-clericalism and distrust in the forces of law and professional authority potentially situate him in a sympathetic relation towards his female characters and towards members of ethnic minorities who are oppressed by these institutions. This is often, but not always, the case.

Those who seek connections between Polanski's life and work might see a link between the author's life experience and the ideas he espouses in his films. Thus, rationalism and anti-clericalism found in his films might be regarded as a consequence of his traumatic contacts with priests, nuns and religious Poles during the Second World War which made him doubly marginalised and persecuted: as a Jew and as a non-Catholic. Similarly, one can explain Polanski's distrust of political and legal systems from his having lived during the war when any law was barbaric; distrust would also be due to his later trouble with authorities in Poland and the USA, leading to his life as a perpetual exile. On the whole, the values he espouses on screen pertain to his position as a cultural traveller – somebody who is well aware of the relative nature of human opinions and ideas. However, Polanski's films also reveal a low degree of ideological consistency. This feature we can partly attribute to his artistic activity having lasted for over half a century, during which time the artist most likely has changed at least some of his views. Another factor is his nonchalant attitude to film, as mentioned at the beginning of this chapter, as a political tool. His films are indeed driven by stories, not ideas and, unlike his more politically-minded colleagues, he is not afraid to use a certain politically incorrect idea or stereotype to make the narrative work.

6

ADAPT TO SURVIVE AND EXPRESS ONESELF:
POLANSKI'S ENCOUNTERS WITH LITERATURE

If I pick a novel and make it into a film it's because I like it, and I always try to be as faithful as I can.

Roman Polanski

[Polanski] is a gifted filmmaker with a genius for pointing a camera. He didn't need to borrow Shakespeare's robes when he had so many of his own.

Kenneth S. Rothwell

In literature there are never any clear boundaries. Everything is dependent on everything else and one thing is superimposed on top of another. It all ends up as a complicated intertextual game, like a hall of mirrors or those Russian dolls.

Arturo Pérez-Reverte, *The Dumas Club*

Roman Polanski began his career as a director and scriptwriter of the films he directed. In due course, however, he increasingly relied on material written by other people. Firstly he invited other authors to cooperate on original scripts, later he turned to novels and plays. Following *Tess* Polanski's career is characterised by a predominance of films based on novels and plays; his last five films have all been adaptations. However, despite the high proportion of adaptations in his overall artistic output, the director's declaration of his desire to be faithful to the literary originals and a wide acknowledgement that his approach to literature is, if not slavishly faithful, at least not subversive, he is not regarded as a director specialising in this type of film. It does not matter if Polanski picks up Shakespeare's *Macbeth* or a postmodern bestseller, *Lunes de fiel* by Pascal Bruckner, the final result is regarded as 'his' film in which the words written by someone else serve only as a vehicle to convey his personal vision.

In this chapter I will try to establish what assures this authorial stamp and how the director tries to reconcile the different objectives and interests of cinema and literature. In order to do so, however, it is worth recollecting that the word 'adaptation' is not confined to the literary/film discourse. Its use is very wide, including in the field of biology where it means an inherited or acquired modification in organisms that makes them better suited to survive and reproduce in a particular environment. The art of film adaptation is not very different to the biological one – the source used by the filmmaker, be it a novel or play, must be able to survive in a new environment, even at the price of becoming unrecognisable in the new 'body'.[1] Accordingly, there is no uniform way of adapting literature to film. Adaptations depend on an almost unlimited number of factors, including the time and place where they are conducted and the type of audience the director or producer has in mind. For this reason, in the recent writings on this subject authors depart from the traditional question of 'fidelity/ betrayal' of a literary original by a film, and propose to treat film and literature as equal partners, existing in a complex and unstable web of relationships with other texts. Following the terminology of Gérard Genette, inspired by the work of Mikhail Bakhtin and Julia Kristeva, Robert Stam proposes to treat adaptation as a relation between the 'hypertext' to an anterior text, the 'hypotext', which the hypertext transforms, modifies, elaborates or extends (see Stam 2000: 65–6). Nevertheless, among the infinite possibilities offered by adaptation, or to use Bakhtin's terminology, 'multidimensional dialogism between film and literature', we can identify certain prevailing approaches, using as a criterion similarity and difference between the hypertext and the hypotext. Dudley Andrew identifies three of them, which he describes as 'borrowing', 'intersecting' and 'transforming sources'. The first term refers to adapting masterpieces or works which due to frequent reappearance claim the status of myth, such as *Tristan and Isolde*, *A Midsummer Night's Dream* or *Don Quixote*. In this case adaptation hopes to win an audience through the prestige of its borrowed title (see Andrew 1992: 422). The 'borrower' of the masterpiece typically makes little attempt to be faithful to the original, or at least his fidelity is very selective. The opposite of 'borrowing' is 'intersecting'. 'Here the uniqueness of the original text is preserved to such an extent that it is intentionally left unassimilated in adaptation'

(Ibid.: 422). Examples of intersection include Robert Bresson's *Journal d'un curé de campagne* (*Diary of a Country Priest*, 1950), Jean-Marie Straub's *Chronik der Anna Magdalena Bach* (*Chronicle of Anna Magdalena Bach*, 1968) and Pier Paolo Pasolini's *Medea* (1970) (Ibid.: 422–3). In the third type of adaptation (which is closest to the way Polanski uses literature), the task is to reproduce in the film something essential about the original text but without sacrificing the specificity of the film. The fidelity can be assessed in relation to the 'letter' and to the 'spirit' of the adapted text. The letter, argues Andrew, can be emulated in an almost mechanical fashion. It includes aspects of fiction generally elaborated in any film script such as the characters and their inter-relation, and the geographical, sociological and cultural information that provides the fiction's context (Ibid.: 423). More difficult is fidelity to the spirit, to the original's tone, values, imagery and rhythm. Some authors find it impossible, as film and literature are two very different signifying systems. Others, however, such as E.H. Gombrich and Nelson Goodman, argue that the problem of adaptation can be solved by introducing the category of matching. Adaptation in this perspective becomes 'a matter of searching two systems of communication for elements of equivalent position in the systems capable of eliciting a signified at a given level of pertinence' (Ibid.: 425). This, however, means that in order to produce a film faithful to the spirit of a particular literary text, the filmmaker might be forced to sacrifice its letter, for example by making extensive cuts or moving the action of the adapted text to a different period. In the light of this opinion it is not surprising that many critics regard Kurosawa's *Kumonosu-jo* (*Throne of Blood*, 1957) as the most faithful adaptation of Shakespeare's *Macbeth*, despite the fact that the film does not include a single word written by Shakespeare (see Anderegg 2000: 163).

In her 'A Note on Novels and Films' Susan Sontag is close to Gombrich and Goodman when she recognises not only the equivalence of particular novels and films, but also the matching of great novelists with great filmmakers, and some cinematic styles with literary genres. She claims that in D.W. Griffith the cinema had its Samuel Richardson, the cinema of Eisenstein and Kurosawa is an equivalent of literary epic, and some avant-garde short films which were made in France in the 1920s, such as Jean Renoir's *La Petite marchande d'allumettes* (*The Little Match Girl*, 1928), an equivalent of poetry (see Sontag 1994b: 244). Furthermore, Sontag claims that both novels and films can be divided into 'analytic'/ psychological and 'expository'/anti-psychological. The first kind of films, represented by directors such as Carné, Bergman, Fellini and Visconti and writers such as Dickens and Dostoevsky, are concerned with revelation of the characters' motives. The second kind, exemplified by the work of Antonioni, Godard and Bresson and the literature of Stendhal, refrain from psychologising; their characters are opaque, 'in situation' (Ibid.: 245). These categories seem to me very useful in capturing some important features of Polanski's cinema.

TWO TYPES OF OUTSIDERS, TWO TYPES OF SUBJECTIVISM

Although Polanski always pronounces his desire to be faithful to the novels and plays he screens, he also emphasises that his faithfulness is not at the price of creating 'uncinematic' films – films that look like filmed plays or novels, or betray their literary origin by, for example, including the images of the act of writing, as was the case in Bresson's *Diary of a Country Priest*. Accordingly, he seeks novels and plays which have significant cinematic potential and in the process of adaptation tries to conceal their literary character. He changes or reduces the amount of dialogue, in the case of adapting plays chooses settings that are unavailable for the theatre, such as the sea, and extensively uses specifically cinematic techniques, such as close-ups, crane shots and rapid change of location. However, as we can read in Arturo Pérez-Reverte's *El Club Dumas* (*The Dumas Club*, 2003), in literature, as indeed in any other discipline of art, everything is dependent on everything else. This, of course, affects adaptation; the change of one aspect of the literary origin influences many others, sometimes even the alleged essence of the adapted work. We could observe it in Polanski's take on *Macbeth* – the drastic reduction of Shakespeare's dialogue was equated by some critics with the destruction of the integrity of the adapted work.

The protagonist of my book chooses literary material not only on the grounds of its applicability to the cinematic medium as such, but also according to its suitability to 'his cinema' – namely, his beliefs, values and sensitivity; this gives the impression that his adaptations are not very different to his films based on original scripts. However, as I discussed earlier, some of his beliefs and interests do not change and others undergo a significant transformation. In particular, throughout his entire career Polanski perceives the world as full of conflict and cruelty, even absurd (see Chapter 2). On the other hand, until a certain moment in his career, marked by directing *Tess*, his cinema had been that of a psychologist, preoccupied with the uniqueness of his character's vision. Later, he became more concerned with outside reality or, to put it differently, with what the perceptions of his central character have in common with those of other people (see Chapters 2 and 3). I will suggest that both the constant elements and the changes in his interest are reflected in his choice of literary pieces and the way he reworks them.

Polanski always favoured books with a distinctive central character (as suggested by the titles derived from the names of their protagonists – *Rosemary's Baby, The Tenant, Macbeth, Tess, The Pianist, Oliver Twist*), a character whose vision, conduct and fate differ from what can be regarded as the norm. Their fate is unlike others because typically they are 'borderline' characters who do not fit easily into any prevailing social categories. Tess is both a member of the aristocracy and of the working class but she is not an accepted member of either. At the beginning of her story she is neither a child nor a woman. Trelkovsky is a Pole living in Paris, therefore he is not regarded as either a true Frenchman or a Pole. Władysław Szpilman, the main character of his autobiography *The Pianist*, is a Jew, but his position as a famous pianist separates him from most of his compatriots. Moreover, having been written in 1945, *The Pianist* offers the perspective of somebody who was better aware of what was happening to the Jews than most of his present-day countrymen.

Polanski typically strengthens the impression of the protagonists' difference from society, including their isolation from those closest to them, as conveyed in the literary hypotexts. He achieves this effect through a constant focus on his protagonist, who is frequently seen on his or her own. Thus, in comparison with the original memoirs, the part of Szpilman's account presenting his lonely struggle to survive in Warsaw, destroyed by the insurrectionists and occupiers, is extended in the film, while the scenes showing him with his family are condensed. The most persistent image of Tess is on the road, in transit, unlike the other characters who lead more stable and sedentary lives. Road signifies Tess's real and cultural journey: moving between places, people, social classes and lifestyles, and assuming that real and cultural nomadism is the sign of our times, her modernity.

When Polanski's heroes and heroines are with other people, he shows them both watching and judging others and being watched and judged. However, he values the perceptions and judgements of his protagonists differently to those of secondary characters. When Tess and Władysław Szpilman are shown with members of their families, they appear superior because the behaviour of their relatives is naive or morally dubious. Take the scene in *Tess* when the mother informs the heroine about their noble roots. Not only is Tess unimpressed by the news but she is rightly sceptical about the version of the family history passed to her. When Władysław's brother, Henryk, tells cruel jokes about life in the ghetto,

Władysław remains reticent in full knowledge that Henryk's sarcastic outbursts are only adding to the already heavy atmosphere.

When Tess is looked at by others, their gazes typically prove harmful or at least defective. Take the lusting or loving gazes of Alec which lead to him raping (or seducing) Tess and her subsequent miseries, Angel's gaze which constructs Tess as a 'pure' (simple and virginal) country girl or the judgemental or scrutinising glances of the fellow parishioners which make Tess ashamed of her affair with Alec. Szpilman is rarely looked at by the Germans, but we are aware that their gaze would be disastrous. According to the usual ghetto scenario, those who attracted the attention of the occupiers were singled out to die. In the later part of the film Szpilman is most often looked at by Poles who help him to survive in the destroyed city. The contrast between their elegant appearance and that of emasculated Władysław is so great that the Poles are as ashamed as if their look was pornographic. Whenever Polanski uses multiple focalisation (multiplying points of view), its principal purpose is to facilitate identification with the main character, rather than move between the minds of various characters as is the norm in Hollywood cinema. Such an emphasis on the protagonist results in 'underplaying' secondary characters; they become less complex than in the literary original, their role typically reduced to bringing misery and causing the downfall of the hero. We observe it particularly in *Tess*, when it seems like the whole world is conspiring in her demise (see Constanzo 1981: 75).

To make the viewer identify with one character in the film, rather than have his loyalties and interests dissipated among several personas, also affects Polanski's decisions regarding whom to make the protagonist and whom to make the narrator or 'chief observer' in his films. He tends to merge these two roles even if this means departing from the letter of the adapted text, as is the case of his screening of *The Dumas Club*. The narrator of Pérez-Reverte's novel is Boris Balkan, a writer, literary historian and translator who throughout most of the book remains a distant and disengaged narrator of god-like knowledge about the characters, including the protagonist, Lucas Corso. *The Ninth Gate*, by contrast, does not have a narrator understood as somebody who directly addresses the audience. Instead, Corso – without losing his position as the main character – becomes the medium through which the viewer perceives the reality represented.

Although Polanski always focuses his films on outsiders, there are two types of outsiders in his films. In his adaptations which preceded *Tess*, the characters experience the world differently because they see and hear things which do not exist. In *The Tenant*, based on the novel by Roland Topor and *Rosemary's Baby*, adapted from Ira Levin's book, Polanski shows distortions in the objects that his characters see; their rooms change shape and the characters stop recognising themselves in the mirror. Some of these distortions can be regarded as faithful renditions of literary descriptions. However, in comparison with the literary original Polanski's films tend to widen the gap between the protagonist's perception and that of other people. For example, he included in *The Tenant* a scene in which Trelkovsky goes to a mass to commemorate the death of Simone Choule. In both the book and the film Trelkovsky leaves the church before the service is finished. However, in the book (where the scene happens before Trelkovsky moves to Mademoiselle Choule's old apartment) he does this because of his long lasting fear of death and due to cold. There is no indication that he is hallucinating. In Polanski's film, by contrast, Trelkovsky leaves the church frightened by the content of his subjective and already pathological vision.

Similarly, Polanski puts a question mark over the correctness of his characters' visions where in the book there is no doubt about the status of his or her perceptions. This is particularly true in the case of the heroine of *Rosemary's Baby*. Ira Levin makes it clear that his is a story of a woman used by devil worshippers to produce a Satan. Polanski's film is much more ambiguous in this respect. His Rosemary might be a mentally sound woman confronted by a situation which challenges her rationality, or a hysterical woman who loses her objectivity due to her pregnancy and isolation. Polanski creates this ambiguity by presenting objects pertaining to the character's sick state of mind, such as knives, meat and certain sounds, which nevertheless can be regarded as simply 'being there', irrespective of whether somebody looks at them or not. It is the position of filmmaker that affords him such ambiguity. Rick Altman observes that:

> In literature, a clear distinction must be made between inside views of characters (providing privileged access to their thoughts or feelings) and more distant treatment limited to description of external features. In Hollywood film [and other types of film as well], however, no such distinction holds; similar images serve both purposes. There is no automatic method of deciding – as there is in most novels – whether the face we see is simply an object of someone else's gaze, speech or thought, or whether it is the locus of a thought process that perceives, processes, and thus swallows up the other characters in the film. On the contrary, the lack of clear difference between internal and external views means that the same footage is easily constructed in more than one way. (Altman 2002: 136–7)

Mia Farrow in *Rosemary's Baby* (1968)

In Polanski's later films the focus is still on the character's perception of the world, but this time the character's perception is correct, presented as it is in the literary hypotexts. It could be argued that the point of films such as *Death and the Maiden*, *The Pianist* and *Oliver Twist* is to acknowledge and celebrate the resilience of a character who did not lose his sanity in adverse circumstances (see Chapter 2).

From the perspective of the two types of subjectivism portrayed by Polanski in his films (that of a madman and that of a perceptive outsider), I will regard *Tess* as a watershed. In contrast to *The Tenant* and

Nastassia Kinski in *Tess* (1979)

Rosemary's Baby, we do not find here distorted objects or purely subjective sounds. The film is also remarkably ascetic in terms of transposing to screen the symbolic and metaphysical layers of its literary original (see Constanzo 1981: 76–7). As Peter Widdowson remarks, 'Tess is superimposed on a realistic "period" background' (Widdowson 1993: 101), including authentic nineteenth-century farm machinery and early railroad cars (see Polanski 1984: 378). On the other hand, Polanski's Tess comes across as completely detached from her background and driven by an inner voice, rather than rational reasoning, not unlike a somnambulist. Her detachment, in the words of Peter Widdowson, is 'a characteristically ahistorical existential alienation in which the particular and specific historical conjuncture is finally immaterial' (Widdowson 1995.: 101). In this sense she has more in common with Carol in *Repulsion* than with Hardy's Tess. This alienation is conveyed by Nastassia Kinski's acting; she plays the role in a 'passive, dreamy, almost trance-like state' and speaks like 'a zombie' (Ibid.: 103). Moreover, in the second half of the film, Tess's isolation is conveyed by the use of soundtrack: surrounding her with an 'almost unnatural quiet' (Niemeyer 2003: 142). This quiet is unnatural because it originates from inside Tess, rather than outside reality. Again, in this sense Tess is the sister of Carol, who was surrounded by 'her sounds' and 'her silence'.

Regarding Polanski's take on adaptation and his whole approach to filmmaking, *Tess* is a borderline work also, because it marks a transition that is best captured by Sontag's categories of 'expository'/ anti-psychological/Stendhalian cinema and 'analytic'/psychological/ Dostoevskian-Dickensian cinema. I suggest that Polanski's earlier adaptations, including *Tess*, in common with the majority of his films that were produced in this period based on original scripts, are made in the Stendhal mode. These films, including *The Tenant*, *Rosemary's Baby* and *Macbeth*, as well as *Knife in the Water* and *Cul-de-Sac*, tend to show the characters in situations rather than revealing their motives for action. Dialogue is used sparsely, the main characters remaining a mystery from the beginning to the end. By contrast, in the later part of Polanski's career, identified with films such as *Bitter Moon*, *Death and the Maiden*, *The Pianist* and *Oliver Twist*, cinema à la Dickens prevails. The director's main objective here is to reveal characters' motives and thoughts. In *Bitter Moon* and *Death and the Maiden*, the characters' motives are, in my opinion, overexposed through lengthy discussions or monologues. For this reason Polanski's later films are sometimes described as 'literary', in contrast with the earlier films which were often labelled as 'pure cinema'.

It is likely that the cause of the metamorphosis from expository to analytical cinema in the case of Polanski is his turning to the literature of a particular type, exemplified by Dickens's *Oliver Twist*. However, I believe that Polanski's growing interest in literature is more a symptom of his desire to find a vehicle to create a cinema that attempts to understand and explain human actions, rather than one which respects the mystery of every individual, and which invites viewers' identification, rather than distance. As he himself admitted when shooting *Tess*, he became interested in different types of emotions to those that captivated him earlier in his career. He describes these emotions (great love, utter hatred, extreme fear and desire to survive) as 'simple and essential' (Kennedy 1979: 62), therefore shared or at least understood practically by everybody. It could be suggested that these simple and essential emotions are conveyed if not better then at least more easily by 'Dickensian cinema' than by the 'underplayed' 'Stendhalian one'.[2]

SUBJECTIVISM AND ABSURDISM

A concentration on subjective and idiosyncratic perceptions concurs in Polanski's films with conveying an absurdist outlook on life. The link

Jon Finch and Francesca Annis in *Macbeth* (1971)

between subjectivism and absurdism is especially visible in Polanski's *Macbeth*. Shakespeare's *Macbeth* lends itself to different interpretations: one drawing attention to external, another mental conflicts; one perceiving the story of Macbeth as a testimony to the world's absurdity, another as spreading a message of the order and ultimate justice permeating history. Polanski chose to see *Macbeth* as a subjective and absurdist work.

The subjectivism of Polanski's adaptation is conveyed by presenting the greater part of the play's soliloquies as voice-over narration, revealing Macbeth's thoughts. Such an approach, as Herbert Eagle observes, might be motivated by a desire not to disrupt realism by having the characters so clearly address the audience (see Eagle 1994: 135), but also by Polanski's decision, as Nigel Andrews suggests, to blur the boundary between 'inner' and 'outer' drama (see Andrews 1972: 108), and establish Macbeth as the medium through which we see the external events. Furthermore, we often see Macbeth in profile, placed at the edge of the frame, which renders the world as an object of his vision (see Wexman 1987: 81). Kenneth Rothwell also argues that when there is a disparity between Macbeth's perception and that of the other character, the audience shares the former, even if it is incorrect or impossible, as in the scene when he sees Banquo's ghost (Rothwell 1999: 158) or when his head is severed from his body and he experiences 'the terminal spasms of sensory apprehension' (Rothwell 1999: 160). The fact that we accompany Macbeth even after his beheading also testifies to Polanski's interpretation of *Macbeth* not so much as a tale about Macbeth, but as Macbeth's own story, his autobiography.

Polanski opts for an absurdist *Macbeth* by portraying history not as a road towards a better future, but as a vicious circle of crimes and miseries. Take, for example, the repetitive character of crowning the king – each crowning follows the brutal killing of the previous king, first Duncan, then Macbeth. Another example is the friendly visits by people who later betray their hosts or their guests. This happens when Ross visits Lady Macduff who is subsequently murdered on Ross's orders, and when Macbeth encourages two men to kill Banquo and his son and later shows them no gratitude but sends them to their death. Most importantly, Duncan's younger son, Donalbain, in a scene invented for the ending of the film, is shown approaching the witches' den, as Macbeth did previously – a clear hint that 'the cycle of envy and usurpation will go on' (Johnson 1972: 45).[3] In contrast to these cruel or ominous events, the happy moments, such as when Lady Macbeth greets her husband in utter joy, are rare and always precede particularly bloody events, as if they were an exception to the rule that human life is a misery.

In line with Camus's rule that the 'divorce between man and his life, the actor and his setting, truly constitutes the feeling of Absurdity' (Camus, quoted in Esslin 1968: 23), the absurdism of Polanski's *Macbeth* is strengthened or fully revealed by depicting Macbeth as being aware of the cruel mechanisms of history and deep down loathing them. The sign that his Macbeth is not an over-ambitious usurper, or a vehicle for his wife's plans but a 'visionary' who sees the future and reluctantly follows his fate, is the lack of change in his expression (which some critics, wrongly in my opinion, attributed to Jon Finch's limited acting skills). Throughout the film he comes across as reserved and almost morose, as if from the beginning he has been aware of his own imminent demise and the general futility of human existence. When he is talking to other characters, including those closest to him, such as his own wife, he often does not look at them, but looks far away, as if he cannot share his thoughts with them. Again, he is so distant because he possesses the knowledge that they lack. This knowledge about life's ultimate futility, as Herbert Eagle suggests, ennobles him (see Eagle 1994: 139). Similarly, Macbeth's cruelty is presented not as a sign of his weakness, but rather of his strength, his ability to suppress his sympathies, overcome his disgust with violence and death, and carry on with his duties until the very end.

Favouring a subjectivist–absurdist *Macbeth* links Polanski's interpretation with Jan Kott's[4] reading of Shakespeare's history plays in general and of *Macbeth* in particular (see Johnson 1972: 45; Wexman 1987: 81; Rothwell 1999: 156–7). Kott maintains that Shakespeare perceives history as absurd because each of Shakespeare's History plays, including *King John*, *Richard II*, *Henry IV*, *Henry V*, *Henry VI* and *Richard III*, begins with a struggle for the throne or for its consolidation, and each ends with the monarch's death and a new coronation. Moreover, in each of the Histories the legitimate ruler drags behind him a long chain of crimes. He has to murder his enemies and his allies, as well as possible successors and pretenders to the throne. But he is not able to execute them all, so in the end he is murdered by the new pretender, which begins the new cycle of violence. Kott maintains that *Macbeth* presents the same mechanism of the struggle for power as others of the History plays, but conveys it somehow differently. Not only are crime and murder more extreme and concrete in *Macbeth*, but the work of history is shown here through the personal experience of Macbeth himself. Macbeth, according to Kott, differs from other protagonists of Shakespeare in his realisation of the inevitability and absurdity of history and in his deep inner rejection of the world's mechanisms (see Kott 1967: 74–7). To put it differently, according to Kott, we can list *Macbeth* as an absurdist play not only because of a plot that points to the world's absurdity but also because of its existentialist protagonist.

However, Kott's reading is of course not the only possible interpretation of *Macbeth*. It can for example be rendered not as a play about the absurdity of history and the tragic fate of an admirable individual crushed by its cruel mechanism, but as about the justice of history which punishes unhealthy ambitions and betrayal, and brings in the end order and decency. Roger Manvell, for example, argues that *Macbeth* is not a tragedy but a 'high melodrama', as Macbeth does not have the greatness of character of Hamlet and King Lear (see Manvell 1979: 152–3). The 'melodramatic' interpretation of *Macbeth* is proposed in Akira Kurosawa's *Throne of Blood*. The Japanese Macbeth, called Washizu, is too mediocre, barbaric and irrational a man to be granted a vision in the literal or metaphorical sense. Consequently, the most important events appear to take place without his participation and he remains a puppet in the hands of women: the demon who foretells his future and his ambitious wife, Asaji. This dependence on women in the extremely patriarchal, medieval Japan renders his social position as particularly low. Obviously, such a man is not fit to be king. Because Washizu and Polanski's Macbeth are such different characters, Kurosawa's film has a very different ending to Polanski's – Washizu is killed by his own people, who perceive him as a traitor and a weakling. Washizu's death means the restoration of moral and social order, rather than the beginning of a new cycle of violence and disorder, as was the case in Polanski's film. Not surprisingly, the subjectivity and absurdism of Polanski's *Macbeth* is particularly striking when compared to Kurosawa's film.

Highlighting the subjective vision of Macbeth does not preclude naturalistic representation of his physical and cultural environment. Polanski's *Macbeth* works concurrently on naturalistic and psychological planes. The effect of naturalism is achieved by representing Shakespeare's 'weird sisters' as very corporeal beings and by means of meticulous reconstruction of medieval customs and imagery. During the shooting three real castles were used, and the king's companions, as guests of Macbeth, sleep in a dirt-floor courtyard among piles of hay and animals (see Eagle 1994: 133). As Polanski himself put it: 'Whatever I did in the film I based on different research and on different opinions of scholars. There's three hundred years of scholarship... and every gesture, every line in the play has some reference to be found and can be interpreted according to different theories. And that's what inspired us when we were writing the script' (Polanski, quoted in Middleton

1979–80: 92). Such naturalism, however, is an exception in the tradition of adapting *Macbeth* or even Shakespeare generally,[5] and can be regarded as an attempt to subvert the original text by purging *Macbeth* of its literalness and bringing the play into 'our' material world. Again, such interpretation is in line with Kott's reading of Shakespeare as 'our contemporary' – somebody who would not be surprised by the Holocaust or Stalinist atrocities.

The same meticulousness can be detected in *Tess* and *Oliver Twist*. Both films contain a great deal of detail about English landscape and life in Victorian England. Again, the director went to great lengths to assure the authenticity of costumes, interiors and exteriors. Their naturalism can be regarded as an element that originates in Polanski's outlook on life, in which cruelty and suffering take place in concrete, everyday, mundane reality and are caused entirely by human actions.

INTERNATIONALISATION, AUTOBIOGRAPHY AND OPTIMISM

Bloody Hollywood.

Arturo Pérez-Reverte, *The Dumas Club*

I have mentioned several times that Polanski always wanted to make films for as international an audience as possible. In his original work this ambition forced him to eschew or limit drastically any references to national cultures. The same rule of internationalisation applies to some of his films that are based on novels and plays. The clearest example is *Bitter Moon*. Its literary source, Pascal Bruckner's novel *Lunes de fiel*, is deeply rooted in the French culture of a particular period: the second half of the 1970s. It summarises and assesses the experiences and attitudes of those of the intelligentsia who were born in the 1940s, to which Bruckner himself belongs, and whose views and ideals were formed largely by the student rebellion of May 1968. This group of people, as portrayed by Bruckner, became very disillusioned by the late 1970s, irrespective of the political stance they had taken a decade earlier. The reaction of the main character of the novel, named Franz, to his disappointment is to show utter contempt for both the political left (with which he previously identified) and right, adopting instead an extreme individualism. Bored with French culture and his own social milieu, he seeks fulfilment in an affair with a Jewish woman ten years his junior. This affair allows him to open up to a new society, and is a substitute for the rebellion of his youth because his traditional-minded, right-wing and xenophobic family disapprove of any 'outsiders' in their circle. Moreover, it is a way to move beyond the borders of good taste in sex and in life as a whole and to explore his self. Franz and his lover, named Rebeka, are juxtaposed with Didier and Béatrice, a couple belonging to Franz's generation. As they were less politically involved in their youth, they are not so disappointed by the changes that have taken place in France after 1968. Nevertheless, in common with Franz, they feel boredom and an inner void, and try to assuage their middle-age crisis by giving in to certain fads and snobberies, such as fascination with Indian culture. Bruckner demonstrates that neither Franz's, nor Didier and Béatrice's life-changing scenario bring fulfilment and meaning – all his characters end up as bankrupts (see Lubelski 1993).

Polanski retained the skeleton of the relationships between the two couples, but disposed of their French cultural baggage, assuming that it would have an appeal only to the relatively narrow group of viewers interested in the complexities of French politics and culture. The cultural differences between the characters in the novel are in Polanski's film of a different nature – referring to their nationalities, not political positions. Franz has changed into Oscar an American; Didier and Béatrice become an English couple, Nigel and Fiona. Paradoxically, the only non-French dramatis personae of Bruckner's novel, Rebeka, becomes Mimi, the only French character in Polanski's film. Such transformation allowed the director to explain both the peculiarities of and differences between the characters and the attraction they feel for each other. Oscar in Polanski's film, similarly to Franz in *Lunes de fiel*, comes across as keen to experiment with sex but this is linked to his nationality (American) and particularly his being influenced by American writers, such as Henry Miller and F. Scott Fitzgerald. Nigel and Fiona are represented as sexually and emotionally repressed, which parallels Didier and Béatrice's boredom with each other but this is because they are English, or more exactly English and upper middle-class. These cultural differences are strengthened by the differences in age and professional status. Oscar is the eldest of the four characters and older than his literary equivalent. The difference in age between him and Mimi is significantly greater than that between Franz and Rebeka, which was a mere ten years. It looks as if Oscar is at least double Mimi's age when they meet for the first time and at least twenty years older than Nigel and Fiona. The knowledge that comes with experience, combined with erudition attained through contact with literature, has replaced Franz's bitter wisdom, which had been achieved by studying the meanderings of French politics.

One would expect that the rejuvenation of the three main characters, and retaining one older, was dictated by the desire not to alienate young viewers (who in the last two decades have constituted the vast majority of cinema-goers in the Western world), while at the same time making the film appeal to 'mature' audiences. The changes in representation of the central couples make his characters also similar to certain easily recognisable cinematic and cultural stereotypes in a wider sense, such as the cynical middle-aged man who 'knows about women' and treats them as sexual toys, familiar from westerns and *films noir*. Moreover, the physical resemblance of Peter Coyote to Leonard Cohen, who in his songs and in his life epitomised the promiscuous ageing but still attractive lover, strengthens this association. Similarly, both Fiona and Nigel as upper-class English people whose sexual desires are repressed have their equivalents in many other films including those in which Hugh Grant and Kristin Scott Thomas played before and after appearing in Polanski's movie – *Maurice* (1987), directed by James Ivory, *Angels and Insects* (1995), directed by Philip Haas and, most of all, *Four Weddings and a Funeral* (1993), directed by Mike Newell.

Thanks to all the characters being able to speak English, and Oscar's lack of fluency in French, English becomes the common denominator in the communication between the four main characters and the language of the whole film. The translation of one set of cultural differences between the characters into a different set can be regarded as a confirmation of Goodman's thesis that what is important in a faithful adaptation is not the equivalence of elements between novel and film, but of the position that elements occupy vis-à-vis their different domains. Consequently, in many cases the film adaptations which change more aspects of the original appear more faithful to it than those which change fewer.

Modifying the original text in the way described above also had a side effect: it invited critics to seek an autobiographical dimension in *Bitter Moon*, which probably would not have happened if Polanski had retained the characters in their original cultural milieu. In the 'self-exiled' American artist who experiments sexually with a naive woman half his age, a role played by Polanski's wife, Emmanuelle Seigner, they saw Polanski himself (see Kennedy 1994: 14). The director has resolutely denied such a parallel, but his denial hardly affected viewers' perception of the film. As I argued earlier in Chapter 1, the author of the film does not have full control over any autobiographical effect of his work. Ultimately, it is the viewer who decides what links the film with its author, being governed in his decision by information derived from various sources, not all respectable, such as the tabloid press.

A similar method of increasing the international appeal of a film, such as occurred in *Bitter Moon*, can be detected in *The Ninth Gate*; this is the most selective adaptation in Polanski's career, as is suggested by the film's very title being completely different from the title of the novel, which is *The Dumas Club*. The main character changed from a mature and disillusioned intellectual and polyglot into a young and rather naive adventurer who has significant problems with reading Latin. One French reviewer even compared him to the careless Tintin (see Vachaud 1999: 37). He also changed his nationality from Spanish to American (and his first name from Lucas to Dean), which ensured that English was the language spoken by all the characters. Thanks to these transformations, Johnny Depp could star in the film, which no doubt increased the film's appeal to younger viewers. The predicted habits, interests and intellectual capacity of young audiences were also the most likely factor influencing the decisions regarding what to cut out from the book and what to amplify in the film. *The Dumas Club* has two parallel plots, both related to Corso's search for rare books. One, as the title suggests, concerns the manuscript of *The Four Musketeers* by Alexandre Dumas, the other *The Ninth Gate to the Kingdom of Shadows*, a fictitious book allowing its possessor to call up the devil. *The Dumas Club*, in common with much of the fiction described as 'postmodern' (see Sontag 1994c: 293), is a product of the blurring of the boundary between 'two cultures': the literary–artistic and the scientific. The passages devoted to presenting the actions and motivations of the characters are juxtaposed with pages describing the literary methods of popular writers of previous epochs, such as Dumas, and the techniques used to preserve and check the authenticity of the old books. It takes issue with the relation between low and high art, particularly the dislodging of literature by film and television[6] and the question of authorship and translation – all problems pertaining to postmodern discourses. Moreover, it mixes fact (in the form of the biography of Alexandre Dumas, for example) with fiction and spoof, which again is a very postmodern technique. Accordingly, to appreciate *The Ninth Gate* in its textual richness requires some knowledge and engagement in postmodern discourses and techniques.

Polanski's strategy of adaptation was to give up completely on the plot of searching and researching Dumas's works, and to amplify the motif of looking for copies of *The Ninth Gate* and its apparent creator – the devil. This was meant to ensure that the film had an appeal for fans of horror, which is arguably a larger constituency than that of lovers of Dumas's books, or even any kinds of books. Moreover, as much as possible the filmmaker sheds the intertextual baggage of Pérez-Reverte's novel. Hence, in comparison with its hypotext (the novel), Polanski's film is much less a postmodern work of art. Moreover, its postmodernity, as Philip Strick and Tadeusz Lubelski note, results less from citing literary texts and more from Polanski's conscious or unconscious references to his own works, especially to one of his most successful films: *Rosemary's Baby* (see Lubelski 2000; Strick 2000). *The Ninth Gate* accounts for autobiographical reading in one more way: as an exercise in the style of an 'old master', who has lost interest in plots and ideological messages but has retained a passion for beauty. In this respect it is similar, as some reviewers noticed, to *Eyes Wide Shut* by Stanley Kubrick (made in the same year), as in both films the exquisite, baroque form contrasts with, or even underscores, a rather frivolous content (see Nesselson 1999; Fendel 1999). Both films are also self-reflexive in so far as they explore the difference between living and dreaming (and by extension watching films, as film is often compared to a dream), and their plots revolve around a young man who seems to engage in an illicit activity on behalf of an older man. Needless to say, this man who dislocates his desires to the voyeuristic delectation of a younger man can be regarded as an alter ego of the film director.

We can also talk about internationalisation with reference to *The Pianist*. However, before discussing how Polanski catered for international tastes in this film and how and with what result he inscribed into it his autobiography, something else should be mentioned. As demonstrated by critics' and viewers' responses to such literary adaptations as *Sophie's Choice* (1982) by Alan J. Pakula, *Europa, Europa* (1991) by Agnieszka Holland and particularly Steven Spielberg's *Schindler's List* (1993), when a film refers to the Holocaust, the template against which its faithfulness is assessed largely shifts from the book to the historical truth itself. The historical event becomes the principal hypotext for the filmic hypertext, while the literary material is merely a means to achieve a 'truthful' or 'right' representation of this extraordinarily event. This is also the case with *The Pianist* – its main frame of reference is the war history of European Jews, not Szpilman's memoirs. It is judged primarily as an attempt to 'adapt' the Holocaust to the medium of cinema.

It is widely agreed that the Holocaust poses serious problems to the cinema and especially to mainstream film. There is no space here to discuss or even present all of these problems but it is worth listing some. Firstly, the Holocaust was an horrific event that caused an insurmountable amount of misery and culminated in the deaths of more than six million people. Not to represent the atrocities equals ignoring or misrepresenting history but to show them in a graphic way brings a risk of exploiting the tragedy of the victims of the Nazis for the thrills of the viewers, and of replacing history and its memory with simulacra. The challenge for the filmmaker, therefore, is to invent a new language able to 'represent the unpresentable'. Secondly, for the vast majority of the 'characters' in the Holocaust there was no happy ending. Most perished and even those who survived the ghettos and camps were shattered by the loss of their relatives and friends, and their own traumatic experience. For this reason the story of the genocide of European Jews is the opposite of the Hollywood narrative that favours an individual character who achieves victory in the end. Thirdly, unlike the Hollywood film whose characters are neatly divided into good and bad guys, from a moral point of view the Holocaust constituted a very complex universe, predominantly because its victims were implicated in the destruction of their compatriots and in their own annihilation, for example by being selected for the *Sonderkommando* (special commando) whose role was to help the SS to kill prisoners in the gas chambers (see Levi 1988; Bauman 1989; Borowski 1992). Finally, the ultimate objective of mainstream film is profit, and many custodians of the memory of those who perished in the ghettos and gas chambers object to the use of their history for commercial purposes.

The challenge to create a faithful cinematic representation of the Holocaust while adapting it to the tastes and habits of the mainstream audience was fully realised in the context of Spielberg's *Schindler's List*, based on Thomas Keneally's novel *Schindler's Ark* (1983). The critics' and historians' uneasiness about *Schindler's List* had much to do with the popularity of the film – it was the greatest international blockbuster tackling this subject, made by the most commercially successful Hollywood director of modern times. The detractors of Spielberg's endeavour identified in it all the features listed above, which can be described as unrepresentativeness, melodramatisation, commercialisation, moral simplification and 'simulacrum-isation' of the Holocaust, as well as its inflating of the rescuer's role at the expense of the victims (see Bresheeth 1997: 201–2; Hillberg, quoted in Rawlinson 1999: 119) and its depiction of the Holocaust through 'German eyes'. This was accompanied by another criticism: of representing the Jews according to anti-Semitic stereotypes, as passive, feminised, greedy and puny (Ibid.).[7] It is worth adding here that many critics compared *Schindler's List* with Claude Lanzmann's acclaimed documentary *Shoah* (1985), regarding the latter as the definitive (faithful and unbiased) film about the Jews' annihilation. However, this opinion was robustly rejected in Poland, where *Shoah* was received as not much more than anti-Polish propaganda.

I will suggest that Polanski managed to find a formula that allowed him to avoid the most serious criticisms that were directed at Spielberg and achieve some of the effects accomplished by both Spielberg (including international commercial success) and Lanzmann, without subscribing to Lanzmann's anti-Polish sentiments. There were several components to the film's success in this respect. The largest part of the recipe was probably, you might say, Polanski himself.[8] Being a Holocaust survivor gave him the moral right to make money out of this subject, or at least no critic known to me has had the courage to question the commercial dimension of his endeavour. It also afforded him a special credibility to embark on this project, one which probably no other living director enjoys. Hence, although the story he depicts in *The Pianist* is that of an individual's survival, therefore typical of Hollywood, Polanski was excused for using it on the grounds that it also pertains to his personal and unique circumstances. Similarly, as a Jew who lost his mother in the gas chambers and who himself brushed with death on numerous occasions during the war, Polanski could not be accused lightly of making a film which undermines Jewish suffering or is anti-Semitic. The choice of Szpilman's memoirs as the basis for the film ensured that a Jew, rather than a 'good German', as in *Schindler's List*, or a 'good Pole' or a 'good communist', as in many earlier Polish films tackling this subject, is the main protagonist of the film. In fact, there are Jewish characters in *The Pianist* which conform to anti-Semitic stereotypes, such as the guests in a café where Szpilman is playing the piano, checking whether their coins are made of real gold; however, they are minor characters, more than offset by the decent members of the Szpilman family. Similarly, the alleged Jewish passivity during the war, which allowed Spielberg to view the Holocaust as a moral battle between good and bad Germans, with Jews and Poles passively waiting for its outcome, is contradicted by Polanski whose film refers to various acts of resistance undertaken in the ghetto (such as producing underground newspapers) and includes scenes of the Jewish uprising of 1943. At the same time by showing a 'good German' and several 'good Poles' as secondary characters, Polanski ensured that his film would not be offensive to any of the nations portrayed, and would be favourably received internationally, including in his native Poland (see Mazierska 2005).

Polanski's own memories of life in the ghetto were also seen to guarantee the film's authenticity. Reports from the set mentioned, for example, that the director asked the costume designers to change some details in the costumes of German policemen on the grounds that they did not conform to his recollections of the war. This meticulous reconstruction resembles Lanzmann's approach to the representation of the Holocaust: 'the details are what matters' (Loshitzky 1997: 105). In common with Lanzmann's film and in contrast to *Schindler's List*, which was shot in black and white, *The Pianist* was made in colour. Again, Polanski's choice was explained by his desire to produce a realistic film, rather than a simulacrum or a pastiche of previous cinematic styles, to which Spielberg was sentenced; Spielberg had, by his own admission, 'no colour reference to this period' (Loshitzky 1997: 109). Moreover, as mentioned in Chapter 3, colour allowed the director of *The Pianist* to represent the changes that occurred in the ghetto during the time that Szpilman lived there – with the place's gradual loss of colour due to various forms of deprivations suffered by its inhabitants. The similarity of Polanski's movie to *Shoah*, and by the same token, its authenticity or truthfulness, lies also in there being a documentary about the making of the film, entitled *A Story of Survival*. Accompanying the DVD version of *The Pianist,* this documentary deploys certain techniques that make it strongly resemble *Shoah*. I refer here particularly to Polanski and the co-producer of *The Pianist*, Gene Gutowski, talking about their own war experiences and to the moments where Polanski demonstrates to his actors what to do. In such scenes the viewer is invited to treat him not as a director, but as a Holocaust witness who re-enacts certain scenes which took place in the past – as did Lanzmann's interviewees. When there was a disparity between Polanski's and Szpilman's recollections of certain events and Polanski chose his own, this was treated not as a betrayal of a literary source, but as proof that his portrayal is a more reliable representation of the Holocaust. For example, in Szpilman's memoirs he avoids being sent to the death camp by running away from the Umschlagplatz on the order of a Jewish policeman. In the film version, however, Szpilman is told not to run, but to disappear from the square slowly. The reason is, as Polanski explains in *A Story of Survival*, that he himself was once allowed to leave the Umschlagplatz by a Polish policeman, but was ordered not to run, presumably to avoid unnecessary attention.

Some aspects of Polanski's film, however, are unfaithful to both men's memories, but conform to Hollywood conventions of representing the Second World War or indeed, any historical subject. For example, *The Pianist* uses English as the language spoken by the film characters, irrespective of whether they are Polish Jews, Poles or Germans, only adding some German words for the 'sound effect'. This decision had consequences regarding the casting of the film – Polanski used a largely English cast, including Adrien Brody in the leading role, with Polish actors playing only minor parts. Such a convention not only undermines the realism of the film but leaves out from its discourse an important aspect of the oppression suffered by the victims of the Nazi regime: the linguistic one. As was noted by many of those who went through ghettos and concentration camps, hearing a language foreign to them was often a frightening experience, and not understanding the language of the 'masters' could equal a death sentence (see Levi 1988). By making all characters uniformly speak English, an opportunity was lost to represent the Polish language (which Szpilman's family spoke) as the language of the victims of Nazism, rather than its perpetrators, as was the case in some powerful recollections of the Holocaust, such as Lanzmann's *Shoah* or the memories of Primo Levi.[9] Nevertheless, it is worth mentioning that in Poland Polanski was generally excused for having Szpilman speak in English. Most critics ignored the language issue and those few who addressed it regarded his decision as natural on the grounds that his film was addressed to an international audience (see Płażewski 2002: 15). It seemed as if Poles were so grateful for their most famous director's decision to return home that they forgave him his return being on his own terms. *The Pianist* also omits the problem of the 'grey zone' that existed between the victims and the perpetrators (see Levi 1988: 22–51). Although we see the members of the Jewish police who brutally herd their compatriots to the trains for Auschwitz, their choices and decisions are not interrogated. Moreover, the 'grey zone' of the Nazi collaborators is overshadowed by the 'virtuous zone' of the fighters and the decent Szpilman family.

Polanski also takes liberties with the messages conveyed in Szpilman's memoirs. In particular, although both book and film are stories of survival and can therefore be viewed as optimistic, the optimism of Polanski's film is greater and less qualified than that of the book. We can see this most clearly if we compare the ending of the book with that of the film. The last chapter of Szpilman's memoirs, meaningfully entitled 'Nocturne in C sharp minor', finishes with the following words:

Barney Clark in *Oliver Twist* (2005)

> I must begin a new life. How could I do it, with nothing but death behind me? What vital energy could I draw from death? I went on my way. A stormy wind rattled

the scrap-iron in the ruins, whistling and howling through the charred cavities of the windows. Twilight came on. Snow fell from the darkening, leaden sky. (Szpilman 2003: 187)

These words awaken the feeling of an Earth deserted by people and ghosts, with Szpilman being its last inhabitant, one who sees no point in prolonging his existence. Such an image bears association with existentialism and absurdism, both paradigms being obsessed by the image of the end of humanity.

Polanski, by contrast, finishes his film on an upbeat note by showing Władysław playing the piano to a receptive concert audience. The ending resembles the beginning of the film in which we also saw Szpilman playing the piano – this time on the radio. By using a circular narrative Polanski, not unlike Spielberg, offers a closure to the Holocaust, ignoring the breach that this event caused in Jewish and Polish life, as well as human history in the broadest sense. The claim that *The Pianist* is a 'feel-good' film is confirmed in *A Story of Survival*, where several principal members of the cast, including Polanski himself, repeat that *The Pianist* is about hope. In the documentary Polanski even muses about what personal characteristics make a person a likely survivor, thus coming dangerously close to the proclamation that the millions of Jews who perished during the war bore some responsibility for their doom. Although I object to edifying self-preservation as a moral virtue, I am inclined to forgive Polanski and treat his pronouncements less as a moral manifesto than a form of self-defence for a man who on numerous occasions has been reproached and who has reproached himself for surviving.

The autobiographical dimension can also be detected in *Oliver Twist*, again largely through associations of Oliver's life with that of Polanski during the war. Philip Kemp observes that 'perhaps drawing on his own traumatic childhood memories, Polanski brings a searing intensity and sense of angry helplessness to the early scenes of Oliver's treatment in the workhouse' (Kemp 2005: 80). Polanski confirms this opinion, claiming that in the orphanage adjoined to the factory in the Kraków ghetto he used to make paper bags, a similar task to the work of disentangling pieces of rope that occupies the children in Dickens's workhouse (see Loustalot 2005: 37). He also reminisces that during the war he used to live in a village that resembled a Victorian village, went hungry for days and had legs sore from walking. However, most of all he suffered as a result of missing his parents and feeling lonely (Ibid.: 35). Oliver's curiosity and fascination with the 'big wide world' parallels that of the young Polanski, who ran away from the countryside to Kraków, as is documented in his autobiography *Roman*. Furthermore, overcrowded, vermin-infested

Victorian London, where people die of hunger and disease on the streets, brings memories of the ghetto, as rendered by Polanski in his autobiography and in *The Pianist*. Polanski's Dickens adaptation, even his purging of some characters and episodes whose function is to sentimentalise the story (such as the death of Oliver's mother) makes the final product resemble more the impassive, matter-of-fact tone of *Roman*.

To conclude, I will reiterate the opinion that Polanski uses literature to create films that share many features with his work based on his original scripts and also reflect his outlook on life (first absurdist, then more optimistic), and his approach to filmmaking as a cultural activity that transcends national barriers. Paradoxically, Polanski's literary adaptations strike one as being more personal, even autobiographical films than those which are not. To put it bluntly, literature, for Polanski is not only the means to tell a story but also the means to tell one's own story in a way that will captivate millions.

7

MATRIX OR EMPTY VESSEL: POLANSKI'S USE OF GENRE

It has rightly been said that all great works of literature found a genre or dissolve one – that they are, in other words, special cases.

Walter Benjamin

This book argues that Polanski is the author of his films: he is in control of every aspect of them and his oeuvre possesses a significant degree of consistency. Genre is often contrasted with *auteurism* but critics also convincingly argue that certain filmmakers specialising in genre films, such as John Ford, Alfred Hitchcock or Douglas Sirk, can be considered *auteurs*. However, it is equally true that their prominence results not from their simple repetition of existing formulas but from their inventing of new recipes which are subsequently followed by other filmmakers: they are special cases. My objective in this chapter is to establish whether there are such special cases among Polanski's films.

Before examining how the notion of genre informs Polanski's filmmaking, it is worth briefly explaining this term. Despite its familiarity to ordinary viewers, or perhaps because of it, the term 'genre' is loaded with problems. Firstly, it is a very complex concept, comprising almost every aspect of the film, including visual imagery, plot, characters, setting, modes of narrative development, music and stars (see Cook 1985: 58). Secondly, as Rick Altman argues, its methodological usefulness is problematic, because in a sense every film is a genre film – all contain an element of action, crime or a love story and encourage the viewer to laugh, cry or be afraid. At the same time, there are no genre films (understood as pure examples of a given species), because each movie is a hybrid of many genres. Consequently, delineating the boundaries of genres and establishing what is the main genre and what is a sub-genre ultimately depends on the subjective view of a critic (see Altman 2002). Nevertheless, there is a broad consensus among critics that although genres develop, merge with other genres and even die out, in each period in cinema history we can establish whether a film neatly fits a particular genre, finds itself outside its limits, or attempts to destabilise its rules. This is also a question I will ask in relation to Polanski's films.

GENRE FILM AS A REBELLION AGAINST THE CONSTRAINTS OF POLISH CINEMA

Polish authors are in the forefront of those who regard 'genre' as the main perspective through which to examine Polanski's films (see Jackiewicz 1977; Stachówna 1994; Hendrykowski 1997; Jankun-Dopartowa 2000). This is understandable when bearing in mind that in Poland after the Second World War musicals, thrillers, melodramas, horrors and comedies stood out from the mass of films produced. Paradoxically, what made them so visible was the actual decline of Polish genre cinema during this period, a result of the lack of pressure on filmmakers to produce profitable films and directors' ambitions to produce 'personal' films. Polish critics themselves hindered the development of genre films with their ideologically motivated loathing of transplanting American formulas onto Polish soil, proclaiming that artistic cinema was irreconcilable with the pursuit of generic conventions. There was also a widespread view that certain genres were impossible to reconcile with postwar Polish reality. For example, police films and thrillers were almost condemned by these critics to incredulity and ridicule because there was nothing worth stealing in Poland, police cars were too slow to give an exciting chase, and political kidnappings did not happen because any change in the political system was impossible. Moreover, the genre aspect of many comedies, melodramas and epics was overlooked because their deployment of genre conventions was regarded purely as a means to engage with important ideological issues. Hence, *Przygoda na Mariensztacie (An Adventure at Marienstadt*, 1954), directed by Leonard Buczkowski, was seen not as a musical but a film about building a socialist society. The comedy aspects of Munk's *Eroica* and *Bad Luck* were played down in order to view them as films taking issue with Polish national myths. Comedy was treated only as a means to expose the inadequacy of romantic ideology to the realities of twentieth-century Poland. Similarly, war films, the only genre which flourished in Polish cinema, especially in the 1950s and 1960s, were regarded either as authorial endeavours (for instance, Wajda's films) or as product of a cinematic movement (the Polish School).

In the context of Polish films made in the late 1950s and early 1960s, *Knife in the Water* was an oddity. For one, although the film looked like a thriller, it was of an unusually high standard: its structure, cinematography, editing, sound and music were all impeccable. Its professionalism and elegance starkly contrasted with the amateurish efforts of contemporary Polish thrillers. Moreover, unlike the films of Wajda, Munk or Has, it did not engage in the discourse on Polish history and nation in the way that their films did, and it lacked characters in which viewers could invest their sympathy. Thus *Knife in the Water* was both an atypical generic Polish film and an unusual Polish authorial/art film. Not surprisingly, it confused critics and politicians who saw in this a political allegory and a product foreign to the cinematic tastes of Poles (see Polanski 1984: 156–7; Stachówna 1987).

In *Knife in the Water* Polanski did not attempt mechanically to transpose foreign genre formulas onto Polish soil. On the contrary, he emptied his film of the crucial component of a thriller: the murder. Although the boat where the narrative is set is a classic cinematic location for murderous encounters, and the lake, river or sea a perfect grave for those who do not die a natural death, the director does not follow tradition here. In terms of plot, his yacht is an 'empty vessel', where little happens. This lack is connected to another feature which takes *Knife in the Water* out of the paradigm of a thriller: the absence of characters able to commit such a hideous crime or execute the punishment of it. The male characters Andrzej and the student are both too mediocre individuals to kill their adversary as did, for example, the unscrupulous Tom Ripley in *Plein Soleil* (*Blazing Sun*, 1960) by René Clément, with which *Knife in the Water* is often compared. By not including a murder in his debut feature Polanski fulfilled several objectives. Firstly, he avoided the lack of realism of Polish thrillers that resulted from their directors' failure to reconcile the violent murder represented with the viewers' off-screen knowledge that in communist Poland such incidents do not happen. Secondly, the lack of murder gave the director an advantage over the audience who, lured by the suggestive title of the film and its atmosphere of anxiety, expects a dramatic incident by the film's end. By the same token, the director escaped an important problem of genre films: predictability. Thirdly, it provided *Knife in the Water* with an authorial signature. In the majority of Polanski's genre films and certainly in the best of them, the crucial component of the genre film is missing: thrillers lack murders, comedies lack happy endings, *film noir* is shot in colour. It feels as if Polanski uses a genre as an empty frame to fill with the objects of his interests. For this reason critics frequently add the prefix 'anti' to the genre such as anti-comedy or anti-thriller, or argue that the films may look generic but in reality they are not (see Jankun-Dopartowa 2000).

Another motif in *Knife in the Water*, which will reappear in Polanski's later films, is the 'double'. I referred to this device in the earlier parts of the book, drawing attention to such functions as conveying an absurdist outlook on life (see Chapter 2) and the double vision (see Chapter 3). Dual protagonists are also a typical feature of genre films (see Altman 2000: 24) but Polanski makes his characters similar to each other in a different way to what we encounter in westerns or gangster films. The sheriff and the outlaw are alike in their strong but contrasting moral stances and their extremism, which situates them on different sides of the barricade and renders their reconciliation impossible. Polanski's characters on the other hand constititute a pair not because of their extremism and polarisation, but because of their mediocrity and physical proximity. Jackiewicz compares them to animals belonging to the same species (see Jackiewicz 1977: 144). Often they only have each other against a hostile or indifferent world, and therefore avoid attempts to destroy each other and instead establish a quasi-symbiotic relationship. We observe this on many occasions in *Knife in the Water*. Andrzej becomes exasperated with the student who questions his authority, but puts up with his behaviour as he has nobody else on the yacht to impress with his talents or even to talk to. At one point Andrzej even tells the student: 'You are an asshole but I like you anyway', as if confirming that there are very few people with whom he is able to enter into a meaningful relationship.

Using the conventions of genre cinema also helped Polanski to communicate with an international audience, which was always an ambition of his. After all, film genres share certain fundamental characteristics (resulting, as many authors argue, from sharing their basic structure with myths) which allow them to travel in space and time, be understood by audiences in different countries and of different ages.[1] Not surprisingly, Polanski was approached to make an American remake of his Polish debut film, but regarded this idea as ludicrous (see Polanski 1984: 179).

MODERNISATION

If using generic convention was for Polanski a way to overcome the parochialism and incompetence of Polish cinema, and to communicate with foreign viewers, his urge to turn to genre actually increased when he left Poland and began searching for opportunities to make films abroad. At this time (the mid-1960s), European and French cinema in particular, where Polanski hoped his future would lie, was dominated by the French New Wave. The director of *Knife in the Water*, in his own words, was dismayed by the 'amateurism and appalling technique of films belonging to this movement' (Polanski 1984: 164). I would suggest that such a poor opinion of the French New Wave testifies to Polanski's allegiance to genre cinema. He dismissed the films made by Truffaut, Godard or Rivette not because they failed some litmus test of 'professional cinema' (an absolute litmus test of 'professional cinema' does not exist) but because they were so different from generic films. Polanski also tacitly confirmed that he links professionalism with genre cinema when he singled out the early films by Chabrol, the representative of the French New Wave most influenced by generic rules, as an exception to the 'amateurism and low quality' rule (Ibid.: 164).

Accordingly, Polanski's early films that were made abroad – *Repulsion*, *Cul-de-Sac* and *A River of Diamonds* – are all genre films. However, we observe in them the same desire to supersede generic conventions, which informed the content and style of *Knife in the Water*. The very title of *Cul-de-Sac* bears association with a certain type of American gangster cinema or *film noir*, which can be described as a 'siege film'. Through titles such as *Criss-Cross*, *Double-Cross*, *Desperate*, *The Desperate Hours* and *Dead End* this genre conveyed the fatalism of the world portrayed. As Ivan Butler observes, *Cul-de-Sac*'s 'plot is conventional, the criminals-break-in-and-terrify-occupants formula of a hundred thrillers' (Butler 1970: 91). Such films include *Key Largo* (1948), directed by John Huston, and *Dead End* (1937) and *The Desperate Hours* (1955) by William Wyler. However, from the very beginning there is something not quite right in Polanski's film. The music is too playful for a proper gangster film (see Chapter 4) and the choice of the characters is strange. Richard the main crook is American, thus not quite fitting into an English criminal milieu of gangsters who have good manners and do not kill their opponents unless it is absolutely necessary. Neither does he suit the film's physical environment of the medieval castle situated in the middle of nowhere, as he is an urban dweller. Moreover, he is not a powerful individual driven to a life of crime by the limitations of his humble class origin and the injustices of bourgeois society, as is the case with gangsters in traditional American films; he is instead a man with little authority and initiative of his own. All of his power derives from his connection with a mysterious boss, Mr Katelbach, whom Richard treats with utter reverence.

Stripping Richard of independence, Polanski ensured that he belongs as much to a Kafkaesque and Beckettian universe as to the gangster mythology. Nor does Richard's English companion, Alfred fit the gangster stereotype: he is incapacitated by his injury and has the appearance of a withered, myopic, ineffectual intellectual or, as Grażyna Stachówna suggests, a lower-class clerk (see Stachówna 1994: 186). Jack McGowran, a noted stage actor specialising in works by Samuel Beckett, who physically resembles Charles Hawtrey, a regular actor in the *Carry On* films, brings absurdist overtones to his performance as Albert, thus loosening the link between his character and the classical cinematic gangster.

Their hosts also do not correspond to the familiar stereotypes. As Virginia Wright Wexman observes, George and Teresa are more the outsiders among the bourgeoisie (which normally constitutes the gangsters' nemesis in gangster film) than are the gangsters (see Wexman 1987: 34). Teresa's social background is low, as George reveals when boasting to Richard that he saved her from poverty, and she has a penchant for the reckless and cruel behaviour that is associated with gangster life. George's distance from the middle class is conveyed by his choice to live far away from the city and by his discomfort during the visit of his old acquaintances. He decides not to seek their protection against Richard – which most characters in a gangster film would use as an opportunity to escape – because he feels more attuned to Richard than to his old friends who prove more barbaric, philistine, disruptive and fake than the gangster. George's choice of friends and enemies demonstrates that the social divisions immortalised in the siege narratives of Huston and Wyler are inadequate in the 1960s. Modern society, suggests Polanski, is too heterogeneous and fluid to fit into the simple categories embraced by this genre.

Due to George's conflict with his own social class, the traditional finale of the film, employing a gangster-on-the-run formula, which normally reaffirms the superiority of the orderly capitalist society over the rules of its transgressors, does not provide the reinstatement of equilibrium but its ultimate disruption. By killing Richard, George acknowledges that his escape from the mundane life of his factory and bourgeois marriage was a failure. The utopia has been destroyed and the old world has caught up with him. The last scene of the film, in which George utters the name of his first wife 'Agnes', confirms his defeat.

The difference between Polanski's film and a typical 'siege film' can be conceptualised in terms of the contrast between European and Hollywood cinema. The slow pace of action, criticised by some reviewers, the scarcity of dramatic moments, the loosened chain of cause and effect, the presence of episodes which do not advance the narrative but provide insight into the characters' minds (the characters being interesting in their own right, rather than vehicles of the plot), the significance of landscape, the absurdist sense of humour – all features pertaining to *Cul-de-Sac* – are associated with European cinema. To put it metaphorically, together with uprooting Richard from America to England, Polanski transplanted a Hollywood genre onto European soil. Interestingly, the impression that *Cul-de-Sac*, despite its theme, is a very European film already appeared at the stage of scriptwriting. In his biography Polanski reminisces that when he showed the script of *If Katelbach Comes* (the initial title of *Cul-de-Sac*) to its potential French film producer, Pierre Roustang, Roustang urged him to curb his 'Middle European sense of humour' (Polanski 1984: 165).

The overall result is a film regarded by Polanski as the best in his career and one of the most outstanding gangster films ever made. Polanski's approach to genre in *Cul-de-Sac* was not very different to Jean-Luc Godard's in *À bout de souffle* (*Breathless*, 1959). In his classic, Godard also used a gangster-on-the-run formula to create a very personal and idiosyncratic film. For example, as with *Cul-de-Sac*, although to an even greater extent, the chain of cause and effect is loosened and the physical environment (Paris) receives particular prominence. Moreover, Godard, not unlike Polanski, casts a foreign actress (the American Jean Seberg) as an immoral and beautiful female lead – a woman who lures men to their doom without blinking an eye. Comparing these two films one is surprised by how much the paths of these directors diverged in the following years.

Other works in which Polanski modernises existing conventions by putting across his thematic and stylistic interests are his horror films: *Dance of the Vampires*, *The Tenant* and *Rosemary's Baby*. There is a controversy among critics as to whether the first film is a parody of a vampire genre or a comedy set among vampires (see Butler 1970: 128; Jackiewicz 1977: 144; Wexman 1987: 57; Stachówna 1994: 171–3). Polanski himself insisted on treating his film as the latter (see Delahaye and Narboni 1969: 30). It seems that he chose such a label because the term 'parody' not only undermines the originality of his creation but also misses the crucial characteristic of the world created in this film: it is grotesque. The film invites laughter not by mimicking and ridiculing situations typical of the horror genre, or at least this is not its main source of comedy; rather it becomes humorous through the clash between the visual universe it purports to depict, which bears associations with fairy tales and comic books, and the naturalistic behaviour of its inhabitants. Take for example Alfred, who is frightened to push a wooden stake into the body of a vampire on the instruction of his master, Professor Abronsius. Such concerns are typically dismissed in traditional vampire movies but in real life most people are frightened to treat human corpses in this way – religious taboos prevent humans from violating those who have been buried. Another example of this clash is making one of the vampires homosexual and another a Jew. In traditional horrors the social and cultural differences between vampires are concealed: they represent one homogenous category (usually the Eastern European male aristocracy) but Polanski rationally assumes that if vampires are chosen randomly from the population of humans, they represent an average sample of humanity in terms of gender, ethnicity, class and sexual orientation. Accordingly, he makes Chagal the Jewish vampire fight for a better coffin and a more dignified place to rest than the humble shed allocated to him by Count von Krolock. Even the American subtitle of the film, 'Pardon me, but your teeth are in my neck', reflects the collision between the horrific and the banal. The juxtaposition of the extraordinary and the trivial, the horrific and the funny in *Dance of the Vampires* is reminiscent of Polanski's short films and of *Cul-de-Sac*, and prefigures *Macbeth* and later horror films by this director. However, although it is typical of Polanski's cinema, it is rare in horror films. S.S. Prawer also argues that *Dance of the Vampires* was unique in its time, pioneering a new trend of horror films, characteristic of the 1970s, thanks to being open-ended and therefore 'unsafe' to the viewer – as opposed to the earlier horror movies which tended to 'jolt us out from our everyday life, transporting us into problems which are clearly not our own' (Prawer 1980: 60). He quotes the last sentence in the film, in which the narrator informs us that Professor Abronsius carries away with him the evil he tried to destroy, as proof that the menacing force presented in *Dance of the Vampires* is not contained, but 'points onwards in time and outwards into our own world' (Ibid.: 61).

Prawer's assessment that Polanski's horror is unsafe can also be made with regard to *The Tenant* and *Rosemary's Baby*. In these films the horror is brought, as Prawer puts it, into 'our own world': the universe of apartment blocks, department stores and cafés (see Prawer 1980: 60–61; Wells 2000: 83). These films are also insecure in an additional way to what we see in *Dance of the Vampires*: by questioning the viewer's rationality (see Houston and Kinder 1968–9; Prawer 1980: 77; Wells 2000: 83). Prawer therefore links *Rosemary's Baby* to the concept of *le fantastique* as defined by Tzvetan Todorov: 'hesitation experienced by a person who only knows laws of nature, confronting an apparently supernatural event' (Todorov, quoted in Prawer 1980: 149). As I argued in Chapter 3, at the centre of discourse on

The Tenant and *Rosemary's Baby* is the problem of correct vision. The viewer is invited to decide whether Rosemary's and Trelkovsky's perceptions are sound. The puzzle, especially in *Rosemary's Baby*, is not solved. Unlike in such psychological horrors as *Das Kabinett des Dr Caligari* (*The Cabinet of Dr Caligari*, 1919), directed by Robert Wiene, or Hitchcock's *Psycho* (1960) and Powell's *Peeping Tom*, the psychological ambiguity is sustained until the end of the film. Polanski achieves this largely thanks to the way he uses off-screen space – making us fascinated not by what we see but what we are not allowed to see (see Chapter 3). The epistemological ambiguity impinges on the representation of ontological and moral issues. As a result of not being assured of who has privileged access to reality, we do not know whether Rosemary's baby is a devil's progeny, or a stillborn child. Are Trelkovsky's neighbours monsters who create a web of conspiracy around him to force him to take his own life, or ordinary people who like to have peace in their house? Is he a good man or somebody whose conscience is tarnished by an unspoken desire for Simone Choule's death? And, ultimately, do Polanski's characters fear the external world or their own psyches and bodies? The best testimony to the existence of double meaning are the contrasting interpretations of his horror films. In

Roman Polanski in *Dance of the Vampires* (1967)

particular, critics of *Rosemary's Baby* are divided among those who regard this film as the story of 'the devil in New York', those who see it as a study of hysteria in pregnant women and those who, like me, regard this film as open to both interpretations. Here also lies the film's mastery and their modernity, resulting from Polanski's realisation that in the contemporary world anxiety resulting from inability to decipher our world has largely replaced the old fear of devils and vampires.

Mia Farrow in *Rosemary's Baby* (1968)

DEMYTHOLOGISATION

In the opinion of many, particularly American critics, the most successful of Polanski's encounters with genre cinema is *Chinatown* (see Wexman 1987; Horowitz 1990; Lyons 1993). It invokes the private investigator/ private eye (PI) or hard-boiled detective film (which is often regarded as a sub-genre of *film noir* or the gangster movie) by being set in 1937 Los Angeles and replicating many of the narrative formulas used by older directors. The best-known is the deceptive mission given to the private detective by a client, known from films such as *The Maltese Falcon* (1941), directed by John Huston, and *The Big Sleep* (1946), directed by Howard Hawks. Moreover, Polanski refers to earlier examples of this genre intertextually, by casting the director of *The Maltese Falcon* in the important role of Noah Cross, with himself playing Cross's employee, thus hinting that he is Huston's humble pupil willing to learn from an old master.

After westerns, the private-eye film is the genre most associated with American cinema and the popular culture of this country at large, which partly explains why *Chinatown* attracted so much attention and praise from American critics and film historians. At the same time, one encounters an opinion that there is something profoundly un-American in the cynicism and despair which permeates the social vision put across in this genre (see Eaton 2000: 58). Others argue that it captures the mood of America in its bleakest moments (see Horowitz 1990: 53), which are rare. To an even greater extent than the western, the PI film has a close link with literature. The majority of classic films of this genre are based on novels written by authors like Dashiell Hammett, Ross Macdonald and Raymond Chandler, and typically little time passed between the publishing of the novel and its first film adaptation. The founding novel of the genre, *The Maltese Falcon* by Dashiell Hammett, made it to the screen in the Roy Del Ruth version the year after it was published in 1930 and was filmed twice within a decade (see Lyons 1993: 44). The golden years of the PI film belong to the golden years of Hollywood between the early 1930s and the middle of the 1950s. Two intertwined factors contributed to its decline after this period: the foundering of literature that used to provide cinema with characters and plots, and the change in the socio-political situation which rendered private investigators an anachronism (to which subject I return in due course). Accordingly, *Chinatown* was an attempt to revive the PI genre over twenty years after its decline. It was not a unique attempt; in 1973 Robert Altman directed *The Long Goodbye*, based on Raymond Chandler's novel of the same title published in 1953 and regarded as his elegiac masterpiece (see Lyons 1993: 44). Both films received critical acclaim and are often compared with each other by critics (see Lyons 1993; Stewart 1974–5). *Chinatown* appears to hold a higher place in the history of American cinema[2] and in Polanski's career than *The Long Goodbye* does for America and Altman.

According to the myth embedded in hard-boiled fiction and the PI film, the private detective occupies a position on the margins of the law. He may be a former member of the police force but in the course of the story comes into conflict with his former colleagues. He is relatively poor, but preserves honour and integrity. In fact, his low economic and social status is related to his idealism, as he acts not for financial rewards but to bring justice to society. On his quest for justice he discovers not only a single guilty individual but a corrupt society in which wealthy and respectable people are linked with gangsters and crooked politicians. John Cawelti maintains that there are two different tendencies within the hard-boiled myth. One constructs the private detective as vigilante avenger who judges and punishes the villain himself. In the second, more sophisticated tendency, the detective causes the self-destruction of the offender or simply forces him to confess his crimes. In both cases, however, he wins (see Cawelti 1992: 501). The private detective's chief antagonist both in literature and in film is a beautiful woman. Her menacing side is related to her involvement in crime and to her mystery. Being a professional investigator, the private detective cannot accept that the woman is hiding something from him. At the same time, her beauty and enigma attract him. This conundrum is usually solved by the punishment or even destruction of the woman by the detective – such is the fate of females in *The Maltese Falcon* and in *Farewell, My Lovely* (1944), directed by Edward Dmytryk.

The classic PI films are made in black and white. *Chinatown*, by contrast, is shot in colour. However, the range of colours, dominated by shades of grey, yellow and brown, is limited and their tones are muted, all of which produces an almost monochromatic effect. The melange of colours, which resembles the tones of the desert, goes along with the film's theme of a city devoid of blood, of vital forces, due to the lack of water. Secondly, it produces a nostalgic effect, acknowledging its debt to earlier representations. The effect of representation of representation is corroborated by the camerawork. Garrett Stewart observes that the meticulously compositional style of cinematographer John Alonzo comes to look like a series of deceptive 'frame-ups' (Stewart 1974–5: 26).

The main character, Jake Gittes, initially also deviates from the PI norm, as – to use Chandler's phrase – he is hardly 'a man in a lonely street'. On the contrary, he is extroverted, chatty and much better-off than a typical private detective. Donald Lyons describes him as a 'fastidious dandy unvaryingly attired in crisp three-piece suits with complementing breast-pocket handkerchiefs' and 'a stylist whose smokes come from a gold case, office liquor cabinet is of inlaid wood, as are the interiors of his Buick' (Lyons 1993: 52). His affluence is related to the 'matrimonial work' in which he specialises: spying on unfaithful spouses and their lovers. Such a job does not have the dignity of chasing dangerous criminals which was the métier of the protagonists of Chandler and Hammett. Gittes is aware of this, as testified by his angry outburst in a barber's shop, where a customer questions his way of earning money. The lower moral status of Polanski's character in comparison with his literary and cinematic predecessors, in the opinion of Cawelti, is conveyed by his name, which does not have the aura of Philip Marlowe's knightliness and chivalry or the thoroughness and hardness of Sam Spade. Instead, Gittes connotes 'selfishness and grasping and has a kind of ethnic echo very different from the pure Anglo of Spade, Marlowe and Archer' (Cawelti 1992: 502).[3]

Nevertheless, circumstances intertwined with professional pride allow Gittes to move to the territory normally reserved for a private detective in a classical *film noir*. He tries to investigate a mysterious woman, Evelyn Mulwray, and her husband Hollis, and their alleged matrimonial problems bring him into contact with the puzzle of water disappearing from Los Angeles. Consequently, he attempts to find out and expose those responsible for its lack. On both accounts he fails dismally: he does not learn the truth about Evelyn and Hollis until it is too late, and he does not bring to justice the all-powerful and sinister Noah Cross. Gittes not only proves ineffectual but his actions lead to ends that are contrary to those intended. Thus Polanski questions, if not destroys, the myth of the private detective as judge and avenger, instead exposing him as an agent of the very evil he tries to

Jack Nicholson and Faye Dunaway in *Chinatown* (1974)

destroy. The ultimate message of the film is that the world or at least America would be better off without people like Gittes. In this respect, *Chinatown* is a more pessimistic film than *The Long Goodbye*, because Marlowe in Altman's movie does not worsen a bad situation and in the end even achieves a modest victory.

By rendering an individual who fights the system more powerless and disorientated, and the 'system' stronger, more corrupt and elusive than in any earlier films of this type, *Chinatown* perfectly captured the mood of the time it was made, which was marked by such events as the oil crisis, Watergate and the dominance of post-Fordist economy, which eroded the power of trade unions (see Horowitz 1990: 53). Many critics regard it as a film that lays bare the inadequacies and malaise of modern America (see Stewart 1974–5; Horowitz 1990) or as an allegory of the entire Western world, in which even the most well-meaning individual is disempowered and disorientated. Although Polanski did not write the script of *Chinatown*, it was thanks to his contribution to the story that such a dark prognosis was offered. Robert Towne, credited with the script, wanted it to end on a more positive note, with Evelyn Mulwray killing her father (see Horowitz 1990: 53). *Chinatown*'s pessimism is increased by the fact that, despite his various shortcomings, Gittes comes across as an honest and charismatic man, partly because Jack Nicholson brings to the role the memory of his earlier films in which he played ordinary men who were also heroes, such as *Easy Rider* (1969), directed by Dennis Hopper.[4]

The demythologising effect of *Chinatown* would not appear so strong if it were not rooted in the history of Los Angeles. Drought was and still is a perennial problem for Los Angeles, and its history can be conjured up as a narrative of the struggle between those in control of the city who wanted to provide the water to its citizens as cheaply as possible, such as Hollis Mulwray, and those such as Noah Cross who tried to use the shortage of this essential commodity to exploit the city's inhabitants (see Chapter 3). Critics even pointed out that there is a strong parallel between Mulwray and William Mulholland, superintendent of a private water company which was purchased by the city in 1904 and the designer of the largest aqueduct in the world, linking the Owens Valley on the edge of the High Sierras with Los Angeles (see Eaton 2000: 23–6). Including the problem of water (which is a symbol of life itself) in the film's narrative bestowed upon *Chinatown* an epic dimension unknown to classical hard-boiled detective dramas, in which the conflict typically revolves around a precious but superfluous and esoteric object, such as the Maltese Falcon in Huston's classic. The epic dimension of *Chinatown* is augmented through such cinematic means as Panavision and wide-angle lenses, which allowed for expansive establishing shots with strong foreground/background interplay (see Bordwell 2002: 18).

Moreover, *Chinatown* has an aura of foreboding that bears similarity to classical tragedies. Everything of importance that happens here is forecast either through a similar event that took place in different circumstances or by a material sign. An example of the first type of prognosis is Gittes's disappointing career as a policeman in Chinatown where he tried to save a woman but instead his assistance injured her, possibly fatally. The same happens to Evelyn, who also dies in Chinatown as a result of Gittes's misguided attempt to help her. Her death is announced by the sound of a car's horn, activated by her head hitting the steering wheel. She does it twice in the film, the first time serves as a premonition of the future, fatal event. Evelyn dies from a bullet in the head which penetrates her eye, the eye that has a birth defect – a flaw in the iris.

There are also signs conveyed by names, such as Noah Cross, named after the man who built a boat to survive the flood in the biblical story. Of course, naming the greatest villain in the film not only Noah but also Cross, testifies to Polanski's acute sense of irony. Classical tragedy is also invoked by certain narrative motifs associated with well-known myths such as the motif of incest that refers to the story of Electra.[5] As in a classical tragedy, the characters fail to read the signs correctly; only when it is too late are they able to understand their mistakes. Their belated knowledge that if they had been able to 'see' things correctly they would have been safe increases their and the film viewers' sense of defeat and disappointment.

In *Chinatown* the director's personality appears invisible, as if he 'sacrificed' himself to the PI genre. To an extent this is true. For example, the director was persuaded to give up on music written by Phillip Lambro and accept the score of a Hollywood veteran Jerry Goldsmith, which added romanticism to the atmosphere of the film (see Wexman 1987: 92). In other aspects, inserting into the film Polanski's idiosyncratic *Weltanschauung* and style helped to modernise and revitalise the dying genre. I refer here, particularly, to the motif of the well-meaning individual who becomes a tool of evil – which we find in Polanski's earlier films, such as *Dance of the Vampires* and *Rosemary's Baby*. Most importantly, however, the perception results from the fact that the PI formula, with its interest in the complex relations between private transgressions and public crimes, and its emphasis on the question of correct vision, perfectly matched Polanski's interests. The feeling that *Chinatown* is such a 'pure' genre product, untarnished by the director's idiosyncrasies, makes the counter-myth offered in this film even more convincing.

PASTICHES

In the films made in the 1960s and 1970s Polanski tended to reinvigorate genres suffering crisis, but in the 1980s he made two films which almost slavishly followed existing recipes: *Pirates*, which I shall discuss in detail, and *Frantic*. Not surprisingly, neither film is regarded as Polanski's masterpiece and *Pirates* was labelled the worst film in the director's entire career, which has contributed to its subsequent neglect by historians. As Polanski himself admitted, *Pirates* was the fulfilment of a long cherished dream. As a child he loved films about corsairs such as *The Black Pirate* (1926), directed by Albert Parker and *Captain Blood* (1935), directed by Michael Curtiz, and he wanted to recapture the pleasure of watching them by making one of this kind (see Boutang 1986: 217; Galion 1986: 31). The gestation process of *Pirates* was also very long. The project was first announced in 1976 as a vehicle for Jack Nicholson in the role of Captain Red and Polanski as his sidekick. Yet it was rejected by most of the major Hollywood companies, such as United Artists, Paramount, Universal and MGM, before finally being produced by the Tunisian financier, Tarak Ben Anmar. It looks to me as if Polanski's nostalgia for old pirate films and the gap between *Pirates'* conception and birth account for its main flaws.

Nostalgia for past films is the impulse of many successful genre films of the last four decades, such as *The Godfather* (1971), directed by Francis Ford Coppola, *Star Wars* (1977), directed by George Lucas, the spaghetti westerns of Sergio Leone, *Pulp Fiction* (1994), directed by Quentin Tarantino, and even, as I previously mentioned, *Chinatown*. However, as John Cawelti notes, attempts to evoke nostalgia in films merely by imitating past forms do not generally work because the imitations simply become obsolete. A truly successful nostalgia film must give us a sense of contemporaneity, as well as of the past (see Cawelti 1992: 506). Linking the movie with the present day, however, is a more difficult task for creators of pirate films than for those who work in other film genres. To begin with, a swashbuckler is by its nature a nostalgia film as its action takes place in the seventeenth century in an exotic location, and historic accuracy is not its objective. Instead it tries to evoke the myth of some famous buccaneer without suggesting that he possessed the features attributed to him by the film or even that he lived at all. As pirate films do not take their myths seriously, it is next to impossible to demythologise them. Moreover, from the beginning of their history, films about corsairs were furnished with features that normally signify a revisionist attitude to the genre tradition, such as humorous burlesque.

Taking into account these factors it does not come as a surprise that the golden era of pirate film coincides with the golden era of Hollywood; its principal examples including *Captain Blood*, *The Sea Hawk* (1940), directed by Michael Curtiz and *The Crimson Pirate* (1952), directed by Robert Siodmak. After the 1950s the number of pirate films dwindled and few of them captured the critics' attention. It seems that potential authors were put off by the conundrum of how to make a modern or postmodern pirate film when a classical pirate film has in any case many features which in other genres would be regarded as testimony to their modernity or postmodernity, as well as overcoming the problem of the high cost of pirate films. At the same time the genre did not die out completely because of its great cinematic potential thanks to its focus on the movement of ships and human bodies, colourful locations and picturesque costumes and props.

The most successful or widely discussed contemporary pirate films, such as *Pirates of the Caribbean: The Curse of the Black Pearl* (2003), directed by Gore Verbinski, and *Cutthroat Island* (1995), directed by Renny Harlin (which was a commercial flop), diverge significantly from the formula of the 1930s and 1950s in terms of plot construction, characters and moral messages. Thus *Pirates of the Caribbean* hinges the plot not on stealing the loot, but returning it, and both this film and *Cutthroat Island* give stronger roles to female characters than in traditional swashbucklers, changing them from passive objects of male desire to active agents trying and succeeding in shaping their own fates. In *Pirates of the Caribbean*, the leading lady, in a tight dress given to her by her father, pronounces that she cannot breathe and falls into the water, thus literally and metaphorically rejecting patriarchy. Moreover, she falls in love not with the pirate who saves her life but with a blacksmith whom she has known from her childhood. In *Cutthroat Island* even the principal corsair is female. The authors of these films also attempt to update the male characters. In Verbinski's hit the main buccaneer, Jack Sparrow, played by Johnny Depp, in his speech and behaviour imitates Keith Richard of The Rolling Stones. This brings to the film nostalgia of a type not normally associated with the antiquated world of buccaneers but a more contemporary nostalgia for the modernism of the 1960s.

In contrast, *Pirates* failed the test of contemporaneity largely by founding the characters on outdated and narrow stereotypes. Captain Red, whose very name is an almost too obvious homage to Captain Blood, is an Englishman who became a pirate out of greed. He is more likeable than the Spaniards from whom he steals the ship and its treasures because he is less hypocritical and snobbish, but this does not make him a true hero.

Moreover, to advance his position or preserve his life, he is prepared to organise a mutiny on a ship and even to eat his best friend. Because of this very limited characterisation and the lack of shading in Walter Matthau's acting, the viewer fails to sympathise and engage with Red's adventures. On the other hand, Captain Red's French sidekick, Jean-Baptiste (Cris Campion), addressed by his master as 'the Frog', adheres to the model of a noble buccaneer who did not join the pirates out of greed but for a more selfless cause, in his case a hatred of Spaniards. However, his noble intentions make little practical difference as he slavishly follows his senior companion. He fights alongside him, steals when he steals, and remains with Red when everyone else abandons him. His blind loyalty to his mentor renders him immature or even stupid, rather than providing him with an extra dignity, and it reduces the scope for surprises, so important in action films. The female lead, Dolores, played by Charlotte Lewis, is even more conventional. Her actions are limited to singing, playing the mandolin and sharing her admiration for Jean-Baptiste with her older female companion – as opposed to revealing to him her love which contemporary heroines tend to do. Moreover, in line with the old-fashioned rendering of women in pirate films, Polanski emphasises Dolores's virginity as her main asset and the object of male interest. On several occasions men attempt to rape her but fail thanks to Jean-Baptiste's intervention. Dolores herself pronounces that she would rather be killed than raped – although she does little to fight off the men who try to steal her virginity. Even more stereotypical and lifeless are the opponents of Polanski's buccaneers: the Spaniards. One critic has compared them to the ghost-like bewigged figures in Peter Greenaway's *The Draughtsman's Contract* (1982) (see Strick 1986: 316). On the whole, all the characters are just the vehicles of the plot rather than characters in their own right.

Another weakness of the film is a certain overcrowding of action that paradoxically produces the effect of its deficit. There are many dramatic events such as a mutiny on the galleon, Red's and Jean-Baptiste's escape from jail, or the pirates' carnivalesque celebration on an island where Red's regular crew has its base. However, there is no hierarchy among these events and the film lacks the main attraction of the genre: the sea battle. This problem is exacerbated by (unusual for Polanski) uninventive camera angles and old-fashioned handling of fight sequences. Moreover, there are not enough lyrical moments to allow any respite from the dynamic events and to build up the tension. Consequently, *Pirates* lacks momentum and feels repetitive. The ending, with Captain Red and Jean-Baptiste drifting on a raft in the middle of the ocean, is a mirror-image of the film's beginning; this alludes to Polanski's earlier films and is recognised by his fans as his authorial signature. However, it does not work in an action film and in this case is a lost opportunity to add a last sparkle to a flat film. A reviewer in *Variety* describes it as an 'unexciting nonending' (Lor. 1986: 16). Furthermore, unlike Polanski's earlier films which used a circular narrative to convey the tragedy of characters who failed to change their lives, here we do not get the sense of great misfortune. Throughout the film, the corsairs behave as if they take for granted that sooner or later they will end up adrift on a raft; the sea is their home and their destination.

The *Neptune*, a full-size replica of a seventeenth-century Spanish galleon, built specially for the film (and later transported to Cannes), is stunning, but in its importance for the narrative lies another weakness of *Pirates*: it is used too much. While the best pirate films tend to balance the life at sea with a sedentary existence on land, which gives the opportunity to reveal the advantages and pitfalls of a corsair's life, Polanski's film writes off the possibility of life on terra firma for his protagonists. Moreover the land, especially the island populated by Red's friends and crew, has the same aura of temporariness as the ship. The lack of sea–land dialectic reduces the scope for suspense and surprise and adds to the impression of the repetitiveness and frivolity of the film.

Although in some aspects *Pirates* fits well with Polanski's earlier films, some important elements of his style are missing. For example, Polanski, who used to be a master of counterpoint, irony and ambiguity, in this film gives up on any innuendo as if he is losing trust in the intelligence of his audience. The cardinal rule of *Pirates* is that a meaning conveyed by image is reinforced by dialogue or monologue and often by music. The author of the score, Philippe Sarde, shows no sign of any desire to break new ground in the style of scores for pirate movies.[6] The music slavishly imitates the mood of each scene. Like Walter Matthau's acting, it is written on a single note, usually, as Philip Strick observes, trumpeting loudly over the gunfire (see Strick 1986: 317).

One can detect in *Pirates* some references to the present. The encompassing greed and cynicism of both the pirates and the Spanish sailors and the political hypocrisy of the latter can be regarded as a metaphor of the crude materialism and moral proselytising of the epoch of Ronald Reagan and Margaret Thatcher. However, it requires a considerable effort on the part of the viewer to link the reality on screen with that of the 1980s, which can be explained by Polanski's conceiving *Pirates* as a 'reaction against the many heavy, message-laden films' (Fainaru 1987: 28). Moreover, even if the film is read as a socio-political allegory, it is one devoid of critique. As was already said, the film takes greed and selfishness for granted, and even tries to add charm to Red's single-minded pursuit of gold.

Pirates was not a successful nostalgia film at the time it was created, and the passage of time has only added to its obsolescence through unfavourable comparison with later examples of this genre, especially *Pirates of the Caribbean*. In this sense Polanski was as unlucky with *Pirates* as he was lucky with *Chinatown*. It could be argued that the greatest virtue of this film was to demonstrate to directors such as Gore Verbinsky how much the pirate film must move away from old recipes to reach new generations of viewers.

COMEDY AND TRAVEL CINEMA

One is surprised by a variety of genres that Polanski has used in his career. Although we note that he has a predilection for horror films, he also made a thriller, a gangster film, a PI film, a war (or Holocaust) film, a melodrama, a pirate film and a children's film. Yet, whatever film he makes, he typically furnishes it with features pertaining to two genres. One of them is comedy. Polanski's films provoke laughter, although they cannot straightforwardly be called 'comedies'. If we apply a dictionary definition of comedy, such as 'stage-play of light, amusing and often satirical character, chiefly representing everyday life, and with a happy ending' (Neale and Krutnik 1990: 11), we realise that Polanski's films are excluded from this category because they invite not only laughter, but also sadness, anger and repulsion. It is best to regard them as tragicomedies. As I have suggested, humour in Polanski's films does not result from his desire to produce funny situations and amusing characters; it is rather a consequence of the author's absurdist sensibility. Polanski sees the world as at the same time funny and sad, humorous and horrific. Often the dramatic events only work as catalysts to unearth a grotesque and absurd layer of reality. Nothing conveys this proximity of the tragic, horrific, pedestrian and the comical better than his dialogue, which reveals the discord between the gravity of the character's situation and their trivial or esoteric preoccupations, as well as their lack of understanding of each other. For example, Richard in *Cul-de-Sac*, who comes across as a ruthless simpleton, gets very offended when George accidentally destroys Alfred's glasses. When Teresa asks Richard, who is preparing a shallow grave for Albert, why he is digging, he answers sarcastically that it is his hobby. When in the final scene of *Rosemary's Baby* Minnie Castevet brings Rosemary a cup of tea, telling her it will make her better and Rosemary asks suspiciously what is in it, Minnie replies that it is plain Lipton tea.

The laughter in Polanski's films also derives from his detached, often unsympathetic look at the protagonists; they are exposed to the view of other characters and the camera gaze at moments when they would like to be left alone. Laughter is almost never jovial and it usually contains a dark side because the director, in a Rabelaisian fashion, invites us to laugh at human inadequacies, such as physical disabilities and clumsiness (the hunchback in *Dance of the Vampires*, the man with the cut-out tongue in *Pirates*, or the turkey-like figure of George in *Cul-de-Sac*), vulgarity (eating a rat and urinating in the bath-water in *Pirates*), misfortune (the wounded and semi-conscious Albert trapped in the drowning car in *Cul-de-Sac*), and even cruelty (Teresa lighting strips of paper between the toes of sleeping Richard in *Cul-de-Sac* or a macabre joke told by Władysław Szpilman's brother in *The Pianist*). Some critics argue that Polanski treats his characters as if they are animals rather than human beings (see Chapter 2; Jackiewicz 1977; Stachówna 1994) – animals, it is worth adding, who are living in a jungle. Polanski's humour sometimes also plays on ethnic prejudices, including anti-Semitism. For example, the funny and horrific idea that Minnie Castevet, who comes across as a nosy Jewish woman, is also a witch feeding on babies' blood, bears similarity with the folk tales perpetuated by the Catholic church, about Jews eating babies and drinking their blood. Consequently, laughter is often combined with embarrassment, with viewers' realisation that they too are cruel, prejudiced or at least full of *Schadenfreude*. Moreover, on the whole, Polanski's films are pessimistic. They do not have happy endings, in which cheerful emotions ultimately dominate over dark feelings (take, for example, the final scenes in *Cul-de-Sac* or *Rosemary's Baby*). In this respect he can be likened to the creators of the Theatre of the Absurd, as well as to such directors as Ingmar Bergman and Jean-Luc Godard.

The second element used by Polanski is the motif of travel. His characters are on the move, relocating to new houses and apartments or travelling for business or recreation. Moreover, even if they are in one place for some time, they give the impression of not belonging there or are treated as newcomers and outsiders. Polanski's films nevertheless depart significantly from the classical, American paradigm of road cinema, where the characters are mostly young, male and rebellious, the journeys are fast and have a well-defined itinerary, and characters are neatly divided between those on the move and sedentary types. His travellers belong to all possible social strata, epochs and, so to speak, walks of life. Among them we find the Polish nouveaux riches, Krystyna and Andrzej, the international book dealer, Dean Corso but also Tess and Władysław Szpilman. Few move fast; the majority travel slowly and with an effort. Almost all types of transport are shown in Polanski's films: private cars, buses, trains, ships, yachts, bicycles, horses and horse carts, sledges, even coffins sliding down staircases and slopes covered with snow. Many of his characters ramble on foot, covering large distances and carrying heavy luggage. In some films, such as *Tess* and *Frantic*, the world comes across as a web of roads, rather than assemblages of dwellings. Taking a trip is rarely for the sake of travel, and is usually a means to a different end: finding a safe place to live, a job, solving a mystery or escaping old friends and problems. In this way the impression is created that travelling is a universal condition, a human way of life, rather than an exception from the settled existence. Similarly, the director favours the vision of a traveller and an outsider: somebody who looks at reality through the window of a car or a train and does not take his view for granted, but pays utmost attention to the buildings and people passed, even holes in the pavement. Moreover, his perceptions are unstable, but change according to the distance and angle of his position.

Lionel Stander and Jack MacGowran in *Cul-de-Sac* (1966)

Often, paradoxically, travel in Polanski's film underscores the characters' inability to change their lives, their powerlessness in relation to external circumstances and their own limitations. Take, for example, the final scene in *Knife in the Water*, when Andrzej and Krystyna are sitting in their car signifying their entrapment in their phoney and burnt-out marriage, Captain Red and Jean-Baptiste drifting on a raft in the middle of the ocean, looking for a ship which could save them from starvation, or Evelyn Mulwray's attempt to leave Los Angeles which brings about her death. *Cul-de-Sac* is filled with movements which do not progress the action, but on the contrary halt it. Teresa appears to be always at a run, chasing the hens or hunting for men, Richard moves with a full force, often pushing or pulling a heavy object, George walks around as if trying to find a place for himself but instead always crashes into something. This activity is even multiplied and accelerated when George's guests arrive, filling the huge castle with a buzz. The connection between travel and passivity or impotence is reinforced by the previously mentioned device of finishing the films in the way they began, as well as by an abundance of defunct means of transport and defective moving objects, such as broken cars, kites, rafts, dead horses, hens. Polanski does not idealise journeys in his films but neither does he bemoan (perhaps with the exception of *Tess*) his characters' nomadic life and the culture based on mobility. In contrast to road movies, in Polanski's films travel does not constitute a 'problem' to be solved and it is hardly discussed by the characters.

The way Polanski uses the subject of travel links him to some European filmmakers. Kristin Thompson and David Bordwell compare *Knife in the Water* to *Viaggio in Italia* (*Voyage to Italy*, 1953), directed by Roberto Rossellini (see Thompson and Bordwell 2003: 461), as both films dispense with narrative closure. Polanski's earlier films were also likened to the work of Bergman, Antonioni and Godard, all of them directors who utilise the motif of journey in their narrative and iconography. We can also observe a similarity between the way Polanski depicts mobility and the way that is typical for 'Swinging London' films. As Moya Luckett observes, the mobility of the female heroines of 'Swinging London' films typically does not testify to their freedom but, on the contrary, to their constraint, displacement, homelessness, confusion and lack of stable identity (see Luckett 2000: 239–41). Furthermore, Polanski's participation in the film *The World's Most Beautiful Swindlers*, in which criminal intrigues are used to examine the relation between people and their environments, supports my claim that he specialises in depicting travel.

Despite the longevity and omnipresence of the motif of travel in Polanski's films, his overall allegiance to this paradigm, in common with

CONCLUSION:
THE CINEMA OF
A CULTURAL TRAVELLER

My book has argued that Polanski's cinema can be interpreted as a product of cultural travels. In the conclusion I will summarise the reasons why I am using this label. Firstly, his films are set and shot in many different countries, mirroring Polanski's own, often enforced journeys. Among them we find Poland, France, England, Spain, South America and the USA, as well as a number of mythical locations, such as Transylvania, which is traditionally the homeland of vampires. Polanski's films are likewise set in different epochs, bearing witness to the director's wide historical and literary interests, as well as his conviction that cinema is a magical vehicle or, as one author put it, 'the poor man's luxury liner' (Newnham, quoted in Norris Nicholson 2006) that can transport him to any destination imaginable. Polanski not only appropriates the role of a 'virtual travel agent' but treats it with utmost seriousness. We can often learn more about the details of costumes, farming equipment and customs of particular groups of people from his films than from tourist guides. While travelling around the globe and through different historical periods Polanski appears to trace what various cultures have in common; hence the saturation of his films with references to cultural archetypes, such as biblical tales, Greek myths, and stories conveyed by proverbs. Here we can also find one of the reasons for his affinity to circular narration; in this way the director demonstrates that although human history reveals itself in an infinite number of scenarios, certain types of them permeate even the most distant societies and cyclically return.

Curiosity about the cultures encountered through his journeys is accompanied by Polanski's unwillingness to elevate the cultures where his roots lie, namely Jewish, Polish and French, either as locations of the narratives or as sites of moral norms. On and off screen the director distances himself from any type of nationalism, regarding it as the way to overestimate oneself unjustly and consequently underestimate fellow human beings. The interest in many cultures without favouring a particular one and the mythical dimension of many of Polanski's films, is one of the reasons why his films appeal to international audiences. The viewers do not need to possess a specific historical or ethnic knowledge to understand his narratives and characters.

Secondly, the term 'cultural traveller' refers to Polanski's cinematic erudition, his talent to pick, mix and develop the ideas invented by his predecessors. In this way he uses the films of his compatriot Andrzej Munk, with whom he shares an affinity for the circular narrative and for characters whose life is dominated by rituals; of Alfred Hitchcock, to whom he is linked by his fascination with the horror of the everyday, and of Luis Buñuel, who, like him, is a surrealist. Similarly, Polanski appropriates elements of various literary, artistic and philosophical traditions, most importantly absurdism and surrealism. Yet again, mere recycling is never Polanski's objective. He does not limit himself to crudely imitating or paying homage to his favourite writers such as Samuel Beckett or painters such as René Magritte. Instead, he transports elements from their work to his own cinematic landscape and juxtaposes them with new and unexpected elements. Thanks to this feature Polanski's films come across as very coherent, and therefore we can situate them in the modernist rather than postmodernist paradigm where quotations tend to be transported to the new text verbatim.

Polanski's talent for creatively elaborating the works of other authors is particularly visible in his literary adaptations. He always chooses works with great potential to appeal to international audiences and increases their universal appeal by making changes to the narrative structures and characters. Moreover, he foregrounds those aspects of the book that pertain to the discourse on travel. In a most basic sense, the stories he finds in the books, change after his intervention into narratives of travel and learning about new places, new people, as well as becoming journeys of self-discovery. In this way we can describe *Tess*, *Bitter Moon* and *Macbeth*.

I also regard Polanski's cinema as that of a cultural traveller because of his specific approach to the characters and the situations in which they find themselves. He chooses characters who enter cultural conflict, either due to being immigrants among the indigenous population, speaking a foreign language or using a strange accent, coming from a different social class or representing a different generation than the people who surround them, or due to these factors combined. Polanski's heroes and heroines tend to be alone in an alien world, a world whose meaning they cannot comprehend, among people who disapprove of their difference and eccentricity (or ex-centricity). Sometimes they internalise cultural conflict, trying to reconcile their new social role with their old habits and values

– their old identity. The director always appears to be on the side of the outsiders, condemning their adversaries for xenophobia, intolerance, cruelty and hypocrisy. I will argue that this position makes him particularly sympathetic to women and children because they are expected to conform to rules created by others (the men and their elders) that disadvantage and marginalise them. It could be said that Polanski tends to view women and children as foreigners even in their own countries. Tess and Oliver Twist are the best examples of this attitude. Similarly, Polanski reveals a deep scepticism for such products of culture as religions and political ideologies. He shows that they are instruments of power of certain groups of people over other groups, as well as the means of legitimising their power. Similarly, the values that Polanski most strongly espouses in his films, of rationalism and individualism, can be regarded as a product of his ideological disillusionment that results from first-hand experience of the workings of ideologies in different societies and cultures.

Furthermore, Polanski appears to favour the concept of human identity as being always 'on the move', always changing. Identities of some of his characters such as Trelkovsky in *The Tenant* change dramatically in the course of action. In their mind they become somebody different from whom they were before. Such a transformation can be attributed at least partly to the cultural atmosphere that surrounds them, the clash between their values and those of their hosts. Polanski shows that the pressure of culture, although invisible, can be immense, affecting the very core of a human being – making a good person bad, the strong weak, and changing a brave man into a coward. The realisation that circumstances rather than any inborn and individual features affect human decisions most is the reason why Polanski tends to criticise the system, the ideology, the cultural pattern, as opposed to putting the whole blame on the individual. The director also universalises the condition of an individual character, making us realise and question our own habits and values. Having said that, we should equally acknowledge his eye for exceptionally generous, courageous and nonconformist individuals, and the tenderness with which he portrays them, such as the heroine of *Tess*, Rosemary in *Rosemary's Baby* and Wilm Hosenfeld in *The Pianist*. Perhaps because Polanski directly experienced extreme situations, he is able to appreciate fully the uniqueness and importance of their attitudes and behaviour for humanity.

In the light of what has been said so far it is not surprising that Polanski's favoured type of genre is the travel movie. However, unlike classical road cinema where travellers constitute a tiny minority of society and form a homogenous group consisting of young male rebels, in

Polanski's films they belong to the society's mainstream and represent all classes and age groups. They use all possible means of transport: cars, trains, ships, planes, carts, bicycles as well as their feet. Travelling is thus rendered as a universal condition and the purposes of travel in his films are almost identical to the goals of human life itself: to survive, to find a home, to earn one's living, to escape serious problems or avoid boredom. The idea that not being able to move fast is tantamount with being a loser already appears in Polanski's first film *The Bicycle* and is reiterated in his most recent film *Oliver Twist* – both films featuring young men who bear strong similarities with Polanski himself. Because travelling for Polanski is not very different from living, his films lack the mournful or ecstatic tone associated with road cinema. Equally, the discourse on travel is closely linked with the autobiographic character of Polanski's cinema.

Favouring travel as a narrative mode affects the cinematography and iconography of Polanski's films. As I have said, the director employs the subjective and changing vision of a traveller. Moreover, roads and the sea constitute privileged sites in his films. Towns and villages are usually represented as assemblages of roads, and even the houses in his films do not appear to be stable but behave like labyrinths or corridors, tempting or forcing the characters to leave their apartments and move somewhere else, often to a different ontological order, via the wardrobe that connects the natural with the supernatural.

Polanski also uses comedy but even his funniest films are not ordinary comedies because of their tragic dimension. And humour in Polanski's films is rather a consequence of the author's absurdist sensibility, through which human life is perceived as lacking in harmony and is instead full of conflict and sadness. Comedy also marks Polanski's detachment from the characters and their situations, his looking at them from the distance of somebody who encountered during his peregrinations so many strange and horrific events that nothing surprises or outrages him any more. On the whole, humour testifies both to Polanski's critical attitude to reality and to his appetite for life, and hence to his desire to escape from the horrors and move on, until he finds a better place, rather than in melancholy ponder for ever on life's injustices.

Travel discourse has been compared to colonial discourse due to both being based on a duality of 'us' and 'them'. The 'us' is always equated with those in charge of the gaze, 'them' with the objects of this gaze. 'Them' tend to be construed as uncivilised, barbaric or at least primitive and provincial, 'us' as worldly and civilised (see Elsner and Rubiés 1999). On the other hand, as Susan Sontag observes, travel can be used as a way to overcome colonialist attitudes by 'learning that there are different ways of being civilised and civil' (Sontag 2002b: 283). My final argument is that although in Polanski's films we frequently encounter a detachment characteristic of the colonial traveller, the films are also an immense source of knowledge about what divides people living in different places and times and what they have in common. Through his cinematic journeys Polanski demonstrates that, although people might be different in their interests, aspirations and tastes, they are very similar in their suffering, misery, deprivation and loneliness – all being frequent outcomes of cultural conflicts. Consequently, in a subtle way Polanski's films teach us how to be civilised and civil, as well as to understand better those who failed the test of civilisation.

APPENDIX: FILMOGRAPHY (WITH TECHNICAL DETAILS AND SYNOPSES)

Rower (*The Bicycle*)
Poland, 1955
Direction: Roman Polanski
Screenplay: Roman Polanski
Black and white
Cast: Adam Fiut, Roman Polanski
(Print lost)

A teenage boy is lured to an out-of-town bunker by a man who promised to sell him a bicycle for a bargain price. There the man robs the boy and beats him up.

Morderstwo (*Murder*)
Poland, 1957
Direction: Roman Polanski
Screenplay: Roman Polanski
Cinematography: Nikola Todorov
Production company: PWSF
Black and white
Runtime: 1.5 min.

A man enters the room and inserts a knife in the chest of a sleeping man. When the man dies, he leaves the room.

Uśmiech zębiczny (*Teethful Smile*)
Poland, 1957
Direction: Roman Polanski
Screenplay: Roman Polanski
Cinematography: Henryk Kucharski
Production company: PWSF
Black and white
Runtime: 1.5 min.
Cast: Nikola Todorov (Peeping Tom)

A man is going down the stairs in an apartment block. He stops and looks through a window at a young woman in the bathroom who is drying her hair in such a way that her face is covered by a towel. The man gazes at her bare breasts with delight, but stops when a man opens the apartment door to put the milk bottles out. He continues to go downstairs, but returns to the window when the man is back indoors. This time, however, he sees not the woman but an older man brushing his teeth who directs his wide smile towards the window.

Rozbijemy zabawę (Let's Break the Ball)

Poland, 1957
Direction: Roman Polanski
Screenplay: Roman Polanski
Cinematography: Marek Nowicki, Andrzej Galiński
Production company: PWSF
Black and white
Runtime: 9 min.

A dancing party in the open air, attended by young people, is disrupted by a group of thugs.

Dwaj ludzie z szafą (Two Men and a Wardrobe)

Poland, 1958
Direction: Roman Polanski
Screenplay: Roman Polanski
Cinematography: Maciej Kijowski
Editing: Roman Polanski
Music: Krzysztof Komeda
Executive producer: Ryszard Barski
Production company: PWSF
Black and white
Runtime: 15 min.
Cast: Jakub Goldberg (A man with a wardrobe), Henryk Kluba (A man with a wardrobe), Roman Polanski (Thug), Stanisław Michalski (Thug)

Two men carrying a large wardrobe with a mirror rise out from the sea. They put it on the beach and dance before taking it into the town. Here problems occur: they are not allowed to board a tram with the wardrobe, neither can they get a seat in the café or a room in the hotel. They meet a pretty girl who seems to be friendly but leaves when they return to collect the wardrobe. At an almost empty stadium they encounter a gang of thugs who bait them and then beat them, as well as destroying the wardrobe mirror. Next they get into conflict with the watchman in a storage yard. Eventually they return to the beach, passing a boy who builds sandcastles, completely oblivious to their existence, and plunge into the sea, carrying the wardrobe with them.

Gdy spadają anioły (When Angels Fall)

Poland, 1959
Direction: Roman Polanski
Screenplay: Roman Polanski

Cinematography: Henryk Kucharski
Editing: Roman Polanski
Music: Krzysztof Komeda
Production company: PWSF
Black and white and colour
Runtime: 21 min.
Cast: Barbara Kwiatkowska (The old woman in her youth), Roman Polanski (An old woman giving a parcel to a man leaving for war), Henryk Kluba (German deserter), Andrzej Kondratiuk (The son of the old woman), Ryszard Filipski, Andrzej Kostenko, Henryk Kucharski (Customers in the public lavatory)

An old woman who works as a public toilet attendant reminisces about her past. She dreams about the cavalryman with whom she fell in love, of her son, and of the death of her beloved one. The flashbacks of her private past intermingle with the country's history and the numerous military conflicts that Poland suffered. Her recollections, shot in colour, are interrupted by the black-and-white reality of her unglamorous work: men urinating and hurriedly leaving. In the end an angel – her lover – arrives, crashing through the roof and taking her with him.

Lampa (The Lamp)
Poland, 1959
Direction: Roman Polanski
Script: Roman Polanski
Cinematography: Krzysztof Romanowski
Production company: PWSTiF
Black and white
Runtime: 8 min.

Night. In a workshop, lit by oil lamps, a man is repairing dolls. The same workshop, possibly some years later, is fitted with electricity. The man carries on with his work, as before. When he leaves the workshop, there is a failure in the electrical installation, causing a fire that destroys the dolls.

Le Gros et le maigre (The Fat and the Lean)
France, 1961
Direction: Roman Polanski
Script: Roman Polanski, Jean-Pierre Rousseau
Cinematography: Jean-Michel Bousaguet
Editing: Roman Polanski
Music: Krzysztof Komeda
Producer: Claude Joudioux
Production company: A.P.E.C.
Black and white
Runtime: 16 min.
Cast: Roman Polanski (Lean Man), André Katelbach (Fat Man)

A fat man rests in his rocking chair outside a rundown cottage while his thin companion entertains him, rocking his chair, playing music, cooking his meals, shading him from the sun with a parasol, and even cutting his nails and holding a urinal for him. Exhausted by his daily chores, the lean man tries to run away to a large city, but the fat man catches him and subsequently chains him to a goat. When the fat man frees his companion from the chains, the lean man resumes his usual duties with extra joy and gratitude to his master.

Ssaki (Mammals)
Poland, 1962
Direction: Roman Polanski
Script: Roman Polanski, Andrzej Kondratiuk
Cinematography: Andrzej Kostenko
Editing: Halina Prugar, Janina Niedźwiecka
Music: Krzysztof Komeda
Production company: Se-Ma-For
Black and white
Runtime: 10 min.
Cast: Henryk Kluba, Michał Żołnierkiewicz (Men with a sledge)

Two men with a sledge are crossing a snow-covered hill. One of them is on a sledge, the other is pulling him. They change places when the passenger complains of an injury that he is simulating. After a while they change places again over a new pretext. Each is aware that the other is pretending. At last, they start to fight. During their argument a third man appears and snatches the sledge. The men are reconciled and proceed on foot, taking turns in carrying each other. Soon, however, they start to argue again and continue until they disappear over the horizon.

Nóż w wodzie (Knife in the Water)
Poland, 1962
Direction: Roman Polanski
Screenplay: Jerzy Skolimowski, Jakub Goldberg, Roman Polanski
Cinematography: Jerzy Lipman
Editing: Halina Prugar
Production design: Bolesław Kamykowski
Music: Krzysztof Komeda
Sound: Halina Paszkowska
Production company: Zespół 'Kamera'
Black and white
Runtime: 98 min.
Cast: Leon Niemczyk (Andrzej), Jolanta Umecka (Krystyna), Zygmunt Malanowicz (Student)

Andrzej, a well-off film journalist and his wife Krystyna drive to the Mazurian Lakes in their expensive car for a weekend on their yacht. On their way they pick up a student who has jumped out in front of their car. Andrzej suggests to the student that he joins them. Being an experienced yachtsman Andrzej baits and challenges the student who not only knows nothing about sailing but claims that he cannot even swim. At the same time Andrzej tries to impress his indifferent wife whom the young man finds attractive. The power game changes into a more sinister affair when Andrzej first throws into the water the student's flick knife, which is his most precious possession and then knocks the student in himself. The young man disappears beneath the surface alarming Andrzej and Krystyna. She reproaches her husband for his buffoonery and conceit which could cause the young man's death. Andrzej dives into the lake to try to find the student. Soon the young man, who was listening to their quarrel, hidden behind a buoy, returns to the yacht. Relieved, Krystyna comforts him and they make love. The student leaves and Krystyna joins Andrzej on the shore. She tells him about her infidelity, making him decide whether to ignore his wife's words and to go to the police or to believe her version, admitting to being a cuckold.

La Rivière de diamants (*A River of Diamonds*)
Segment in *Les plus belles escroqueries du monde* (*The World's Most Beautiful Swindlers*)
France/Japan/Italy/The Netherlands, 1964
Direction: Roman Polanski
Screenplay: Gérard Brach
Cinematography: Jerzy Lipman
Music: Krzysztof Komeda
Black and white
Runtime: 34 min.
Cast: Nicole Karen (Nicole), Jan Teulings (Teulings), Arnold Glederman (Jeweller)

A young, French woman arrives in Amsterdam where, after some wandering, she befriends a rich, older man temporarily parted from his wife. She visits a shop with expensive jewellery and arranges for a diamond necklace to be sent to her suitor's address. When the jeweller arrives, she asks him to wait, so that she can show the necklace to her husband, and then disappears. Back on the streets of Amsterdam she exchanges the precious piece for a parrot.

Repulsion
UK, 1965
Direction: Roman Polanski
Screenplay: Roman Polanski, Gérard Brach
Cinematography: Gilbert Taylor
Editing: Alastair McIntyre
Music: Chico Hamilton
Sound: Leslie Hammond
Producer: Gene Gutowski
Production company: Michael Klinger and Tony Tender Production
Runtime: 105 min.
Cast: Catherine Deneuve (Carol Ledoux), Yvonne Furneaux (Helen Ledoux), John Fraser (Colin), Ian Hendry (Michael), Patrick Wymark (Landlord), Helen Fraser (Bridget)

Carol Ledoux, a young and beautiful Belgian immigrant, lives in London with her older sister, Helen, and works in a beauty salon. At work she is often dreamy and absent-minded. Although men adore her, she does not reciprocate their sympathy and attention. She cannot stand the presence of Helen's married lover, Michael, in their flat and shows little interest in Colin, a subtle man who would like to be her boyfriend. When Helen and Michael go on holiday to Italy, Carol's condition deteriorates. She becomes so detached from reality that she injures the hand of a customer and the manager of the beauty salon sends her home. Back in her apartment she sees hands coming out of the walls, trying to catch her and she imagines that a man tries to rape her. She barricades the door to prevent any man from approaching her but two men manage to get in: the sleazy landlord and Colin. Carol kills both. When Helen and Michael return from their journey, they find the apartment in a terrible state and Carol lying under the bed, unaware of what has happened.

Cul-de-Sac
UK, 1966
Direction: Roman Polanski
Screenplay: Roman Polanski, Gérard Brach
Cinematography: Gilbert Taylor
Editing: Alastair McIntyre
Production design: Voytek
Music: Krzysztof Komeda
Sound: Stephen Dalby
Producer: Gene Gutowski
Production company: Gompton/Tekli
Black and white
Runtime: 111 min.
Cast: Donald Pleasance (George), Françoise Dorléac (Teresa), Lionel Stander (Richard), Jack MacGowran (Albert), Cecil (William Franklin).

A car is pushed by a man with an injured arm across a causeway linking the mainland to an island. The man is called Richard. Inside sits his companion, Albert, also wounded and exhausted. The men are injured gangsters on the run. Richard, following the telephone wires, reaches an old castle, inhabited by a married couple: George and his French wife, Teresa, and dozens of hens. Richard manages to terrorise the couple. He forces them to bring to the castle his broken-down car, together with Albert who soon dies. Richard tries to contact his boss, a mysterious Mr Katelbach, hoping that he will help him to leave the deserted island but it proves very difficult. Teresa is very scornful of her husband's submissive attitude to the gangster, and herself stands up to Richard, humiliating him when some unexpected guests arrive – George's old friends. On this occasion Richard has to play the role of the couple's butler. The guests irritate George immensely and eventually he orders them to leave.

Katelbach rings informing Richard that he has forsaken him. Richard decides to leave but on his way out is shot by George with a gun, given to him by Teresa. Teresa leaves with one of the guests who has returned to the castle to collect his gun.

George tries to destroy his house and eventually crouches on a rock surrounded by water, calling the name of 'Agnes' – his first wife.

Dance of the Vampires
American title: *The Fearless Vampire Killers*
(*Pardon Me, But Your Teeth are in My Neck*)
UK, 1967
Direction: Roman Polanski
Screenplay: Roman Polanski, Gérard Brach
Cinematography: Douglas Slocombe
Editing: Alastair McIntyre
Production design: Wilfred Shingleton
Costume design: Sophie Devine
Music: Krzysztof Komeda
Sound: George Stephenson
Producer: Gene Gutowski
Production company: Cadre Films/Filmways
Colour
Runtime: 107 min.
Cast: Jack MacGowran (Professor Abronsius), Roman Polanski (Alfred), Alfie Bass (Shagal), Jessie Robins (Rebecca), Sharon Tate (Sarah), Ferdy Mayne (Count von Krolock), Iain Quarrier (Herbert), Terry Downes (Koukol), Fiona Lewis (Magda)

Professor Abronsius, a famous vampire specialist, accompanied by his faithful disciple, Alfred, travels to Transylvania on a sleigh. They stop at a local inn, kept by Shagal and his wife Rebecca. The inn is situated in close proximity to a castle, owned by Count von Krolock, the chief vampire in this region. Shagal's beautiful daughter, Sarah, who is a compulsive bather, attracts Alfred's attention. Sarah is also an object of the interest of von Krolock, who during one of her baths crashes through the ceiling and kidnaps her. Shortly afterwards the frozen and bloodless body of Shagal is found – he too fell victim to a vampire. Later Shagal changes into a vampire himself. Despite all these incidents, pointing to the presence of a menacing force, the villagers pretend that there are no vampires in the neighbourhood, and that all the damage is done by wolves.

Professor Abronsius and Alfred arrive at the castle where they meet Count von Krolock. Von Krolock's son, Herbert, a homosexual vampire, tries to seduce Albert but with no success. Albert hears Sarah's singing but cannot find her until the night of a ball, when dozens of vampires assemble in the castle. Abronsius and Alfred manage to escape in a coffin-sleigh, taking Sarah with them. Sitting on the back of the sleigh, Sarah sinks her teeth into Alfred's neck.

Rosemary's Baby
USA, 1968
Direction: Roman Polanski
Screenplay: Roman Polanski, based on the novel by Ira Levin
Cinematography: William Fraker

Editing: Sam O'Steen, Bob Wyman
Production design: Richard Sylbert
Costume design: Anthea Sylbert
Music: Krzysztof Komeda
Sound: Harold Lewis
Producer: William Castle
Production Company: Paramount/William Castle Enterprises
Colour
Runtime: 137 min.
Cast: Mia Farrow (Rosemary Woodhouse), John Cassavetes (Guy Woodhouse), Ruth Gordon (Minnie Castevet), Sidney Blackmer (Roman Castevet), Maurice Evans (Hutch), Ralph Bellamy (Doctor Sapirstein), Angela Dorian (Terry)

Rosemary Woodhouse and her husband Guy, an actor, visit an apartment in the Bramford, an old-fashioned block of flats in New York, with an intention to rent it. The former tenant, Mrs Gardenia, had passed away. They decide to take it, despite Rosemary's old friend Hutch, attempting to dissuade them from the idea by telling them that the Bramford has a reputation as a site of devil worshippers and baby-eaters. After moving in, Rosemary meets a young woman Terry, who lives with an elderly couple, Minnie and Roman Castevets, who are also the Woodhouses' new neighbours. She claims that they helped her to overcome drug addiction. Terry wears a charm round her neck with tannis root which she received from the Castevets. Soon after their first and only meeting Terry is found dead – she leapt from an apartment window. On this sombre occasion the Woodhouses meet the Castevets.

Minnie and Roman invite Rosemary and Guy to their flat for dinner. Soon they see each other daily and give Rosemary the charm. However, while Guy is completely under their spell, Rosemary finds them intrusive and suspects that they have a bad influence on Guy who has become distant. This impression increases after Rosemary becomes pregnant. On the night of conception Rosemary imagines being raped by Satan in a strange ceremony that includes the Castevets and their circle of friends. The Castevets, overjoyed by the news of their neighbour's pregnancy, persuade her to change her obstetrician, Doctor Hill, for a more famous doctor and their friend, Doctor Sapirstein. Despite his fame, Sapirstein is unable or unwilling to help Rosemary, who suffers continuous pain, looks pale and withered and has an appetite for uncooked meat. Her friends, including Hutch, are alarmed by her appearance. Hutch arranges to see Rosemary but he does not turn up. She learns that he has fallen seriously ill. In Rosemary's opinion the responsibility for his illness, as well as for other recent misfortunes, lies with the Castevets whom she suspects of being Satanists. She becomes very worried about her unborn baby, thinking that they want to use it in their rituals. Soon before the birth she approaches Doctor Hill, telling him about her suspicions. He seems to be sympathetic but while she waits to be taken to hospital, he betrays her to Guy and Doctor Sapirstein, who take her back to the Bramford where she goes into labour. When she recovers consciousness, Rosemary is told that the baby has died. She does not believe it and eventually makes her way to the Castevets' apartment, where the whole group of devil worshippers, including Guy and Sapirstein, gather around a black-draped cradle, celebrating the birth of a son to Satan. After a brief hesitation, Rosemary starts to rock the cradle.

Macbeth
UK, 1971
Direction: Roman Polanski
Screenplay: Roman Polanski, Kenneth Tynan, based on the play by William Shakespeare
Cinematography: Gilbert Taylor
Editing: Alastair McIntyre
Production design: Wilfred Shingleton
Costume design: Anthony Mendleson
Music: The Third Ear Band
Sound: Jonathan Bates
Producer: Andrew Braunsberg
Production company: Playboy Productions/Caliban Films
Colour
Runtime: 140 min.
Cast: Jon Finch (Macbeth), Francesca Annis (Lady Macbeth), Martin Shaw (Banquo), Nicholas Selby (Duncan), John Stride (Ross), Stephen Chase (Malcolm), Paul Shelley (Donalbain), Terence Bayler (Macduff)

Medieval Scotland. Three witches bury a severed forearm. They gradually disappear from the horizon and a landscape after a battle there appears with injured soldiers and horses dying in the mud. The fight took place between King Duncan's forces and those of the King of Norway, supported by the rebellious Thane of Cawdor. After playing a major role in the victory, general Macbeth is rewarded with the post of Thane of Cawdor by King Duncan. However, as the witches forecast that this title was only a stage towards becoming king, Macbeth thirsts for faster advancement. His craving for the crown is fanned by the disappointing news that King Duncan declared his eldest son Malcolm, Prince of Cumberland (and his successor) and by the regal ambitions of his wife, Lady Macbeth. She encourages Macbeth to murder the king the night he stays in their castle. Duncan's body is discovered by a nobleman named Macduff. The blame is put on the king's guards whom Macbeth kills before they are interrogated. Duncan's sons, Malcolm and Donalbain, flee Scotland, fearing for their own lives. Macbeth becomes the new king; the news is brought to him by Ross, who was previously the messenger announcing Macbeth's rise to be Thane of Cawdor.

Macbeth's achievement does not satisfy him, as he is haunted by the prediction that the children of Banquo, another general who fought against the King of Norway, are to inherit the throne. Macbeth arranges for the murder of Banquo and his only son, Fleance. However, Fleance escapes the attack and flees the country. This event is witnessed by Ross who later sends Banquo's murderers, on the order of Macbeth, to jail. Macbeth gives a great dinner for the court and is about to take his seat when he sees the ghost of Banquo (invisible to the guests) and his remarks break up the feast.

Macbeth visits the witches in their den. They warn him to beware of Macduff but assure him that no man born of a woman can harm him and that he cannot be defeated until Birnam Wood comes to Dunsinane, the site of his castle. Back in his castle he is greeted with the news that Macduff has fled to England to join Malcolm. Macbeth orders the murder of Lady Macduff and her children. This is arranged by Ross who pays Lady Macduff a friendly visit and on his departure allows the killers to enter her home. Lady Macbeth starts hallucinating, seeing blood on her hands. Macduff, gathering forces with the escaped Malcolm in England, leads an army against Macbeth's castle at Dunsinane. On his way to Scotland he is visited by Ross who tells him about the brutal killing of his family. Lady Macbeth dies, most likely committing suicide. Malcolm's soldiers camouflage their advance with branches cut from the trees of Birnam Wood, making it appear that the wood is coming to Dunsinane. Macbeth's subjects desert the castle. The castle is attacked and during his final combat lonely Macbeth learns that his opponent, Macduff, was prematurely ripped from his mother's womb by Caesarean section. Macduff cuts off Macbeth's head. Ross takes the crown from Macbeth's head and passes it to Malcolm. Donalbain approaches the witches' den.

Che? (What?)

Italy, France, West Germany, 1972
Direction: Roman Polanski
Screenplay: Gérard Brach, Roman Polanski
Cinematography: Marcello Gatti, Giuseppe Ruzzolini
Production design: Aurelio Crugnola
Music: Claudio Gizzi
Producer: Carlo Ponti
Production company: A Carlo Ponti Production
Colour
Runtime: 113 min.
Cast: Sydne Rome (Nancy), Marcello Mastroianni (Alex), Hugh Griffith (Joseph Noblart), Romolo Valli (Giovanni), Guido Alberti (Priest), Roman Polanski (Mosquito)

Nancy, a young American woman travelling through Italy, avoids being raped by the men who have given her a lift by jumping into a cable car that takes her to a large villa belonging to an elderly millionaire and art collector, Joseph Noblart. It is inhabited by various hangers-on, many of whom are utterly eccentric and decadent. Among them are a mad priest, a group of young men indulging in promiscuous sex and table tennis, an ex-pimp Alex, who gets utter pleasure from destroying their tennis balls and two ladies who parade completely naked except for their large hats. On her arrival Nancy is also semi-naked as her clothes were destroyed by the rapists, and to cover herself she must steal somebody's pyjamas. Superficially the atmosphere in the villa is relaxed but people here have a penchant for cruel games, including sadomasochistic sex, to which Nancy often falls prey. Moreover, people do not keep their appointments, there is no structure to their lives and increasingly Nancy has a sense of déjà vu. After making the acquaintance of most of Noblart's guests, she meets the old man himself. He gets so excited looking at Nancy's 'private parts' (which he asks her to reveal to him) that he has a heart attack and dies. A naked Nancy runs away from the villa, followed by the crowd of its inhabitants, and boards a lorry. She explains to Alex that she must leave, otherwise the film in which she is playing, entitled What?, will never be finished.

Chinatown
USA, 1974
Direction: Roman Polanski
Screenplay: Robert Towne
Cinematography: John A. Alonso
Editing: Sam O'Steen
Production design: Gabe Resh, Robert Resh
Costume design: Anthea Sylbert
Music: Jerry Goldsmith
Sound: Larry Jost
Producer: Robert Evans
Production company: Long Road Productions
Colour
Runtime: 131 min.
Cast: Jack Nicholson (J.J. Gittes), Faye Dunaway (Evelyn Mulwray), John Huston (Noah Cross), Perry Lopez (Escobar), Darrell Zwerling (Hollis Mulwray)

Los Angeles, 1937. Private detective Jake (J.J.) Gittes, who used to work as a policeman in Chinatown, specialises in investigating marital infidelity. A woman pretending to be Evelyn Mulwray hires him to look into the suspected affair of her husband, Hollis Mulwray, the head of the LA Water Department. Gittes follows Hollis Mulwray and learns that he opposes the building of a dam in LA on the grounds that it would risk damaging the town. He also takes pictures of him embracing a young woman, possibly his lover. Soon after this incident Mulwray is found dead as a result of drowning – which is a paradox as LA is suffering a deep drought. Gittes suspects that Mulwray was murdered by his jealous wife. He meets the real Evelyn and they start an affair, which however is marred by Gittes's conviction that she is hiding from him important information. He also meets her father, Noah Cross, a rich and powerful man.

Eventually Jake discovers that not Evelyn but Noah killed Hollis Mulwray, because of his opposition to the dam which would multiply Noah's wealth. It turns out also that the young woman with whom he saw Hollis was not his mistress, but Evelyn's daughter Catherine – the fruit of her incestuous relationship with her father. Trying to protect Catherine from Noah, Evelyn tries to escape from LA to Mexico, but is killed by the police and Catherine is taken away by her father/grandfather. This incident happens in Chinatown, in front of Gittes's eyes.

Le Locataire (*The Tenant*)
France, 1976
Direction: Roman Polanski
Screenplay: Gérard Brach, Roman Polanski, based on the novel *Le Locataire chimérique* by Roland Topor
Cinematography: Sven Nykvist
Editing: Françoise Bonnot
Production design: Pierre Guffroy
Music: Philippe Sarde

Sound: Michèle Boehm
Producer: Andrew Braunsberg
Production company: Marianne Productions
Colour
Runtime: 126 min.
Cast: Roman Polanski (Trelkovsky), Isabelle Adjani (Stella), Shelley Winters (Concierge), Melvyn Douglas (Mr Zy), Jo Van Fleet (Mme Dioz), Lila Kedrova (Mme Gaderian)

Trelkovsky, a clerk and naturalised Pole living in Paris, enquires about an apartment to let. He learns from the landlord, the morose Monsieur Zy, that the apartment is empty but cannot be let while its previous occupant, Simone Choule, a woman who threw herself out of the window, is still alive. Trelkovsky visits her in hospital and meets her friend Stella. Simone, completely covered in bandages, seems to be unconscious but she utters a terrible cry when Stella tries to waken her. Soon Trelkovsky learns that Simone has died and he moves into the apartment. He organises a house-warming party for his work-pals, which triggers hostile reactions from his neighbours. They complain about the noise and ask him to sign a petition to evict another tenant. Moreover, his flat is burgled and the police harass him. Increasingly insecure in his apartment, Trelkovsky becomes obsessed about the previous tenant and starts to imagine that he is Simone. He dresses like her and sports a wig and platform shoes. Eventually he is convinced that his neighbours are conspiring to drive him to suicide. He rushes to Stella and is comforted by her but leaves her flat in the morning, believing that she sides with his neighbours against him. Back in his apartment he jumps twice from the window. In the hospital, Stella finds a figure bandaged from head to toe, except for a mouth that utters a terrible cry.

Tess

France/UK, 1979
Direction: Roman Polanski
Screenplay: Gérard Brach, Roman Polanski, John Brownjohn, based on the novel *Tess of the d'Urbervilles* by Thomas Hardy
Cinematography: Geoffrey Unsworth, Ghislain Cloquet
Editing: Alastair McIntyre, Tom Priestley
Production design: Pierre Guffroy
Costume design: Pierre Lefait, Jean-Claude Sevent
Music: Philippe Sarde
Sound: Peter Horrocks
Producers: Claude Berri, Timothy Burrill
Production Company: Renn Productions/Burrill Productions
Colour
Runtime: 172 min.
Cast: Nastassia Kinski (Tess), Peter Firth (Angel Clare), Leigh Lawson (Alec d'Urberville), John Collin (John Durbeyfield), Tony Church (Parson Tringham), Rosemary Martin (Mrs Durbeyfield)

Wessex, England, the end of the nineteenth century. John Durbeyfield, an impoverished trader, learns from Pastor Tringham that he is a descendant of the aristocratic d'Urberville family. This gives him the idea of sending his eldest daughter, beautiful sixteen-year-old Tess, to the wealthy Stoke-d'Urbervilles, to claim kinship. Alec d'Urberville, whose father bought the title, hires Tess to look after his mother's poultry. Soon Alec seduces (or rapes) Tess and she becomes his mistress. After some time she leaves the farm, returns home and gives birth to a child which dies. She leaves home to work on a dairy farm where she falls in love with Angel Clare, who is a parson's son. Angel reciprocates her affection and asks her to marry him. Tess reluctantly agrees and after their wedding tells him about her affair with Alec. Angel is taken aback to learn about Tess's past. He sends Tess back home and himself embarks for Brazil. Tess begins to work as a fieldhand, but returns to Alec to provide for her mother and siblings, unable to support themselves after John Durbeyfield's death. Angel, moved by Tess's letters, returns to her. First she rejects him but then stabs Alec and runs away with Angel. The couple enjoys a brief respite in an empty house before the police catch them and take Tess to be hanged.

Pirates

France, 1986
Directed by: Roman Polanski
Writing credits: Gerard Brach, Roman Polanski, John Brownjohn
Cinematography: Witold Sobociński
Editing: Hervé de Luze, William Reynolds
Production design: Pierre Guffroy
Costume design: Anthony Powell
Music: Philippe Sarde
Sound: Jean-Pierre Ruh
Producer: Tarak Ben Ammar
Production company: Carthago Films/Accent-Cominco
Colour
Runtime: 124 min.
Cast: Walter Matthau (Captain Red), Cris Campion (Jean-Baptiste, 'the Frog'), Damien Thomas (Don Alfonso), Charlotte Lewis (Dolores), Olu Jacobs (Boumako), Ferdy Mayne (Captain Linares), Władysław Komar (Jesus)

The seventeenth century. Pirate Captain Red and his young sidekick, Jean-Baptiste, known as 'the Frog', float on a raft in the middle of the ocean. So hungry that he is thinking about eating his young companion, Red notices a Spanish galleon, the *Neptune*, on the horizon. As they board the ship, they lose their treasure chest. Red discovers that the ship contains a golden Aztec throne and immediately plans to seize it. He stirs up a mutiny and captures the throne together with the whole galleon from its Spanish captain, Don Alfonso. He also takes hostage the beautiful Dolores, niece of the Governor of Maracaibo. Jean-Baptiste falls in love with Dolores who reciprocates his affection. Red, however, offers her and the rest of the *Neptune's* passengers as hostages to a mercenary called Dutch, who lives on an island where Red's crew awaits their captain.

Don Alfonso manages to escape from the island and recapture the galleon. Red and Jean-Baptiste follow him to Maracaibo where they blackmail the governor to partake in the operation which gives them back the throne. It goes wrong, however, and they end up in jail, awaiting execution. Red's crew frees them and they again start to pursue Don Alfonso. The buccaneers manage to recapture the Aztec treasure, but they find themselves on a raft once more, awaiting new adventures.

Frantic
USA, 1988
Direction: Roman Polanski
Screenplay: Roman Polanski, Gérard Brach
Cinematography: Witold Sobociński
Editing: Sam O'Steen
Production design: Pierre Guffroy
Costume design: Anthony Powell
Music: Ennio Morricone
Sound: Jean Goudier, Jean-Pierre Ruh
Producers: Thom Mount, Tim Hampton
Production company: Warner Bros/A Mount Company Production
Colour
Runtime: 120 min.
Cast: Harrison Ford (Richard Walker), Betty Buckley (Sondra Walker), Emmanuelle Seigner (Michelle), Alexandra Stewart (Edie), David Huddleston (Peter), Robert Barr (Irwin)

Cardiologist Richard Walker, accompanied by his wife Sondra, arrives in Paris from San Francisco for a medical conference. At the hotel his wife disappears and Walker discovers that they have somebody else's suitcase. Walker turns to the hotel staff, the police and the American embassy but nobody is helpful. From the matchbox in the suitcase he gets a telephone number of somebody called Dédé and the name of a nightclub, the Blue Parrot. Dédé is of little help, as Walker finds him dead but he is contacted by Michelle, a girl who mixed up her suitcase with that of the Walkers. She admits that she was hired through Dédé to smuggle something from San Francisco to Paris, most likely by the same people who kidnapped Sondra. They retrieve the suitcase from the airport. Walker is contacted by Sondra's captors who demand the return of a miniature Statue of Liberty from Michelle's luggage in exchange for his wife. Walker, who learns that the cheap souvenir contains a device used to trigger a nuclear bomb, meets the Arab kidnappers and is united with Sondra. Michelle and the Arabs, however, die in a shoot-out. Walker leaves the scene with Sondra, throwing the nuclear device into the Seine.

Lunes de fiel (Bitter Moon)
France/UK, 1992
Direction: Roman Polanski
Screenplay: Roman Polanski, Gérard Brach, John Brownjohn, based on the novel by Pascal Bruckner

Cinematography: Tonino delli Colli
Editing: Hervé de Luze
Production design: Willy Holt, Gérard Viard
Costume design: Jackie Budin
Music: Vangelis
Sound: Laurent Quaglio, Roberto Garzelli
Producers: Roman Polanski, Alain Sarde
Production company: R.P. Productions/Timothy Burrill Productions/Les Films Alain Sarde
Colour
Runtime: 139 min.
Cast: Hugh Grant (Nigel Dobson), Kristin Scott-Thomas (Fiona Dobson), Emmanuelle Seigner (Mimi), Peter Coyote (Oscar), Victor Bannerjee (Mr Singh)

British couple of seven years, Nigel and Fiona, are sailing to Istanbul en route for India. They meet another couple, a young French woman named Mimi and her older crippled American husband Oscar. Both Mimi and Oscar try to seduce Nigel, Mimi with her feminine charm, Oscar with his story. Oscar tells Nigel how he had come to Paris hoping to became a writer and became obsessed with a young woman – Mimi – whom he encountered by chance on a bus. He met her again some time later in a restaurant where she worked as a waitress. They started a passionate love affair, which, however, after some time lost its edge, at least for Oscar, despite enhancing it with sado-masochism. Eventually, Oscar threw Mimi out of his apartment but took her back when she begged him to allow her to be with him. The next stage of their life was marked by mental cruelty on the part of Oscar. Mimi got pregnant with his child and had an abortion. After this incident he left her on a plane to Martinique. Alone, Oscar gave up any ambitions to be a writer and indulged in pleasures of casual sex and alcohol. This life finished when he was knocked down by a car and broke his leg. In hospital he was visited by Mimi, who pushed him out of bed, resulting in his paralysis. His old love became his sadistic nurse. They got married and Mimi gave him a gun for his birthday.

At a party on the cruise Nigel confesses to Mimi to falling in love with her. She, however, dances with Fiona and goes to bed with her. In the presence of Nigel, Oscar shoots Mimi and then himself. United, Nigel and Fiona reach Istanbul.

Death and the Maiden
UK/USA/France, 1994
Direction: Roman Polanski
Screenplay: Rafael Yglesias, Ariel Dorfman, based on the play by Ariel Dorfman
Cinematography: Tonino delli Colli
Editing: Hervé de Luze
Production design: Pierre Guffroy
Costume design: Milena Canonero
Music: Wojciech Kilar
Sound: Daniel Brisseau
Producers: Thom Mount, Josh Kramer

Production company: A Mount/Kramer production
Colour
Runtime: 103 min.
Cast: Sigourney Weaver (Paulina), Ben Kingsley (Roberto Miranda), Stuart Wilson (Gerardo Escobar)

A country in South America, after a dictatorship. Paulina Escobar prepares supper for her husband Gerardo in their beach house, when she hears on the radio that he is to head a government commission to investigate the crimes committed by the previous regime. A storm brews and the electricity cuts out. Gerardo returns home. Paulina hears him thanking a man who gave him a lift. Gerardo explains that it was their neighbour who helped him when he had a flat tyre. It is revealed that Paulina, who was herself a victim of torture, is not happy about Gerardo's acceptance of the position as head of the commission. Soon afterwards the neighbour, Doctor Roberto Miranda, returns with the tyre. While Gerardo and Miranda are talking, Paulina dresses, takes the gun and drives the doctor's car into the sea. Gerardo assumes that his wife has left him and gets drunk with the doctor. Paulina returns home, finds Miranda asleep, hits him and ties him to a chair. She explains that she recognises in him the torturer who used to rape her while playing for her Schubert's string quartet *Death and the Maiden*. Miranda protests his innocence, supported by Gerardo, who tries to untie him. Paulina, however, threatens him with a gun. Paulina wants Miranda to confess to his crimes. First he denies her accusations, claiming that he was working in Barcelona when she was tortured. However, later on, marched to the edge of a cliff, he confesses all and Paulina lets him go.

At a concert of *Death and the Maiden*, Paulina exchanges looks with Miranda, who sits with his wife and children in a balcony.

The Ninth Gate
France/Spain/USA, 1999
Direction: Roman Polanski
Screenplay: John Brownjohn, Enrique Urbizu, Roman Polanski, based on the novel *El Club Dumas* by Arturo Pérez-Reverte
Cinematography: Darius Khondji
Editing: Hervé de Luze
Production design: Dean Tavoularis
Costume design: Anthony Powell
Music: Wojciech Kilar
Sound: Jean-Marie Blondel
Producer: Roman Polanski
Production company: R.P. Productions/Orly Films/TF1 Filmproduction
Colour
Runtime: 133 min.
Cast: Johnny Depp (Dean Corso), Lena Olin (Liana Telfer), Emmanuelle Seigner (Girl with Green Eyes), Frank Langella (Boris Balkan), James Russo (Bernie), Jack Taylor (Victor Fargas), José Lopez Rodero (Pablo and Pedro Ceniza)

New York, the present. Dean Corso, a dealer in rare books, is invited by Boris Balkan to ascertain whether his copy of *The Nine Gates of the Kingdom of Shadows*, a book which allegedly allows contact with the devil, is authentic. Balkan bought the book from Andrew Telfer, who subsequently committed suicide. The dealer agrees to embark on a trip to Europe to compare Balkan's copy with two other existing exemplars. However, before his journey his apartment is burgled and his collaborator, with whom Corso temporarily left the book, is murdered. Corso suspects that the person behind these acts is Telfer's widow Liana, who is desperate to take possession of her husband's volume.

Corso travels to Spain and Paris, where the two remaining copies of *The Ninth Gate* are kept, and consults the famous antiquarians, the Ceniza brothers. He compares the books, discovering that each contains a different set of engravings, signed 'LCF' (possibly meaning 'Lucifer'). The owners of the respective volumes, a decadent aristocrat, Victor Fargas, and Baronness Kessler, are both murdered at the time that Corso is conducting his inspection. His own life is also threatened but he manages to escape thanks to the help of a mysterious Girl with Green Eyes. Corso's investigation leads him to a mansion where Liana Telfer conducts a Satanist ceremony using the engravings from the three copies of *The Ninth Gate*. The event is disrupted by Balkan, who kills Liana and seizes the illustrations. He attempts to use them to call up Satan, but instead himself dies in flames – which proves that at least one of the engravings was not authentic. Corso, guided by the girl (with whom he has sex), obtains the authentic engraving from the Cenizas and enters the ninth gate.

The Pianist

France/Poland/Germany/UK, 2002
Direction: Roman Polanski
Screenplay: Ronald Harwood, based on the book by Władysław Szpilman
Cinematography: Paweł Edelman
Editing: Hervé de Luze
Production design: Allan Starski
Costume design: Anna Sheppard
Music: Wojciech Kilar
Sound: Jean-Marie Blondel
Producers: Roman Polanski, Robert Benmussa, Alain Sarde
Production company: R.P. Productions/Heritage Films/Studios Babelsberg/Runteam Ltd
Colour
Runtime: 149 min.
Cast: Adrien Brody (Władysław Szpilman), Thomas Kretschmann (Captain Wilm Hosenfeld), Frank Finlay (Mr Szpilman, the father), Maureen Lipman (Mrs Szpilman, the mother), Emilia Fox (Dorota), Ed Stoppard (Henryk Szpilman, the brother), Julia Rayner (Regina Szpilman, the sister), Jessica Kate Meyer (Halina Szpilman, the sister)

Warsaw, 1939. A concert at a radio station given by Władysław Szpilman, a famous pianist and composer of popular songs, is disrupted by a bomb blast. The war begins and German forces take control of the city, first imposing restrictions on the movement of the Jewish population, then forcing Warsaw's Jews into a ghetto. The

Szpilmans, Władysław's parents, his brother and two sisters, have to give up their comfortable apartment and move into a small flat. The majority of ghetto Jews experience extreme poverty and hunger, as well as continuous terror. Władysław, however, makes a living from playing in a café visited by rich Jews.

In 1942 the bulk of the ghetto residents, including Szpilman's family, is sent to the death camps. Władysław survives thanks to a Jewish policeman who drags him away from the crowd queuing for a train to Auschwitz. For some time Szpilman remains in the ghetto, working on a building site and then goes into hiding, helped by his Polish friends. From there he observes first the Ghetto Uprising of 1943 and then the 1944 Warsaw Uprising, increasingly suffering hunger and fear. To escape the Nazis, he moves to the devastated part of the city where he hides in an attic. Here he is discovered by a German officer, Captain Wilm Hosenfeld. On learning that Władysław is a pianist, he invites him to perform on a grand piano and brings him food and clothes. After the Germans leave the city, Szpilman leaves his hiding place, covered in a German army coat provided by Hosenfeld, and is almost taken for a Nazi and shot by the Russian soldiers who liberate the city.

Hosenfeld is imprisoned in a camp in Soviet territory. There he approaches a passing Polish ex-prisoner, Szpilman's friend and violinist, to find the pianist and ask him for help. Szpilman travels to the site of the camp with the friend but it no longer exists and the friend does not even know the name of Szpilman's saviour. The film closes at a symphonic concert in which Szpilman plays the piano.

Oliver Twist

UK/France/Czech Republic, 2005
Direction: Roman Polanski
Screenplay: Ronald Harwood, based on the novel by Charles Dickens
Cinematography: Paweł Edelman
Editing: Hervé de Luze
Production design: Allan Starski
Costume design: Anna Sheppard
Music: Rachel Portman
Sound: Jean Goudier
Producers: Robert Benmussa, Alain Sarde, Roman Polanski
Production company: R.P. Productions/Runteam II Ltd/Etic Films S.R.O.
Colour
Runtime: 130 min.
Cast: Barney Clark (Oliver Twist), Ben Kingsley (Fagin), Jamie Foreman (Bill Sykes), Harry Eden (Artful Dodger), Leanne Rowe (Nancy), Edward Hardwicke (Mr Brownlow), Ian McNeice (Mr Limbkins), Mark Strong (Toby Crackit), Jeremy Swift (Mr Bumble)

England, mid-nineteenth century. Ten-year-old orphan, Oliver Twist, brought up by the parish, is taken by Mr Bumble from the orphanage farm to the workhouse. There he is chosen by another boy to ask for a second helping of food. After this episode he is regarded as a troublemaker and sent to work for an undertaker, Mr Sowerberry. His life is bearable until he gets into a fight with an older apprentice, who makes offensive remarks about Oliver's mother. Sowerberry beats him up and locks him in the cellar. The next day Oliver runs away to London and walks for seven days. There he is found by an older boy, Artful Dodger, who introduces him to his master Fagin. Fagin exploits a gang of boys who steal for him. Oliver joins them and learns to be a thief. Soon he is caught when he observes two boys, including Dodger, practising their trade in front of the bookshop and is brought to the magistrate, accused of robbing an elderly man, Mr Brownlow. However, he is cleared by the owner of the bookshop and taken home by Mr Brownlow who is a wealthy and educated man.

Fagin's associate, a sinister burglar called Bill Sykes, anxious that the boy will betray his masters, instructs his mistress, a young prostitute Nancy, to trace the boy. Oliver is recaptured by Nancy and Sykes, and forced to help Sykes and his associate, Toby Crackit, to rob Brownlow's house. The burglary goes wrong and Oliver is wounded. Sykes proposes to kill him but Nancy contacts Brownlow to save Oliver. On learning from Dodger that Nancy helped Oliver, Sykes beats her to death. Fagin, Sykes and Fagin's gang go into hiding. The police, alerted by Brownlow, arrive. Sykes, taking Oliver as his hostage, tries to escape over the rooftops but falls and hangs himself. Oliver returns to Mr Brownlow and enjoys a luxurious lifestyle. Oliver visits Fagin in the police cell before his execution and asks him to join together in prayer but his old master is mad and thinks only about his lost possessions.

NOTES

CHAPTER 1

1 The blurred division between Polanski's life and the fiction he creates is suggested by the title of his autobiography: *Roman*, which refers to the director's first name and signifies the fictional character of his confession. And, in the acknowledgements to the book Polanski writes that so many people invested their time and energy in writing it that 'it feels like cooperative venture, almost like the making of a motion picture' (Polanski 1984: viii), thus adding to the impression that his life is like his films and vice versa.

2 Sontag was interested in the work of Gombrowicz. She wrote an introduction to his acclaimed novel *Ferdydurke* in which she attributed to its author features that, in my opinion, also pertain to Polanski, such as a desire to impose distance between himself and myths central to Polish literature and culture, and thus to create a different type of prose which would not be just Polish but universal, and to create his own legend (see Sontag 2002a).

3 Eaton describes Polanski's accusation of sex with a minor and consequent exile from America as 'a long-overdue revenge drama on the Playboy generation' (Eaton 2000: 9).

CHAPTER 2

1 The episode in which the third man takes possession of the two men's sledge is an illustration of the Polish proverb: *Gdzie dwóch się kłóci, tam trzeci korzysta* (*When two men quarrel, the third man takes advantage*). It is often cited by parents to their children as a way of encouraging them to play peacefully with each other.

2 The motif of doublings can be interpreted as a metaphorical rendering of Jung's concept of the personality as split between the conscious and the unconscious (ego and id), and this perfectly captures the ambiguity of the autobiographical discourse of Polanski's cinema (see Chapter 1). According to Hamid Naficy, doublings are also typical of diasporan cinema (see Naficy 2001: 272–6). However, we can find this motif in many other types of cinema and art in a wider sense, which is neither diasporan nor autobiographical, such as in the books of Dostoevsky (see Lawton 1981) and the paintings of Magritte (see Chapter 3).

3 Jakub Goldberg, who played one of the men with a wardrobe, was, in fact, Jewish.

CHAPTER 3

1 Polanski, together with the whole generation of Polish directors who started their careers in the 1950s, including Andrzej Wajda, revealed a good knowledge of art and were strongly inspired by painting. In the case of Polanski and Wajda, an additional factor was the fact that both studied at art school and at certain periods dreamt about careers in fine arts.

2 Fantomas is the anti-hero of a series of over thirty pre-First World War thrillers written by Pierre Souvestre and Marcel Allain. He is a master of disguise known for the most appalling crimes such as forcing a victim to witness his own execution by placing him face-up in a guillotine.

3 Gertrude Stein, another famous American in modern Paris, is assiduously avoided from the list of writers inspiring Oscar, most likely on account of his misogyny.

CHAPTER 4

1 The score for *Chinatown* is the most discussed among the soundtracks for Polanski's films (see Prendergast 1992: 159–62; Wexman 1987: 92; Ross 1998).

2 Poland, in common with many European countries, has a long jazz tradition, reaching as far back as the First World War. Accordingly, jazz, or at least what was regarded as jazz in the 1920s and 1930s, and which included foxtrot and blue-fox, was used in many Polish films made between the two world wars. Examples are *Szpieg w masce* (*The Spy in a Mask*, 1933), directed by Mieczysław Krawicz, *Pieśniarz Warszawy* (*Warsaw Singer*, 1934), directed by Michał Waszyński and *Piętro wyżej* (*One Floor Higher*, 1937), directed by Leon Trystan. The composer of the majority of the early scores with jazz elements was Henryk Wars, who in 1947 settled in Hollywood and as Henry Vars wrote music for many well-known films (see Włodek 2002).

3 The mythologised account of Polish jazz in the early 1950s, inspired by the authentic history of the jazz band Melomani, led by Jerzy 'Duduś' Matuszkiewicz, is the topic of the film *Był jazz* (*There Was Once Jazz*, 1981), directed by Feliks Falk.

4 Komeda was also interested in the relation between music and other arts; he was an author of a 'Jazz and Poetry' show presented at Jazz Jamboree '60 and later at the Warsaw Philharmonic Hall.

5 The reason was the pressure of the British trade unions which did not allow the employment of a foreign composer in a British film (see Batura 2001: 88).

6 Such segregation indeed took place during the war, particularly in the concentration camps and was later documented in literature and cinema. Particularly worthy of attention are the memoirs of the Polish Jewish composer, violinist and conductor, Szymon Laks, *La musique d'un autre monde* (*Music From Another World*), published in 1948. Laks spent three years in the concentration camps of Auschwitz and Dauchau, published in 1948; and music literally saved his life because as a member of the camp orchestra (violinist, conductor and arranger) he was spared the daily ordeal of physical labour that killed so many around him. The music as a tool of survival in the concentration camp is also the main theme of Leszek Wosiewicz's film *Kornblumenblau* (1988), based on the memoirs of Kazimierz Tymiński. Its title is taken from the German song which the Polish musician plays for the German blockleader, who is obsessed by this tune.

CHAPTER 5

1   One may think here of a Jewish father from the books of Kafka and also of Polanski's own father who was unable either to appreciate Roman's artistic and social talents or to pass on to him any knowledge he himself possessed (see Kiernan 1980; Polanski 1984).

2   It is not an accident, in my opinion, that the majority of books devoted to Polanski's films, including this one, are written by women.

3   One gets the impression that Krystyna's unchanging expression also drove Polanski crazy. The description of his work with the amateur actress Jolanta Umecka, who played Krystyna, constitutes one of the most misogynist passages of his autobiography (see Polanski 1984: 150–1).

4   Feminist historians point out that there is no single category of 'feminist art' in the sense of a homogeneous style or movement. According to Griselda Pollock, in order to classify a piece of work as feminist, one must place it in a socio-cultural context, considering its relations to prevailing styles and ideas in the given culture, and its relations to the audience. Pollock suggests that feminist art is supposed to be an intervention which challenges the dominant definitions of gender and sexual difference and resists ideological norms and aesthetic codes (see Pollock 1992). However, in the case of Polanski's films, which are situated in numerous, often opposite contexts, such as generic/mainstream and art-house cinema, and Hollywood and European film, modernism and postmodernism, the task of considering feminist art in relation to any prevailing styles and ideas is particularly difficult.

CHAPTER 6

1   The analogy between literary and biological adaptation recently provided a subject for the film, suitably entitled *Adaptation* (2002), directed by Spike Jonze.

2   One can notice that the move from Stendhalian to Dickensian cinema is reflected in the changes in Polanski's scriptwriters. On earlier films Polanski worked with Gérard Brach and occasionally with other authors, such as Jerzy Skolimowski, who were closer to Stendhal and Beckett in their approach to narratives and characters than to Dickens. In later films, while still collaborating with Brach, Polanski brought in new scriptwriters, such as John Brownjohn and Ronald Harwood. The films for which Brownjohn and Harwood wrote scripts, including some not directed by Polanski, were made in Dickensian mode.

3   The witches also appear at the end of Orson Welles's adaptation of *Macbeth*, which Michael Anderegg interprets as Welles's endorsement of an absurdist reading of Shakespeare's play (see Anderegg 2000: 166).

4   This is understandable in the light of the fact that Kott was a Pole and his interpretation of Shakespeare, as well as other writings, influenced a large number of Polish artists and intellectuals, especially those of Polanski's generation.

5   Both Kurosawa's and Welles's adaptations underscore their theatrical origins by such elements as theatrical make-up (*Throne of Blood*) and expressionist lighting and mise-en-scène (Welles's *Macbeth*).

6   At one point Lucas Corso realises that he remembers the characters in *The Three Musketeers* as they appeared in the film, not the novel and comments: 'Bloody Hollywood' (see Pérez-Reverte 2003: 80).

7 After *Schindler's List* the most discussed cinematic rendition of the Holocaust was *La vita è bella* (*Life Is Beautiful*, 1997),by Roberto Benigni with critics repeating many of the arguments that had previously been voiced with reference to Spielberg's film (see Bullaro 2005).
8 Polanski's moral right to make a film about the Holocaust and his ability to produce its authentic rendition were acknowledged by many critics in Poland and in the West. For example, David Thompson wrote that *The Pianist* is 'as near-perfect a marriage of subject and artist as could be imagined' (Thompson 2003: 58).
9 Being interviewed, Levi described Polish as 'a truly hellish language, made up of only consonants'. For many non-Polish Jews, including Levi, it was even worse than German because they were able to understand German, while Polish was completely incomprehensible to them (see Frankel 1995–2001).

CHAPTER 7

1 In the late 1950s and early 1960s, Polish cinema did relatively well on the international stage, as demonstrated by the awards received by films such as Wajda's *Kanal* and *Ashes and Diamonds* at the film festivals at Cannes and Venice. However, even these films did not reach mass international audiences, while *Knife in the Water* was shown in the cinemas of Paris and London. The difference resulted from the fact that the viewer had to know Polish history to understand a film by Wajda or Munk whereas to grasp *Knife in the Water* he only needed to know popular cinema.
2 Many books about post-classical Hollywood discuss the phenomenon of *Chinatown*. Recently David Thomson begins his book *The Whole Equation: A History of Hollywood* with an extended discussion of *Chinatown* and pays this film a loving tribute, suggesting that it is the last great 'adult' American picture (see Thomson 2005: 3–16).
3 This 'ethnic echo' might be linked to Gittes's functions in the film as Polanski's alter ego: the non-American director trying to make sense of an unfamiliar world (see Chapter 1).
4 Jack Nicholson also played in the sequel of *Chinatown*, *The Two Jakes* (1990), based on a script by Robert Towne, which he himself directed. However, the film was too mediocre to strengthen the appeal of Nicholson's character. Instead, it pointed to Polanski's input into creating a believable protagonist and fascinating story.
5 However, most critics see in *Chinatown* a rewriting of the Oedipus story, rather than that of Electra, perhaps because in psychoanalysis Electra is reduced to being a 'female Oedipus' (see Linderman 1981).
6 This is understandable taking into account that in 1986 eleven films were released with Sarde's music.

BIBLIOGRAPHY

Adorno, Theodor W. (1973). 'After Auschwitz', in *Negative Dialectics*, trans. by E.B. Ashton (London: Routledge and Kegan Paul), pp. 361–5.

Adorno, Theodor W. (1981). 'Perennial Fashion – Jazz', in *Prisms*, trans. by Samuel and Shierry Webber (Cambridge, MA: The MIT Press), pp. 119–32.

Altman, Rick (2002). *Film/Genre* (London: BFI).

Alvarez, A. (1965). *The Writer in Society: Eastern Europe and the USA*. (Harmondsworth: Penguin Books).

Anderegg, Michael (2000). 'Welles/Shakespeare/Film: An Overview', in James Naremore (ed.), *Film Adaptation* (London: The Athlone Press), pp. 54–76.

Andrew, Dudley (1992). 'Adaptation', in Gerald Mast et al. (eds), *Film Theory and Criticism*, (4th edition Oxford: Oxford University Press), pp. 420–8.

Andrews, Nigel (1972). 'Macbeth', *Sight and Sound*, Spring, p. 108.

Bachelard, Gaston (1994). *The Poetics of Space*, trans. by Maria Jolas (Boston: Beacon Press).

Bagh, Peter von (1965). 'Repulsion', *Movie*, 14, pp. 26–7.

Balcerzan, Edward (1995). 'Jak jest zrobiony *Lokator*?', in Bogusław Zmudziński (ed.), *Roman Polański* (Kraków: Wydawnictwo Dyskusyjnego Klubu Filmowego Uniwersytetu Jagiellońskiego), pp. 124–30.

Barr, Charles (1965). 'Repulsion', *Movie*, 14 (Autumn), pp. 26–7.

Barthes, Roland (1977). 'The Death of the Author', in *Image Music Text*, trans. by Stephen Heath (London: Fontana Press), pp. 142–8.

Batura, Emilia (2001). *Księżycowy chłopiec: O Krzysztofie Komedzie-Trzcińskim* (Warsaw: Alfa-Wero).

Bauman, Zygmunt (1989). *Modernity and the Holocaust* (Ithaca, NY: Cornell University Press).

Benjamin, Walter (1999a). 'Franz Kafka on the Tenth Anniversary of His Death', in *Illuminations*, trans. by Harry Zorn (London: Pimlico), pp. 108–35.

Benjamin, Walter (1999b). 'Max Brod's Book on Kafka and Some of My Own Reflections', ibid., pp. 136–43.

Benjamin, Walter (1999c). 'The Image of Proust', ibid., pp. 197–210.

Bonitzer, Pascal (1981). 'Partial Vision: Film and the Labyrinth', trans. by Fabrice Ziolkowski, *Wide Angle*, 4, pp. 56–64.

Bordwell, David (2002). 'Intensified Continuity: Visual Style in Contemporary American Film', *Film Quarterly*, 3, pp. 16–28.

Borowski, Tadeusz (1992). *This Way for the Gas, Ladies and Gentlemen*, trans. by Michael Kandel (London: Penguin).

Boutang, Pierre-Andre (ed.) (1986). *Polański par Polanski: textes et documents* (Paris: Chene).

Brandes, David (1977). 'Roman Polanski on Acting', *Cinema Papers*, January, pp. 227–9.

Bresheeth, Haim (1997). 'The Great Taboo Broken: Reflections on the Israeli Reception of Schindler's List', in Yosefa Loshitzky (ed.), *Spielberg's Holocaust: Critical Perspectives on Schindler's List* (Bloomington and Indianapolis: Indiana University Press), pp. 193–212.

Brown, Royal S. (1994). *Overtones and Undertones: Reading Film Music* (Berkeley: University of California Press).

Bryll, Ernest (1962). 'Statek kabotynów', *Współczesność*, 7, p. 5.

Bukowski, Krzysztof (1980). 'Muzyka Komedy', *Magazyn Muzyczny Jazz*, 7–8, pp. 8–11.

Bullaro, Russo Grace (2005). *Beyond 'Life is Beautiful': Comedy and Tragedy in the Cinema of Roberto Benigni* (Leicester: Troubador).

Butler, Ivan (1970). *The Cinema of Roman Polanski* (New York: The International Film Guide Series).

Camus, Albert (1955). *The Myth of Sisyphus*, trans. by Justin O'Brien (London: Hamish Hamilton).

Cawelti, John G. (1992). '*Chinatown* and Generic Transformation in Recent American Film', in Gerald Mast et al. (eds), *Film Theory and Criticism*, (4th edition, Oxford: Oxford University Press), pp. 498–511.

Cegiełła, Janusz (1976). *Szkice do autoportretu polskiej muzyki współczesnej* (Kraków: Polskie Wydawnictwo Muzyczne).

Chappetta, Robert (1969). 'Rosemary's Baby', *Film Quarterly*, 3, pp. 35–8.

Coates, Paul (2004). 'Nóż w wodzie/Knife in the Water', in Peter Hames (ed.), *The Cinema of Central Europe* (London: Wallflower Press), pp. 76–85.

Comolli, Jean Luc and Narboni, Jean (1992). 'Cinema/Ideology/Criticism', in Gerald Mast et al. (eds), *Film Theory and Criticism*, (4th edition, Oxford: Oxford University Press), pp. 682–9.

Constanzo, William V. (1981). 'Polanski in Wessex Filming Tess of the D'Urbervilles', *Literature/Film Quarterly*, 9, pp. 71–8.

Cook, Pam (ed.) (1985). *The Cinema Book* (London: British Film Institute).

Crnković, Gordana (1997). 'Death and the Maiden', *Film Quarterly*, 3, pp. 39–45.

Crnković, Gordana P. (2004). 'From the Eye to the Hand: The Victim's Double Vision in the Films of Roman Polanski', *Kinoeye*, 4, 5, 29 November, http://www.kinoeye.org/index_04_05.php.

Cyz, Tomasz (2002). 'Między "słyszę" a "widzę"', *Tygodnik Powszechny*, 29, p. 16.

Davis, Mike (1998). *City of Quartz: Excavating the Future in Los Angeles* (London: Pimlico).

De Lauretis, Teresa (1987). *Technologies of Gender* (London: Macmillan Press).

Delahaye, Michel and Narboni, Jean (1969). 'Entretien avec Roman Polanski', *Cahiers du cinéma*, 208, pp. 23–31.

Deleuze, Gilles and Guattari, Félix (2000). *Kafka: Toward a Minor Literature*, trans. by Dana Polan (Minneapolis: University of Minnesota Press).

Deutscher, Isaac (1968). *The Non-Jewish Jew and other Essays* (London: Merlin Press).

Diski, Jenny (1995). 'Sitting Inside', *Sight and Sound*, 4 (April), pp. 12–13.

Dondziłło, Czesław (1984). 'Nóż w wodzie', *Film*, 28, pp. 14–15.

Dyer, Peter John (1962–3). 'Life Is a Pain Anyway', *Sight and Sound*, Winter, pp. 21–3.

Eagle, Herbert (1994). 'Polanski', in Daniel J. Goulding (ed.), *Five Filmmakers* (Bloomington and Indianapolis: Indiana University Press), pp. 92–155.

Eaton, Michael (2000). *Chinatown* (London: BFI).

Eberhardt, Konrad (1967). 'Horror codzienności', *Film*, 27, p. 4.

Eberhardt, Konrad (1982). 'Skolimowski', in *Konrad Eberhardt o polskich filmach* (Warsaw: Wydawnictwa Artystyczne i Filmowe), pp. 112–31.

Eleftheriotis, Dimitris (2000). 'Cultural Difference and Exchange: A Future for European Film', *Screen*, 1 (Spring), pp. 92–101.

Elley, Derek (1974). 'What?', *Film and Filming*, June, p. 45.

Elsner, Jas and Rubiés, Joan-Pau (1999). 'Introduction', in Jas Elsner and Joan-Pau Rubiés (eds), *Voyages and Visions: Towards a Cultural History of Travel* (London: Reaktion Press), pp. 1–56.

Esslin, Martin (1968). *The Theatre of the Absurd* (Harmondsworth: Penguin Books).

Fainaru, Dan (1987). 'From Hell to High Water', *Cinema Papers*, January, pp. 28–30.

Fendel, Heike-Melba (1999). 'Die Neunte Pforte', *EPD*, 12, pp. 51–2.

Foucault, Michel (1986). 'What Is An Author?', in John Caughie (ed.), *Theories of Authorship* (London: Routledge), pp. 282–91.

Frankel, Ari (1995–2001). Primo Levi Internet site http://www.inch.com/~ari/levi2.html

Frodon, Jean-Michel (2002). '*Le Pianiste*: une dalle de marbre sur le destin d'un survivant du ghetto de Varsovie', *Le Monde*, 26 June.

Furman, Jan (1996). *Toni Morrison's Fiction* (Columbia: University of South Carolina Press).

Gablik, Suzi (1970). *Magritte* (London: Thames and Hudson).

Galion, Yves (1986). 'Pirates: Le fantome d'Errol Flynn', *La Revue du cinéma*, 418 (Juillet-Août), pp. 31–2.

Gelmis, Joseph (1971). *The Film Director as Superstar* (London: Secker and Warburg).

Gershuny, Ted (1981). 'Repulsion', in Frank N. Magill (ed.), *Magill's Survey of Cinema*, Vol. 5 (Englewood Cliffs: Salem Press), pp. 2011–13.

Gombrowicz, Witold (1997). *Dziennik 1953–1956* (Kraków: Wydawnictwo Literackie).

Graffy, Julian (1992). 'Bitter Moon', *Sight and Sound*, 10 (October), pp. 53–4.

Guze, Joanna (1966). 'Polański i inni', *Film*, 42, p. 4.

Hall, Stuart (1988). *The Hard Road to Renewal: Thatcherism and the Crisis of the Left* (London: Verso).

Hall, Stuart (1992). 'The Question of Cultural Identity', in Stuart Hall et al. (eds), *Modernity and its Futures* (Cambridge: Polity Press).

Haltof, Marek (2004). *The Cinema of Krzysztof Kieślowski: Variations on Destiny and Chance* (London: Wallflower Press).

Hamington, Maurice (1995). *Hail Mary? The Struggle for Ultimate Womanhood in Catholicism* (London: Routledge).

Haskell, Molly (1987). *From Reverence to Rape: The Treatment of Women in the Movies*, (2nd edition, Chicago: The University of Chicago Press).

Heilman, Robert Bechtold (1968). *Tragedy and Melodrama: Versions of Experience* (Seattle: University of Washington Press).

Helman, Alicja (1967). *Na ścieżce dźwiękowej* (Kraków: Państwowe Wydawnictwo Muzyczne).

Hendrykowski, Marek (1997). 'Modern Jazz', *Kwartalnik Filmowy*, 17 (Spring), pp. 86–96.

Hinchliffe, Arnold P. (1969). *The Absurd* (London: Methuen).

Horowitz, Mark (1990). 'Fault Lines', *Film Comment*, November–December, pp. 52–5.

Houston, Beverle and Kinder, Marsha (1968–9). 'Rosemary's Baby', *Sight and Sound*, Winter, pp. 17–19.

Humphries, Reynold (2002). *The American Horror Film: An Introduction* (Edinburgh: Edinburgh University Press).

Jackiewicz, Aleksander (1977). 'Polański', in *Mistrzowie Kina Współczesnego* (Warsaw: Wydawnictwa Artystyczne i Filmowe), pp. 142–5.

Jackiewicz, Aleksander (1981). 'Losy reżyserów', in *Latarnia Czarnoksięska* (Warsaw: Wydawnictwa Radia i Telewizji), pp. 258–60.

Jackiewicz, Aleksander (1989). 'Amadeusz w Paryżu', in Moja Filmoteka: Film w Kulturze (Warsaw: Wydawnictwa Artystyczne i Filmowe), pp. 266–70.

Jackson, D.D. (ed.) (1960). The Etiology of Schizophrenia (New York: Basic Books).

James, Nick (1995). 'Death and the Maiden', Sight and Sound, 4 (April), p. 40.

Jankun-Dopartowa, Mariola (2000). Labirynt Polańskiego (Kraków: Rabid).

Johnson, William (1972). 'King Lear. Macbeth', Film Quarterly, Spring, pp. 41–8.

Kałużyński, Zygmunt (2001). Kino na nowy wiek (Wrocław: Siedmioróg).

Kemp, Philip (2005). 'Oliver Twist', Sight and Sound, 10, pp. 80–1.

Kennedy, Harlan (1979). 'Tess: Polanski in Hardy Country', American Film, October, pp. 62–7.

Kennedy, Harlan (1994). 'The Moon's Our Home', Film Comment, January–February, pp. 12–14.

Kępiński, Antoni (1974). Schizofrenia (Warsaw: Państwowy Zakład Wydawnictw Lekarskich).

Kiernan, Thomas (1980). Roman Polanski: A Biography (New York: Delilah/Grove Press).

Klein, Norman M. (1997). The History of Forgetting: Los Angeles and the Erasure of Memory (London: Verso).

Kolasińska, Iwona (1995). 'Kiedy mężczyzna opowiada o tym, co widzi kobieta (Wstręt, Dziecko Rosemary)', in Bogusław Zmudziński (ed.), Roman Polański (Kraków: Wydawnictwo Dyskusyjnego Klubu Filmowego Uniwersytetu Jagiellońskiego), pp. 75–86.

Komeda-Trzciński, Krzysztof (1961). 'Z ankiety "Rola muzyki w dziele filmowym"', Kwartalnik Filmowy, 2, pp. 35–8.

Kott, Jan (1967). Shakespeare Our Contemporary, trans. by Bolesław Taborski (London: Methuen).

Kowal, Roman (1995). Polski jazz. Wczesna historia i trzy biografie zamknięte: Komeda, Kosz, Seifert (Kraków: Akademia Muzyczna w Krakowie).

Kułakowska, Zofia (1961). 'Problem instrumentacji w muzyce filmowej Andrzeja Markowskiego', Kwartalnik Filmowy, 2, pp. 39–45.

Lawton, Anna (1981). 'The Double – A Dostoevskian Theme in Polanski', Literature/Film Quarterly, 9, pp. 121–9.

Leaming, Barbara (1981). Polanski: The Filmmaker as Voyeur (New York: Simon and Schuster).

Levi, Primo (1988). The Drowned and the Saved, trans. from Italian by Raymond Rosenthal (London: Michael Joseph).

Liehm, Mira and Liehm, A.J. (1980). 'Roman Polanski, Jerzy Skolimowski and the Polish Emigres', in Richard Roud (ed.), Cinema. A Critical Dictionary: The Major Film-Makers, vol. 2 (London: Secker and Warburg), pp. 782–7.

Linderman, Deborah (1981). 'Oedipus in Chinatown', Enclitic, 5 (Autumn), pp. 190–203.

Lor. (1986). 'Pirates', Variety, 14 June, p. 16.

Loshitzky, Yosefa (1997). 'Holocaust Others: Spielberg's Schindler's List versus Lanzmann's Shoah', in Yosefa Loshitzky (ed.), Spielberg's Holocaust: Critical Perspectives on Schindler's List (Bloomington and Indianapolis: Indiana University Press), pp. 104–18.

Loustalot, Ghislain (2005). 'Oliver i ja', Film, 10, pp. 34–9.

Lubelski, Tadeusz (1993). 'Gorzkie gody, czyli Amerykanin w Paryżu', Iluzjon, 2, pp. 11–14.

Lubelski, Tadeusz (2000). 'Prawdopodobnie diabeł', Kino, 2 (January), pp. 8 and 59.

Luckett, Moya (2000). 'Travel and Mobility: Femininity and National Identity', in Justine Ashby and Andrew Higson (eds), British Cinema, Past and Present (London: Routledge), pp. 233–45.

Lyons, Donald (1993). 'Laws in the Iris: The Private Eye in the Seventies', *Film Comment*, July–August, pp. 44–53.

Malatyńska, Maria and Malatyńska-Stankiewicz, Agnieszka (2002). *Scherzo dla Wojciecha Kilara* (Kraków: Polskie Wydawnictwo Muzyczne).

Manvell, Roger (1979). *Theater and Film* (Branbury, NJ: Associated University Press).

Marcus, Jane (1981). 'A Tess for Child Molestors', *Jump/Cut*, 26, p. 3.

Maurin, Huguette (1980). 'Les relations des personnages et des lieux dans les films de Polanski', *Revue du cinéma*, 254 (February), pp. 22–31.

Mazierska, Ewa (2000). 'Non-Jewish Jews, Good Poles and Historical Truth in Films of Andrzej Wajda', *Historical Journal of Film, Radio and Television*, 2, pp. 213–26.

Mazierska, Ewa (2005). 'Double Memory: The Holocaust in Polish Film', in Toby Haggith and Joanna Newman (eds), *Holocaust and the Moving Image* (London: Wallflower Press), pp. 225–35.

Mazierska, Ewa and Rascaroli, Laura (2003). *From Moscow to Madrid: Postmodern Cities, European Cinema* (London: I.B. Tauris).

Mazierska, Ewa and Rascaroli, Laura (2004). *The Cinema of Nanni Moretti: Dreams and Diaries* (London: Wallflower Press).

Mazierska, Ewa and Rascaroli, Laura (2006). *Crossing New Europe: Postmodern Travel, European Cinema* (London: Wallflower Press).

McArthur, Colin (1968–9). 'Polanski', *Sight and Sound*, Winter, pp. 14–17.

McFarlane, Brian (1995). 'Death and the Maiden', *Cinema Papers*, August, pp. 43–4.

McKay, George (2005). *Circular Breathing: The Cultural Politics of Jazz in Britain* (Durham, NC: Duke University Press).

Michalak, Bartosz (2001). *Na zakręcie: Agnieszka Osiecka we wspomnieniach* (Warsaw: Bis).

Michałek, Bolesław (1962). 'Sztuczne serca', *Nowa Kultura*, 12, p. 8.

Middleton, David (1979–80). 'The Self-Reflective Nature of Roman Polanski's *Macbeth*', University of Dayton Review, 1 (Winter), pp. 89–94.

Milne, Tom (1976). 'Le Locataire (The Tenant)', *Monthly Film Bulletin*, September, p. 193.

Modleski, Tania (1988). *The Women Who Knew Too Much: Hitchcock and Feminist Theory* (New York and London: Methuen).

Mulvey, Laura (1996). 'Visual Pleasure and Narrative Cinema', in Antony Easthope (ed.), *Contemporary Film Theory* (London: Longman), pp. 111–24.

Naficy, Hamid (2001). *An Accented Cinema: Exilic and Diasporic Filmmaking* (Princeton: Princeton University Press).

Neale, Steve and Krutnik, Frank (1990). *Popular Film and Television Comedy* (London: Routledge).

Nesselson, Lisa (1999). 'The Ninth Gate', *Variety*, 30 August–5 September, pp. 50–1.

Niemeyer, Paul J. (2003). *Seeing Hardy: Film and Television Adaptations of the Fiction of Thomas Hardy* (Jefferson, NC: McFarland).

Norris Nicholson, Heather (2006). 'Through the Balkan States Home Movies as Travel Texts and Tourism Histories of the Mediterranean, c. 1923–39', *Tourist Studies*, 1, pp. 13–36.

Owczarek, Małgorzata (1995). 'Karnawał grozy (*Bal wampirów*)', in Bogusław Zmudziński (ed.), *Roman Polański* (Kraków: Wydawnictwo Dyskusyjnego Klubu Filmowego Uniwersytetu Jagiellońskiego), pp. 100–8.

Perec, Georges (2003). *Life: A User's Manual*, trans. by David Bellos (London: Vintage).

Pérez-Reverte, Arturo (2003). *The Dumas Club*, trans. by Sonia Soto (London: Vintage).

Piekarczyk, Jerzy (2000). 'Dwaj ludzie bez szafy', *Przekrój*, 19, pp. 13–15.

Płażewski, Jerzy (2002). 'Zeznanie przed trybunałem historii', *Kino*, 9, pp. 15–16.

Podobińska, Klaudia and Polony, Leszek (1997). *Cieszę się darem życia: Rozmowy z Wojciechem Kilarem* (Kraków: Polskie Wydawnictwo Muzyczne).

Polanski, Roman (1984). *Roman* (London: Heinemann).

Polański, Roman (1980). 'Kino według Polańskiego' [fragments of Polański's interviews], *Film na świecie*, n. 264–265, pp. 8–58.

Pollock, Griselda (1992). 'Feminism and Modernity', in Maggie Humm (ed.), *Modern Feminism: Political, Literary, Cultural* (New York: Columbia University Press), pp. 362–6.

Prawer, S.S. (1980). *Caligari's Children: The Film as Tale of Terror* (New York: Da Capo Press).

Prendergast, Roy M. (1992). *Film Music: A Neglected Art* (New York: W.W. Norton & Company).

Przylipiak, Mirosław (2004). 'Dekalog/ The Decalogue', in Peter Hames (ed.), *The Cinema of Central Europe* (London: Wallflower Press), pp. 225–34.

Rawlinson, Mark (1999). 'Adapting the Holocaust: *Schinder's List*, Intellectuals and Public Knowledge', in Deborah Cartmell and Imelda Whelehan (eds), *Adaptations: From Text to Screen, Screen to Text* (London: Routledge), pp. 113–27.

Rojek, Chris (1995). *Decentring Leisure: Rethinking Leisure Theory* (London: Sage).

Rorty, Richard (1989). *Contingency, Irony and Solidarity* (Cambridge: Cambridge University Press).

Rosenbaum, Jonathan (1976). 'The Tenant', *Sight and Sound*, Autumn, p. 253.

Ross, Alex (1998). 'Oscar Scores', *The New Yorker*, 9 March, reproduced in Alex Ross: *The Rest Is Noise Articles, a blog, and a book-in-progress by the music critic of* The New Yorker http://www.therestisnoise.com/2004/05/oscar_scores.html

Ross, Alex (2003). 'Ghost Sonata: Adorno and German Music', *The New Yorker*, 24 March, reproduced in Alex Ross: *The Rest Is Noise Articles, a blog, and a book-in-progress by the music critic of* The New Yorker http://www.therestisnoise.com/2004/05/theodor_adorno.html

Rothwell, Kenneth S. (1999). *A History of Shakespeare on Screen* (Cambridge: Cambridge University Press).

Sartre, Jean-Paul (1965). *Nausea*, trans. by Robert Baldwick (Harmondsworth: Penguin Books).

Sass, Louis. A. (1997). 'The Consciousness Machine: Self and Subjectivity and Modern Culture', in Ulric Neissen and David A. Jopling (eds), *The Conceptual Self in Context: Culture, Experience, Self-Understanding* (Cambridge: Cambridge University Press), pp. 203–32.

Sobolewski, Tadeusz (2002). 'Swoimi słowami: Pianista', *Kino*, 7–8, p. 74.

Sontag, Susan (1983a). 'Fascinating Fascism', in *Under the Sign of Saturn* (London: Writers and Readers), pp. 73–105.

Sontag, Susan (1983b). 'Under the Sign of Saturn', ibid., pp. 109–34.

Sontag, Susan (1994a). 'Spiritual Style in the Films of Robert Bresson', in *Against Interpretation* (London: Vintage), pp. 177–95.

Sontag, Susan (1994b). 'A Note on Novels and Films', ibid., pp. 242–5.

Sontag, Susan (1994c). 'One Culture and the New Sensibility', ibid., pp. 293–304.

Sontag, Susan (2002a). 'Gombrowicz's Ferdydurke', in *Where the Stress Falls* (London: Jonathan Cape), pp. 97–105.

Sontag, Susan (2002b). 'Questions of Travel', ibid., pp. 274–84.

Sorlin, Pierre (1994). *European Cinemas, European Societies 1939–1990* (London: Routledge).

Sowińska, Iwona, *Historia polskiej powojennej muzyki filmowej* [work in progress].

Stachówna, Grażyna (1987). 'Nóż w wodzie Romana Polańskiego czyli: jak debiutować w kinie', *Kino*, 8, pp. 4–7 and 24–6.

Stachówna, Grażyna (1994). *Roman Polański i jego filmy* (Warsaw: PWN).

Stachówna, Grażyna (1995). '*Gorzkie gody* Romana Polańskiego czyli Aneks do książki *Roman Polański i jego filmy*', in Bogusław Zmudziński (ed.), *Roman Polański* (Kraków: Wydawnictwo Dyskusyjnego Klubu Filmowego Uniwersytetu Jagiellońskiego), pp. 136–44.

Stam, Robert (2000). 'Beyond Fidelity: The Dialogics of Adaptation', in James Naremore (ed.), *Film Adaptation* (London: The Athlone Press), pp. 54–76.

Stewart, Garrett (1974–5). 'The Long Goodbye from Chinatown', *Film Quarterly*, 2, pp. 25–32.

Strick, Philip (1986). 'Pirates', *Monthly Film Bulletin*, 10, pp. 316–17.

Strick, Philip (2000). 'The Ninth Gate', *Sight and Sound*, 9, pp. 45–6.

Sutton, Martin (1988). 'Polanski in Profile', *Films and Filming*, 9, pp. 23–5.

Sydney-Smith, Susan (2004). 'Romancing Disaster: *Titanic* and the Rites of Passage Film', in Tim Bergfelder and Sarah Street (eds), *The Titanic in Myth and Memory* (London: I.B. Tauris), pp. 185–95.

Szpilman, Wladyslaw (2003). *The Pianist*, trans. by Anthea Bell (London: Phoenix).

Szwarcman, Dorota (2000). 'Muzyka przetrwania', *Wprost*, 46, pp. 122–3.

Tarratt, Margaret (1969). 'Rosemary's Baby', *Screen*, March–April, pp. 90–5.

Thompson, David (1964). 'Noz w wodzie (Knife in the Water)', *Sight and Sound*, 7, p. 61.

Thompson, David (1995). 'I Make Films for Adults', *Sight and Sound*, 4, pp. 6–11.

Thompson, David (2003). 'The Pianist', *Sight and Sound*, 2, pp. 57–8.

Thompson, Kenneth (1986). *Beliefs and Ideology* (Chichester: Ellis Horwood).

Thompson, Kristin and Bordwell, David (2003). *Film History: An Introduction* (New York: McGraw-Hill).

Thomson, David (2005). *The Whole Equation: A History of Hollywood* (London: Little, Brown).

Toeplitz, Krzysztof Teodor (1962). 'Nóż w wodzie', *Świat*, 25 March, p. 12.

Tomasik, Wojciech (2004). 'All that Jazz! On Tyrmand's Challenge to Stalinism', *Blok*, 3, pp. 179–86.

Turowska, Zofia (2000). *Agnieszki: Pejzaże z Agnieszką Osiecką* (Warsaw: Prószyński i Spółka).

Vachaud, Laurent (1999). 'La Neuvième Porte: Tintin et les livres noirs', *Positif*, 463, p. 37.

Wells, Paul (2000). *The Horror Genre: From Beelzebub to Blair Witch* (London: Wallflower Press).

Wexman, Virginia Wright (1987). *Roman Polanski* (London: Columbus Books).

Whitfield, Sarah (1992). *Magritte* (London: The South Bank Centre).

Widdowson, Peter (1993). 'A "Tragedy of Modern Life"? Polanski's *Tess*', in Widdowson (ed.), *New Casebooks: Tess of the d'Urbervilles* (London and Basingstoke: Macmillan), pp. 95–108.

Widłak, Wojciech (1998). 'Koncert fortepianowy Wojciecha Kilara', *Dysonanse*, 2, pp. 2–9.

Williams, Linda (1981). 'Film Madness: The Uncanny Returned of the Repressed in Polanski's *The Tenant*', *Cinema Journal*, 2, pp. 63–73.

Włodek, Roman (2002). 'Pierwszy polski jazzman', *Kino*, 10, pp. 55–8.

Womack, Kenneth (2004). 'Reading the Titanic: Contemporary Literary Representations of the Ship of Dreams', in Tim Bergfelder and Sarah Street (eds), *The Titanic in Myth and Memory* (London: I.B. Tauris), pp. 85–93.

Wróbel, Szymon (2001). 'Biografia jako dzieło sztuki', *Sztuka i filozofia*, 19, pp. 140–63.

Żukowska-Sypniewska, Izabela (1999). 'Poloneza czas zacząć: O muzyce filmowej Wojciecha Kilara', *Kino*, 10, pp. 24–6

INDEX